Fundamentals of College Astronomy

Michael C. LoPresto
Henry Ford Community College

Kendall Hunt
publishing company

Pages 55, 56, 57, 58 from *Mysteries of the Sky: Activities for Collaborative Groups* by Shannon Willoughby and Jeff Adams. Copyright © 2007 by Shannon D. Willoughby and Jeff Adams. Reprinted by permission of Kendall Hunt Publishing Company.

Images on pages 117, 118, 119, 120, 121, 122, 123, 124, 125, 126, 127, 131, 132, 133, 138, 139, 140, 141, 142, 143, 144 have made use of the Exoplanet Orbit Database and the Exoplanet Data Explorer at exoplanets.org. Used with permission.

Images on page 151 courtesy of the Lowell Observatory.

Image on page 238 courtesy of Yerkes Observatory.

Image on page 240 courtesy of Palomar Observatory.

Image on page 247 courtesy of Robert Stein, Physics and Astronomy Department, Michigan State University.

Figures I.2, I.3, I.4, I.5, 1.3, 1.17, 1.20, 2.1, 3.2, 3.4, 5.1, 5.2, 5.4, 5.7, 5.9, 5.10, 5.11, 5.12, 5.15, 5.16, 5.17, 5.18, 5.19, 5.20, 5.22, 5.23, 6.1, 6.2, 6.3, 6.4, 6.5, 6.6, 6.7, 6.8, 6.9, 6.10, 6.12, 6.13, 6.14, 7.1, 7.2, 7.6, 7.8, 7.9, 7.10, 7.11, 7.12, 7.13, 7.14, 7.15, 7.16, 7.17,, 7.18, 7.19 , 8.5, 8.6, 8.15, 9.1, 9.3, 9.4, 9.5, 9.6, 10.1, 10.2, 10.3, , 11.1, 11.3, 11.6, 11.11,, 11.12, 11.13, 11.14, 11.15, 11.16, 12.9, 12.12, 13.3, 13.4, 13.5, 13.6, 13.8, 13.9, 13.10, 13.11, 13.12, 13.13 courtesy of NASA.

Illustrations by Colin Ferguson and Lina Levy.

Website by Steve Murrell.

Cover images © Shutterstock, Inc.

www.kendallhunt.com
Send all inquiries to:
4050 Westmark Drive
Dubuque, IA 52004-1840

Copyright © 2010 by Michael C. LoPresto

ISBN 978-0-7575-8174-8

Contents

Preface (Acknowledgments)

I thank the editors of Kendall Hunt Publishing for encouraging me to take on this project and working through it with me. I especially thank Steve Murrell, fellow astronomy instructor at HFCC, for his work on the website portion of this project and the camaraderie we have experienced as colleagues, teaching physics & astronomy, and friends in recent years.

I also thank HFCC instructor of physics and astronomy at HFCC, James Marks, for his detailed review of the entire text, and artists Colin Ferguson of John Tyler Community College for the portraits, and Lina Levy for the diagrams.

I wrote the initial drafts during a visiting researcher appointment in the Department of Astronomy at my alma mater, the University of Michigan, while on sabbatical from HFCC during the winter and spring of 2010. I thank them for their hospitality during that time.

This work is the result of 20 years of teaching astronomy at HFCC, and would not have been possible without the numerous students who have taken astronomy with me over that time. In gratitude, I dedicate this work to them and to all the students who will study astronomy with me in the future.

Michael C. LoPresto, 2010

Introduction –Sizes and Scales in the Universe

I.1 Overview

There are four basics "scales" at which astronomy is studied. These are (1) the scale of our own planet, Earth; (2) the scale of the solar system in which Earth, 7 other planets and numerous other objects orbit our star, the Sun; (3) the scale of the galaxy, an assemblage of a few hundred billion stars of which our Sun is only one and finally; (4) the universe. Our Milky Way galaxy with its nearest neighbor, the Andromeda galaxy, and the 25 to 30 other galaxies in our cluster, the Local Group are only a few of the countless numbers of galaxies and clusters of galaxies in our almost limitless universe.

Figure I.1 The scales of the Universe.

The four sections of this text are divided with these 4 scales. Chapters 1 and 2 are about observing motions in the sky from Earth, and how the first astronomers developed theories about them. Chapters 3-7 are about the solar system. Chapters 8-10 are about the Sun and the other stars in our galaxy. Chapters 11-13 are about our

Milky Way galaxy and others in our universe and the universe itself, including whether or not we on Earth are its lone living inhabitants.

I.2 The Scale of Earth

At the scale of our planet, Earth, measurements are made in kilometers or miles. At its thickest point, the equator, Earth is about 13,000 km or 8,000 miles across, its *diameter*, and about 40,000 km or 24, 000 miles around, its *circumference*. Earth's lone natural satellite, the Moon, is about a quarter of Earth's diameter, about 3300 km or 2000 miles across and about 400,000 km or 250,000, a quarter of a million, miles away. The distance between Earth and the Moon is 30 times the diameter of Earth. If Earth were a basketball, the Moon would be a baseball about 50 meters or 30 feet, about 30 diameters of the basketball, away.

Figure I.2 Sizes and distances on Earth are measured in kilometers or miles.

I.3 The Scale of the Solar System

The distance between Earth and the Sun is about 150 million kilometers or 93 million miles. Before astronomers even knew how far this distance was, they labeled it an *Astronomical Unit,* or AU for short. Since the distances in the solar system are all so large, they are always measured in AU. Jupiter is just over 5 times as far from the Sun as Earth is, so its orbital distance is 5.2 AU. The most distance planet, Neptune, is about 6 times as far from the Sun as that, at about 30 AU. Even the orbital distances of planets closer to the Sun than Earth can be measured in AU. Venus orbits the Sun at about 0.72 AU and Mercury, on average, at about 0.38 AU.

Figure I.3 Sizes of the planets relative to each other and the Sun (relative distances from the Sun are not to scale).

Even moreso than in the Earth-moon system, the distances between objects in the solar system dwarf the sizes of the objects. Most models of the solar system do not have the relative sizes of the planets and the distances between them on the same scale. If they do they either cannot fit in a room or most of the planets would be too small to see. For example, if the Sun were shrunk down to the size of a softball, the largest planet, Jupiter would be no bigger than a large marble; and smaller planets, like Earth, would be the size of the head of a pin. The distance between the softball and a "pin-head" Earth would be about 50 meters or 30 feet. The distance to the marble-Jupiter would be five times that and the entire solar system would be 4 or 5 km, 2 or 3 miles, across. Most of this model, except for a few marbles, pinheads, and some grains of sand and specks of dust that would represent asteroids and comets, would be *empty space.*

I.4 The Scale of the Galaxy

The stars in the galaxy are even more isolated than the planets of the solar system. The distance between stars is so immense that even the AU is too small a unit to be useful in measuring distances. Even the closest stars to our Sun are over 40 *trillion* km or 25 *trillion* miles away. The most commonly used unit for measuring distances in the galaxy and beyond is the *light-year*. A light-year is *not* a measurement of time, rather it is the distance that light waves moving at a speed of 300,000 km/s or 186,000 miles/s can travel in a year. This is almost 10 trillion km or about 6 trillion, (6,000,000,0000,000) miles. The closest stars are over 4 light-years away and most are much farther away. Our galaxy is estimated to be over 100,000 light-years across.

When trying to build a model of the galaxy on the same scale as a college campus-sized model solar system, with its softball-size sun and marble and pin-head size planets, one campus-sized solar system would be about *two-thousand* miles away from the next one over, with *nothing but empty space* in between.

Figure I.4 Galaxies contain hundreds of billion of stars and can be hundreds or thousands of light-years across.

I.5 Look-Back Time

At these immense distances, even light waves, which can circle our Earth seven times in one second, take years or more to travel between objects. *When you are looking out into space you are also looking back in time.* Nothing observed by astronomers is seen as it is, but rather as it was. The look-back time of any object is numerically equal to its distance. We see the moon with time lag of just over a second, so it is just over a light-second away; the Sun is 8 light-minutes away. The furthest planets are a few light-hours away. We see the nearest stars as they looked 4 years ago, further stars as they looked, decades or centuries ago. The Andromeda galaxy appears as it looked almost 3 million years ago, and other more distant galaxies appear as they looked billions of years ago. The furthest objects in the universe, quasars, thought to be the active centers of galaxies in their early stages of development, appear as they looked over ten billion years go. Perhaps now, quasars are more like our own galaxy, and possibly inhabitants of those distant galaxies see our Milky Way as a quasar. Astronomers really can study the history of our universe because when they look out into space they can actually see the past.

I.6 The Scale of the Universe

Galaxies, containing billions of stars and being hundreds of thousands of light-years across, are so large that within a galactic cluster like our Local Group, the relative scale is similar to that of the Earth-Moon system. If our entire Milky Way Galaxy, about 100,000 light-years across, with all of its several hundred-billion stars, were packed into the size of a basketball, making our Sun and entire solar system barely even microscopic, the Andromeda galaxy, our nearest neighbor galaxy, about 3 million light years away, would be about the same size and about 30 feet away, with the space in between, again, *empty*.

Even on this scale, the size and distance between galaxies in clusters and superclusters of tens, hundreds, and even thousands of galaxies, and ultimately the universe, becomes hard to imagine. The size of the *observable* universe is limited by the age of the universe that has been estimated to be almost 14 billion years. This means that nothing further away than 14 billion light-years can be seen because its light has not yet had time to reach us.

Figure I.5 The Hubble Space Telescope's *Deep Field;* a part of our universe in a section of the sky that appears from Earth to be about the size of a postage stamp.

Review Questions

1. If Earth were the size of a basketball, how big would the moon be? How far away would it be?

2. How large would the Sun be in a model of the solar system that was about as large as a college campus? How large would the largest planets be in such a model? Of what would most of the model be comprised?

3. If the solar system were your campus, where would a campus be that would represent the nearest other solar system? What would be found in most of the space in between the two models?

4. What is an Astronomical Unit? How far is an AU? What is a light-year? How far is a light-year?

5. How large is the galaxy? How large is the observable universe? Why do we say *observable*?

6. List the following objects in order of their size, from smallest to largest: galaxy, moon, planet, star, universe.

7. List the following distances is order of their size from smallest largest: distance across Local Group, distance across our Milky Way galaxy, distance across universe; Earth-Moon, Earth-Sun, Milky Way-Andromeda Galaxy, Sun-nearest star.

8. Compared to their size, which objects are the most isolated from other objects; planets, stars, or galaxies? Explain your answer.

9. Match each distance with the unit best used to measure it (unit may be used more than once).

Diameter of Earth

Distance across galaxy   Astronomical Unit

Earth-Moon   kilometers

Earth-Sun   light-years

Sun –Nearest Star

10. Explain what is meant by *look-back time*.

Tutorial--A Solar System Walk

The Sun's Display case is located on the Eastern-most side of the planetarium's circular wall, on the top floor of the science building.

1. The sun appears to be about the size of a (circle one);

    Golf ball   Baseball   Softball   Basketball

Use the map in the sun's display case to find the all the inner solar system (Terrestrial) planets.

2. The Terrestrial Planets all appear to be the about the size of a (circle one);

    head of a pin   small marble   golfball   a baseball

3. About how far from the sun did you find Earth (circle one)?

    3 inches   3 feet   30 feet   300 feet

Now use the maps in the display cases to begin your venture into the outer solar system.

But first, do not forget to cross the asteroid belt!

4. The asteroids appear to be about the size of (circle one):

small marbles   the heads of pins   specs of dust or gains of sand

They are so small they are microscopic!

5. Once you have found Jupiter, it appears to be about the size of a (circle one):

baseball   golfball   large marble   head of a pin

6. About how far is Jupiter from the Sun (circle one)?

15 feet   50 feet   150 feet   1500 feet

Make sure to visit all the outer solar system (Jovian) planets.

7. Name in order the next three planets you visited: _____

_____

_____

8. The Jovian Planets are all about the size of a (circle one):

baseball   golfball   large or small marble   head of a pin

Now finish your trip by finding the Kuiper Belt and Pluto.

9. Pluto's size is most similar to a (circle one):

Terrestrial planet   Jovian planet   (an) asteroid

In between an asteroid and a terrestrial planet.

10. About how far from the Sun is Pluto? (circle one)

A few tens of feet   A few hundred feet   The better part of a mile
Miles away

Something to think about--In the real solar system the space between the planets is NOT crowded with all the things you see on campus. Rather, interplanetary space is virtually empty; that is why we call it space!

An afterthought--Also, since our campus represents a solar system, it is reasonable to say that the next solar system over, with nothing between our solar system and the next (interstellar space), would be another campus. Where do you think this campus might be?

Next Door   Detroit   Ann Arbor   Chicago   Arizona

Chapter 1-The Motions of the Sky

1.1 Motions of the Stars

The Celestial Sphere

As seen from Earth, the sky can be thought of as a gigantic, imaginary sphere that is centered on Earth and to which all objects in the sky are attached. This is called the *celestial sphere*. Points on the celestial sphere that are directly above specific points on Earth are named for them. For example, the point in the sky directly above Earth's north pole is called the north celestial pole. The point above Earth's south pole is called the south celestial pole. The line directly above Earth's equator at all points is called the celestial equator.

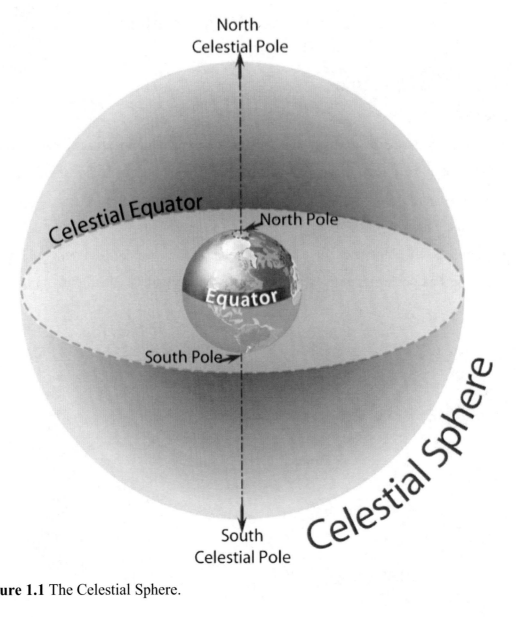

Figure 1.1 The Celestial Sphere.

From an observer's point of view, Earth simply looks like a circular disk that is centered on the observer and extends the same distance in all directions. The disk appears to end at a line called the *horizon*. This is the line where Earth ends and the sky begins. The sky also appears to center on the observer and is in the shape of a dome, or hemisphere. The point in the sky directly above the observer's head is called the *zenith*. The compass points on the horizon, due north, south, east, and west are collectively known as the *cardinal points*.

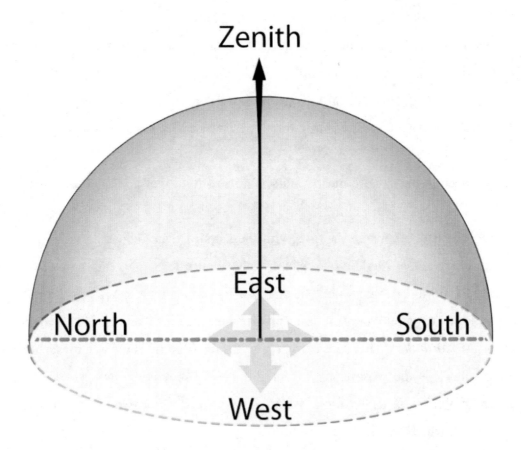

Figure 1.2 View of Earth and the sky from an observer's perspective.

The part of the celestial sphere that an observer will see depends on where they are on Earth. In Figure 1.2 the angle from the zenith down to the horizon is 90°, a right angle. An observer's zenith will always be directly over their location on Earth and they will be able to see any part of the celestial sphere, the sky that is within 90° of their zenith. An observer can see anything that is between their zenith and their horizon. An observer *cannot* see anything that is below their horizon. For instance, an observer at Earth's north pole will look straight up and see the north celestial pole *at* their local zenith. On their horizon, 90° below their zenith, they will see the celestial equator. An observer at Earth's north pole will see the entire northern half of the celestial sphere. All of the stars and other objects that are above the celestial equator will be visible to them. The entire northern half of the sky is visible and the southern half is not visible. An observer at Earth's north pole will *never* see objects that are below the celestial equator. All the objects in the southern half of the sky are below their horizon. The exact opposite is true for an observer at Earth's south pole.

The objects seen in the sky are mostly stars, points of light that appear to be fixed to the celestial sphere. Astronomers group the sky into 88 sections they call constellations. Playing connect the dots with the stars of many constellations makes familiar and easy recognizable pictures in the sky. Figure 1.3 shows the region of the sky around the north celestial pole. The star that appears almost exactly at the north celestial pole, which would make it almost exactly above Earth's north pole, is called *Polaris* or the *North Star*. There are common myths that Polaris is the brightest star in the sky or that it is the closest star to our Sun, but it is neither of these. What is special about Polaris is its location. Being above Earth's north pole, Polaris will always indicate which way is north.

Figure 1.3 A common trick for finding the North Star, *Polaris*, is to use the two outer stars of the Big Dipper's handle as *pointer* stars. A imaginary line drawn out of the Big Dipper's bowl along the line of the pointer stars will point to Polaris, the star at the end of the handle of the Little Dipper.

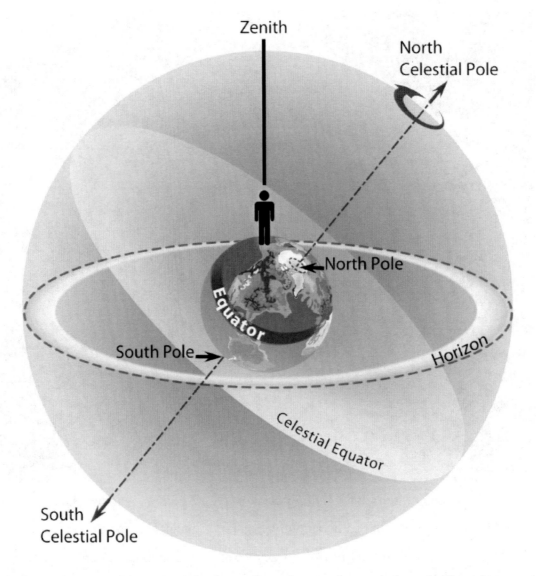

Figure 1.4 View of the celestial sphere to an observer located about halfway between the celestial equator and the north celestial pole.

An observer anywhere on Earth will always see half of the celestial sphere, but only those at the North and South poles see exactly the northern and southern halves of the sky. Much of the world's population lives about half way between Earth's equator and the North Pole. This region is called the *middle-north latitudes. Latitude* is the measurement of how far north or south a location is from the equator. An observer in a middle-north latitude location will look up and see their zenith at a point in the sky that is about halfway between the celestial equator and the north celestial pole. So they will see the north celestial pole about halfway up from the horizon to the zenith in the northern part of the sky and the celestial equator about halfway up from the horizon to the zenith in the southern part of their sky.

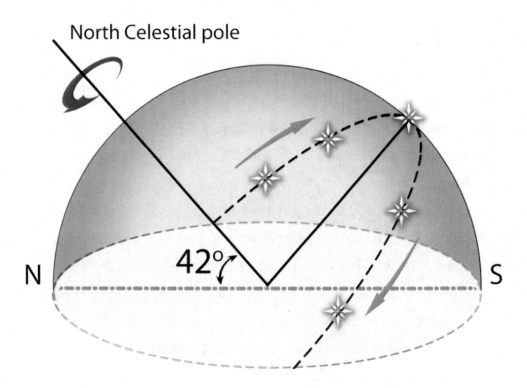

Figure 1.5 View of the sky for an observer at middle- north latitude.

All the stars appear to move in circles around the North Celestial pole from east to west as if they are attached to the celestial sphere. For stars near the North celestial pole, like those in Figure 1.3, their entire circle is above the horizon so they are stars that are visible every night. These are called *circumpolar* stars. Stars further from the north celestial pole will appear from below the horizon, or *rise* in the east, move across the southern part of the sky, reaching their highest angle above the horizon, or their highest *altitude*, when above the point due south on the horizon, then descend toward the west and disappear below the horizon, or *set* in the west. The arrows in Figure 1.5 point in the direction of the motion of the stars.

1.2 Motions of the Sun

Daily Motion

The daily motion of the Sun is similar to the motion of stars. The sun rises in the east and its altitude increases until it is directly above due south on the horizon and then its altitude decreases until it sets in the west. The line from due south to due north, passing through the zenith and dividing the sky into an eastern or rising half and a western or setting half, is called the *meridian*. The time that the Sun crosses the meridian is defined as local *noon*. The amount of time between two noons is our definition of the time measurement, *day*. The hours before the Sun reaches the meridian are called *ante meridiem,* AM being the familiar abbreviation for the morning hours. The *post meridiem* hours, abbreviated as PM, are the afternoon, the hours after the Sun has crossed the meridian.

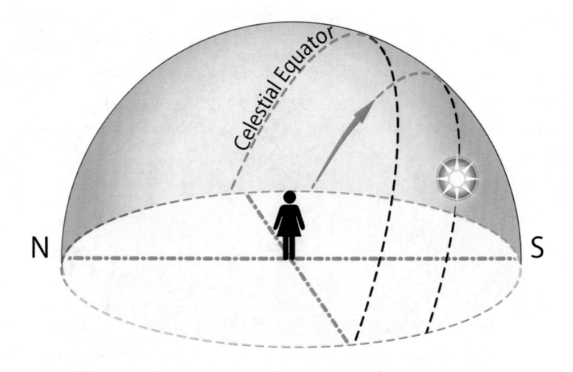

Figure 1.6 Daily motion of the Sun across the sky.

Annual Motion

The difference between the motion of the Sun and that of the stars is that a star's path through the sky will be the same every day, but the Sun's path is slightly different each day. If you observe the rising and setting positions and noon altitude of the Sun on any given day you will not notice much change in the next day or two. However, after about a week or more, you will notice a difference. The noon altitude and the rising and setting positions along the horizon will change. That the sun always rises exactly due east and always sets exactly due west is a common misconception. When the Sun's rising and settings positions are their furthest north of due east and west, the length of Sun's path through the sky is longest; this occurs about June 21, the *summer solstice*. When the Sun is high in the sky, its rays strike the ground more directly and heat the ground more efficiently, causing warmer weather. When the sun is lower in the sky the rays are much less direct. The same amount of solar energy being spread out over a larger area means the ground is being heated less efficiently, resulting in colder weather.

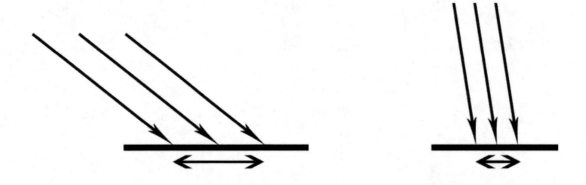

Figure 1.7 The Sun's rays from lower and higher altitudes.

Throughout the days of summer, the Sun's path gradually moves southward and the noon altitude gets lower. Eventually, by about September 21, the rising and setting positions reach *exactly* due east and due west and the Sun is up and down for 12 hours each. This is known as the *autumnal equinox*. Since the Sun's altitude is getting lower, the sun is heating the ground less efficiently and the weather, as is expected, becomes cooler in the fall.

The Sun's daily path will continue to move south, and the noon altitude will continue to decrease until about December 21, the day of the Sun's shortest path and its lowest noon altitude, called the *winter solstice*. After this solstice, the Sun's rising and setting positions will start to move north again and noon altitudes will increase. When the rising and setting positions return to due east and west, the noon altitude will be the same as it was on the autumnal equinox. This is the *vernal equinox* or first day of spring, and occurs about March 21.

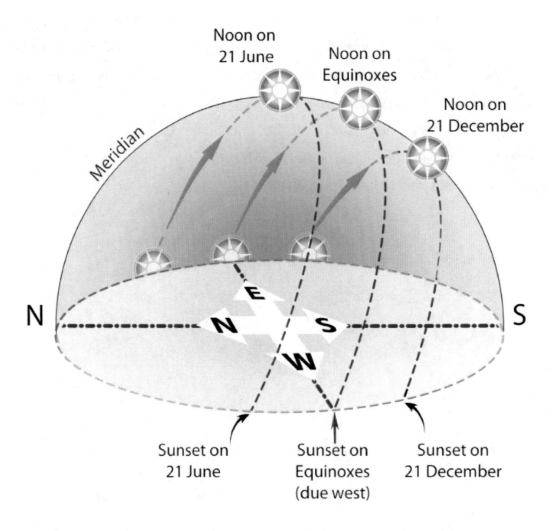

Figure 1.8 Differences in the Sun's daily path through the sky at different times of year.

The amount of time required for the Sun to completely cycle through its changing daily paths is our definition of the time measurement, *year*. So, like the day, the year is also a natural cycle of the Sun. A year is approximately 365 1/4 days. The extra 1/4-day is the reason for leap years. Our calendar is 365 days, so every 4 years a day is added at the end of February to keep our calendar in sync with the Sun.

Even though the Sun reaches its highest altitude of the day at noon usually the warmest temperatures of the day come a few hours later. Also, even though the highest noon altitudes of the Sun for the year occur in late June, usually the hottest temperatures of the year occur later; in July or August. The reasons for these time lags are that the Earth's surface does not heat up instantaneously; it takes time. It also takes time to cool off, so the *coldest* temperatures of the year are usually in January or February, not December when the Sun's altitudes are lowest. The coldest time of day is usually right before sunrise, since the ground has had the entire night to cool off.

The Ecliptic

Each star has a fixed point on the celestial sphere, like cities have a fixed point on Earth. The stars all appear to move across the sky once per day, together with the celestial sphere, but *do not* appear to move *relative* to one another. Since the Sun's path is slightly different each day, the Sun requires not just a point on celestial sphere like each star, but its own *path*. The path extending all the way around the celestial sphere and tilted at an angle of 23 1/2° to the celestial equator, intersecting it at two points, is the Sun's path through the stars. This path is called the *ecliptic*.

On any given day, as the celestial sphere appears to rotate, the Sun moves *with* it. This results in the Sun's daily motion across the sky. By the next day, the Sun will have moved a small amount along the ecliptic and its observed path will be a little different. The Sun appears to moves completely around the ecliptic once in a year.

The points on the ecliptic are named for the northern hemisphere seasons. When the Sun is at its northernmost point, it is high in the northern hemisphere and it is summer there. However, if the Sun is high in the northern hemisphere, it will be low in the southern hemisphere, making it winter there. The reverse is true for the winter solstice. Southern hemisphere seasons are opposite those in the northern hemisphere.

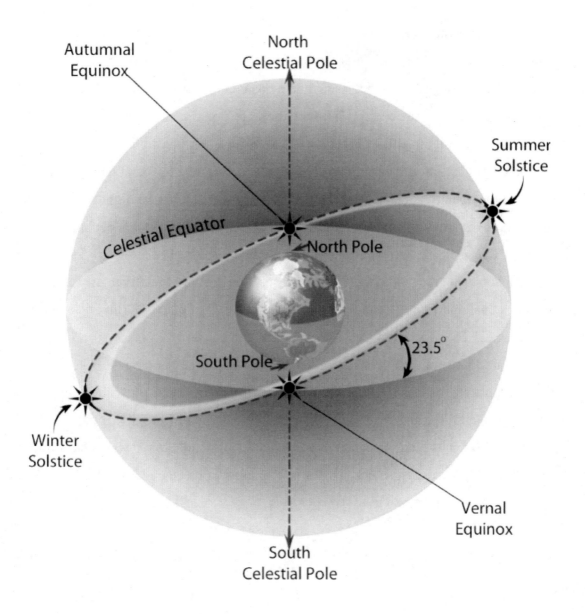

Figure 1.9 The ecliptic on the celestial sphere.

Because of the Sun's apparent motion on the ecliptic, motion around the celestial sphere, the stars visible at different times of year will change. When the Sun is at a given position on the ecliptic, stars and constellations near that location on the celestial sphere will not be seen because they are up *with* the Sun during the day. Those stars are still there, but we cannot see them because their light is washed out by the incredibly bright light of the Sun. The stars and constellations that *will* be seen are those on the opposite side of the celestial sphere from the Sun, the nighttime side. As the Sun moves around the ecliptic throughout the year, different stars become visible at night. This is the reason for constellations being seasonal. The night sky for a given season is opposite the sun's position on the celestial sphere at that time of year. Stars and constellations are visible at their highest altitudes at midnight during *their* season. Seasonal star charts are provided in **Appendix 2**. The stars that lie on or around the ecliptic are known as those of the ***zodiac***. Historically, the zodiac had been divided into 12 constellations, so the Sun spends *about* a month *in* each constellation. Among the 88 constellations into which the sky has been divided in modern times there is actually a 13th constellation, called *Ophiuchus*, that lies along the path of the ecliptic, so technically, it should also be considered a member of the zodiac.

1.3 Explanations for the Motions

Thus far, the observed motions of the stars and the Sun have been explained simply as they are seen from Earth, as if Earth is stationary and everything moves around it. The sky appears to rotate around Earth once per day and the Sun appears to move with the sky each day. The Sun also appears to revolve around the Earth on the ecliptic once per year. This is an Earth-centered or *geocentric* perspective.

There is also a Sun-centered, or *heliocentric*, perspective. From this point of view, daily motion of the sky is attributed to Earth rotating once per day from west to east *underneath* a stationary sky. This causes the sky to appear to move in the opposite direction each day. This is just like riding a merry-go-round. Everything seems to be moving around you in the direction opposite your motion.

The Sun's annual motion can be attributed to Earth revolving in an orbit around the Sun once per year, making the Sun only *appear* to be moving along the ecliptic, causing different stars to be visible at only certain time of the year.

From the heliocentric perspective, the seasonal changes in the Sun's daily path are explained by attributing the tilt not to the ecliptic, but to Earth's rotational axis. As Earth revolves around the Sun once per year, the Earth's axis always stays pointing in the same direction, toward Polaris, causing different parts of Earth to receive different amounts of sunlight.

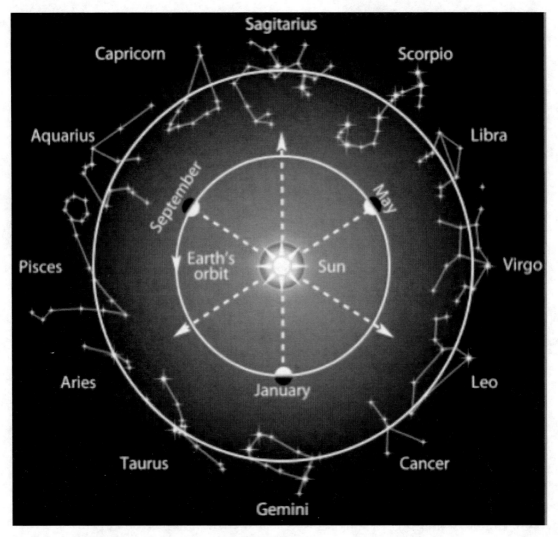

Figure 1.10 Earth's orbit causes the Sun appear to move through the stars.

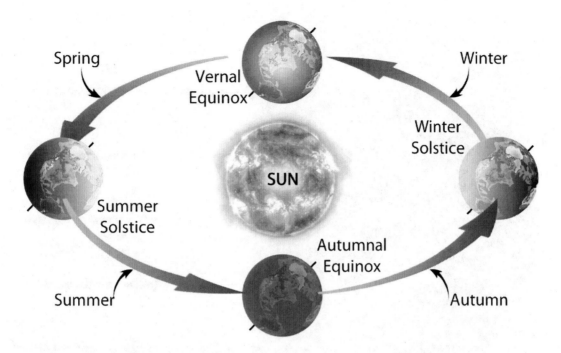

Figure 1.11 As Earth orbits the Sun; its tilted rotational axis causes the seasons (sizes and distances in figure not to scale).

Note the angles of the Sun's rays, the arrows, in Figure 1.12. The North Pole is tilted toward them so the Sun's rays make larger angles with Earth's surface, causing the Sun to appear higher in the sky, so it is summer. Also note that as Earth rotates, the northern hemisphere locations will spend more time in daylight and less in darkness, with the opposite being true in southern hemisphere where it is winter.

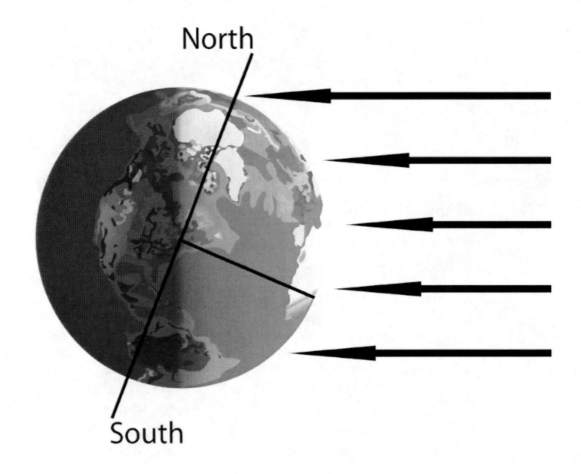

Figure 1.12 A close up of northern hemisphere summer.

1.4 Motions of the Moon

The Moon goes through the most rapid changes in both appearance and position of any object in the sky. The variations in the amount of the Moon's surface that is visible from Earth are called *phases* and the times when the Moon is visible change with the phase.

Lunar Phases

The Moon cycles through its phases in a period of about 29 1/2 days, about a month. The approximately 30-day length of our calendar month is based on the Moon's cycle of phases.

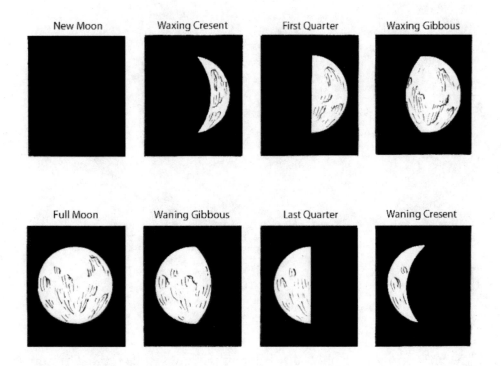

Figure 1.13 Lunar phases.

From the new to full phases, the Moon is getting brighter, so these are called *waxing* phases. The phases from full to new, when the Moon is getting dimmer, are called *waning* phases.

As the Moon orbits Earth, the sides of *both* objects facing the Sun are illuminated; the sides opposite the Sun will be dark. How the Moon will look from Earth in any given position in its orbit depends on how much of the side of the moon facing the Sun, the side receiving light, is also facing Earth.

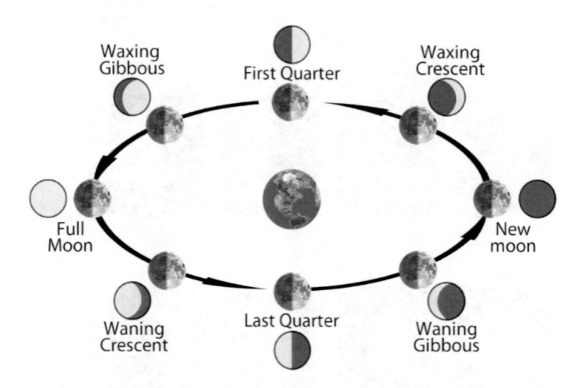

Figure 1.14 The phases of the Moon in the different positions in its orbit. The Sun's rays are coming from the right.

The best way to correctly visualize the phases of the moon from a picture like Figure 1.14 is to hold the page up so that the figure is edge-on on at eye-level and look from behind the image of Earth at the position of the Moon in which you are interested. The amount of darkness and light on the side of the Moon *facing you* should match the phase pictured at that position. See Figure 1.15.

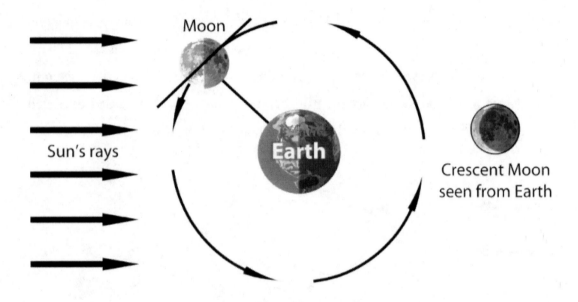

Figure 1.15 Hold the page up edge-on at eye level and look from behind the image of Earth to see which parts of the side of the Moon facing Earth are in darkness, and which are in light.

The times that the Moon will be visible can also be determined from the figures; it is noon at the point on the Earth directly below the Sun. In Figures 1.14, 1.15 and 1.16 that is the point on the far left of the image of Earth. At the point opposite noon, it is midnight. Viewed from above the North Pole, Earth rotates counter-clockwise. This defines the time at all other points on Earth. For instance, at the point halfway between noon and midnight, at the bottom of the image of Earth in the figures, it is 6 PM, and at the point halfway between midnight and noon, at the top of the image of Earth in the figures, it is 6 AM. These are also the times of sunset and sunrise, the positions where an observer would cross from being in daylight to darkness and vice-versa.

The time on this *Earth-clock* that the Moon is directly above, in any phase, is the time that the Moon will be seen *overhead*, at its highest altitude of the day in the southern sky. The moon will be visible from any point on Earth for the 12 hours that the point is facing the Moon, so the rising time of the Moon is six hours before it is overhead and the setting time six hours after that time, 12 hours after it rose. See Figure 1.16.

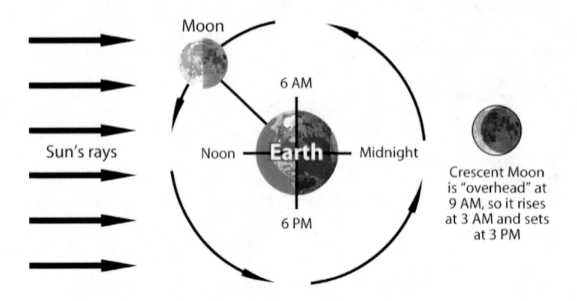

Figure 1.16 Determining the rising and setting times for the Moon.

In Figure 1.16, the Moon is directly above 9 AM on the Earth-clock, so it must have risen at 3 AM and will set at 3 PM.

The Far Side of the Moon

As the Moon orbits Earth, the same side always faces towards Earth. There is a *far side* that no observer on Earth ever sees. Astronauts orbiting of the Moon in the Apollo 8 spacecraft first photographed the far side of the Moon on Christmas Eve, 1968. The reason is that the Moon rotates in exactly the same amount of time that it takes to revolve around Earth, a month. That the Moon not rotating causes this is a common myth.

Figure 1.17 The near and far sides of the Moon.

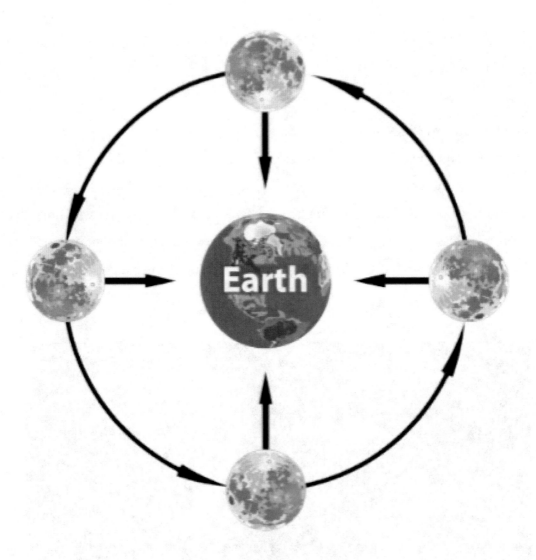

Figure 1.18 The same side of the Moon always faces Earth because the Moon rotates in the same amount of time that it takes to revolve around Earth.

1.5 Eclipses

From Earth, the Sun and the Moon both appear to be about the same angular size, about 1/2°. A fist held out at arm's length has an angular size of about 10°, a thumb about 2°, a finger 1°, and a pinky-finger about 1/2°. A pinky held out at arm's length can block out the Sun or the Moon. This is always true whether the Sun or the Moon are high overhead or close to the horizon. They both seem much larger when close to the horizon, since there are near objects with which they can be compared. This can be tested. No matter how large either object looks, a pinky finger can still cover them both.

The coincidence that the Sun and the Moon have the same angular size is the reason that events known as *eclipses* are so interesting. As indicated by the name, an **eclipse** can occur when the Moon is on or near the ecliptic. If the Moon is on the ecliptic when it is in between the Sun and Earth, the new Moon phase, it will block out the view of the Sun from Earth. This is a *solar eclipse.* If Earth is between the Sun and the Moon, the full Moon phase, Earth's shadow will cover the Moon. This is a *lunar eclipse.*

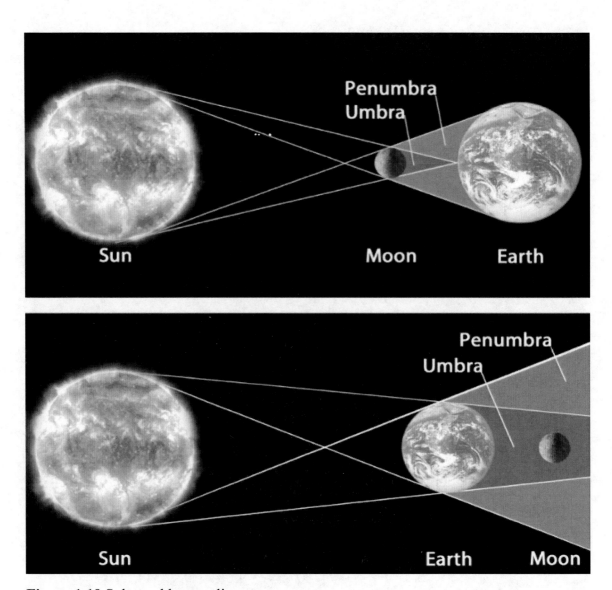

Figure 1.19 Solar and lunar eclipses.

Figure 1.20 A total solar eclipse and a total lunar eclipse.

Eclipses do not occur at every new and full Moon. This is because the Moon's orbit is tilted about 5° from the ecliptic. The ecliptic and the Moon's orbit are shown in geocentric perspective in Figure 1.21. The intersection points are called *nodes*. The line passing through Earth and connecting the nodes is known as the *line of nodes*. When the Sun and Moon are both on the line of nodes at the same time, an eclipse will occur. The Sun traverses the ecliptic once per year, so it will be on the line of nodes twice per year. The Moon orbits Earth once per month, so it will be on the line of nodes 24 times a year. If the Moon crosses a node when the Sun is also at a node there will be an eclipse. If the Sun is not at a node, there will not be an eclipse. Since the Moon travels through the sky must faster than the Sun, it usually comes near enough to a node whenever the Sun is at one, so that eclipses occur about twice per year. The times that the Sun is at or near a node are called *eclipse-seasons*. If the Sun and Moon are at the same node, a solar eclipse occurs. If they are at opposite nodes, a lunar eclipse occurs. If the Sun and the Moon are not exactly lined up, but are close, a partial eclipse occurs.

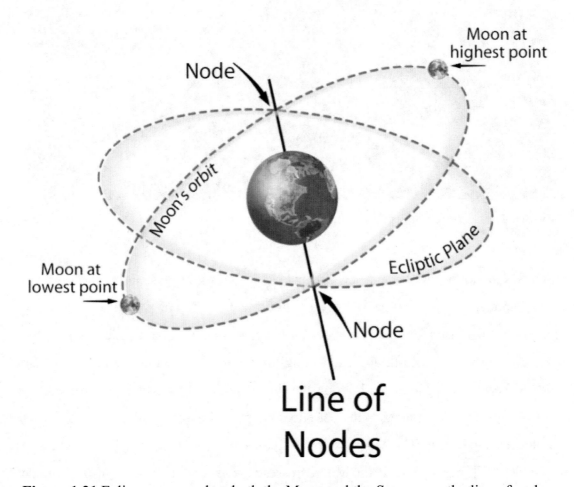

Figure 1.21 Eclipses occur when both the Moon and the Sun are on the line of nodes.

Referring back to Figure 1.19 shows that most people are likely to see more lunar eclipses in their lifetime than solar eclipses. During a lunar eclipse, anyone on the entire night side of Earth, the side facing away from the Sun, can see the full

Moon eclipsed. During a solar eclipse, only people in the specific position on Earth covered by the Moon's shadow will see the eclipse.

1.6 Precession

The motions discussed thus far are *rotation*, an object spinning on an axis, and *revolution*, one object in orbit around another. Rotation is responsible for the daily motion of the sky. Revolution is responsible for annual motion in the sky.

A third motion is called *precession*. Precession is likely most familiar as the motion of a top when it is running out of energy and about to fall. The rotational axis traces out the path of a cone. The north celestial Pole, the point in the sky directly above Earth's north pole, traces out a circular path through the stars about once every 26,000 years. As with other motions, precession could be attributed to either the celestial sphere or Earth. Although it takes 26,000 years, much longer than rotation or revolution, the effects of precession can be noticed in much smaller amounts of time. Since precession actually changes the position of the north celestial pole, the star located at or closest to this point will not always be the same. Polaris is our current North or *Pole Star* and obviously has been ever since it was first named for its position. However, other stars have been the pole star in the past and different stars will be in the future.

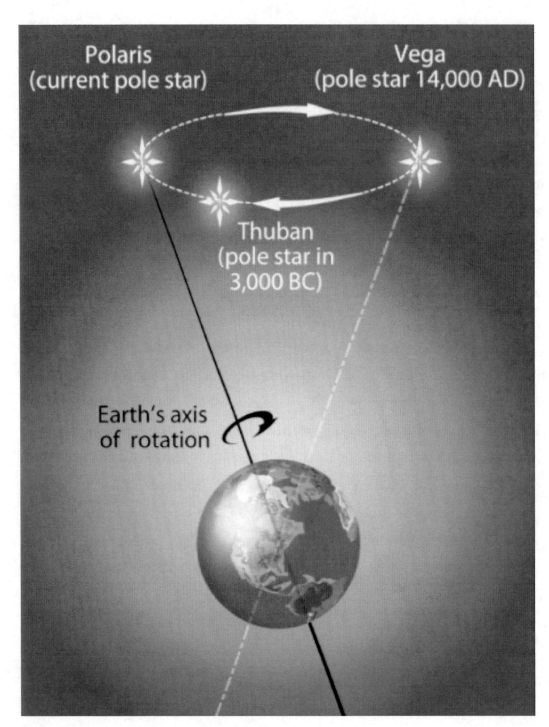

Figure 1.22 Precession

Changing the direction that Earth's axis is pointing also affects our perception of the seasons. Our calendar is based on the observed motion of the Sun. If precession occurred without adjustment of the calendar, the seasons would appear to be occurring in months different from what we expect. For instance, when the calendar reads July, the northern hemisphere is pointed toward the Sun and experiences high Sun angles and long daylight periods, resulting in warm summer weather. After about 13,000 years, half of a complete precession, the northern hemisphere will be pointing away from the Sun at that particular position in its orbit. Summer will still occur, but when Earth is on the opposite side of the Sun. So, according to the calendar, summer will occur in January and winter in July. This effect is noticeable in much less than 13,000 years, so minor adjustments are periodically made in the calendar to compensate for precession.

Review Questions

1. Describe the daily path of most stars. Where do they rise, reach their highest altitude, and then set?

2. Explain what is special about Polaris, the North Star.

3. About how long does the celestial sphere (the sky) appear to take to move around Earth once?

4. Describe the daily path of the Sun; where does the Sun rise, reach its highest altitude, and then set?

5. When does the Sun reach its highest altitude for the day? When will the Sun reach that altitude again?

6. What are the differences between the Sun's daily path in the summer and in the winter?

7. On what day(s) does the Sun rise exactly at due east and set exactly at due west?

8. How long does the Sun take to move all the way around the ecliptic (completely through the zodiac)?

9. During what month will Australia experience its shortest day of the year?

10. Explain how use of the term "Dark Side of the Moon" can cause confusion when referring to the Moon's far side.

11. Refer to Figure 1.19. What kind of eclipse would be observed from the Moon while the Earth is experiencing a lunar eclipse? What would be observed from the Moon while Earth is experiencing a solar eclipse?

12. Does a New Moon occur on the same day of every month on the calendar? Explain your answer.

13. Is the Moon ever visible during the day? Explain why or why not.

14. Explain the effect that precession can have on a calendar.

15. Name the motion responsible for the time measurements: day, week, month, and year.

Tutorial--Mapping the Solar System from Earth

There are two principle points of view in the sky: (1) geocentric (Earth centered) and (2) heliocentric (Sun centered). This exercise is about learning to convert between the two views.

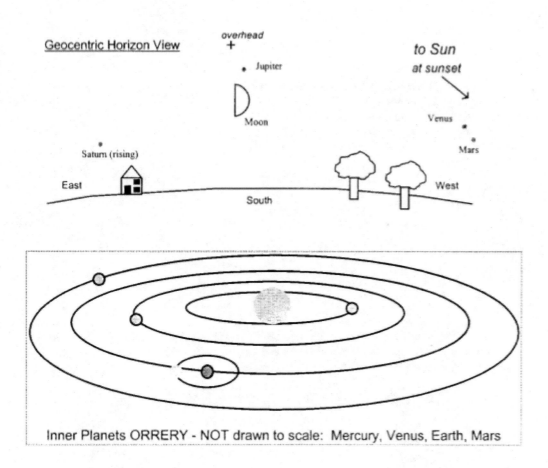

Inner Planets ORRERY - NOT drawn to scale: Mercury, Venus, Earth, Mars

Part I: Rising and Setting Times

As seen from above, Earth appears to rotate counterclockwise. *Figure I-a* shows a top view of Earth and an observer at noon. Note that our Sun appears overhead when standing at the equator.

1. In Figure I-a, sketch and label the positions of the observer at midnight, 6 pm (sunset) and 6 am (sunrise).

Figure I-a: Observer Positions on Earth
[Observer is at Equator]

to Sun

Noon

2. Consider *Figure I-b,* which shows Earth, Moon, Mars, and Venus. At what time would each of these sky objects be overhead? Remember that Earth spins counter-clockwise when viewed from above. [*Hint: Make use of Figure I-a*]

Time Overhead:

Venus: _____

Moon: _____

Mars: _____

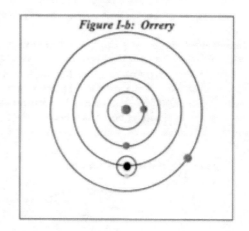

Figure I-b: Orrery

3. If Earth spins in 24 hours, that means that each sky object is visible for about 12 hours. What time will the sky objects shown in Figure I-b rise and set? Complete the table below? *Each member of your team should fill in the data for one sky object.*

Sky Object	Rise Time	Time Overhead	Set Time
Sun			
Venus			
Moon			
Mars			

4. Using complete sentences, explain why our Sun is not visible at midnight. Add a sketch of Earth, Sun, and observer in the space provided to support your explanation.

Narrative	*Sketch*

Part II: Converting Geocentric to Heliocentric

5. *Figure II-a* shows the horizon view of the first quarter Moon and Saturn visible at sunset. On the orrery shown in *Figure II-b*, sketch and label the position of Jupiter, Moon and Saturn. Use an arrow to indicate the direction to our Sun. Start by indicating the position of the observer at sunset. After completing the diagram, complete the table.

Sky Object	Rise Time	Set Time
Sun		
Jupiter		
Moon		
Saturn		

Figure II-a: Horizon View at Sunset (6 pm)

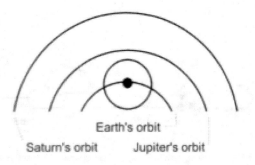

Earth's orbit

Saturn's orbit   Jupiter's orbit

Orrery Not Drawn to Scale !!
Figure II-b

6. If Neptune is visible overhead in the southern sky at sunrise (6 am) sketch the relative positions of Sun, Earth, Neptune, and observer in an orrery in the space below.

Part III: Converting Heliocentric to Geocentric

7. *Figure III-a* shows the position of Mercury, Venus, Earth, Mars, and Moon. On the horizon diagram, *Figure III-b*, sketch and label the positions of Mercury, Venus, Mars, a comet, and Moon at <u>midnight</u>.

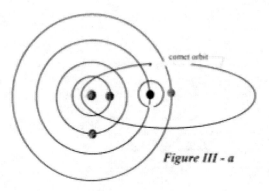

Figure III - a

Figure III-b: Geocentric Horizon View at Midnight

overhead

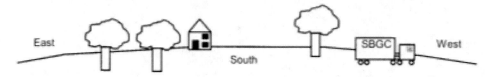

East

South

SBGC

West

8. Venus is often called the *morning star* or the *evening star*. Why is it never seen at midnight?

Chapter 2-The History of Astronomy

2.1 Prehistoric Astronomy

Astronomy is arguably the oldest of the sciences. Stonehenge is only the most famous of many prehistoric ruins all over the world that show that our ancestors were watching the sky.

Figure 2.1 Stonehenge

Why were our ancestors such avid sky watchers? Many of them lived in nomadic tribes that were following food supplies, which also likely meant with warmer weather. If people had waited for weather changes, they may have moved too late. Using the motions in the sky was a more reliable way to keep track of time. The annual reappearance of a certain bright star or a specific positioning of the Sun or Moon could indicate when it was time to move on. It is also likely that they used the positions of certain stars such as the Polaris to navigate.

The advent of agriculture was the beginning of civilization. This allowed people to stay in one place. Watching the sky continued to be just as important so people knew when to plant and harvest crops and when to seek warmer clothing and shelter.

Many ancient civilizations were geographically isolated from one another, and communication, other than through wars and conquest, was limited. As a result of this isolation, there was very little exchange of knowledge and discoveries. Not until about 2,500 years ago did enough information exchange occur to establish *worldviews*, ideas or beliefs shared by a significant number of peoples in different places. The first worldview of science came from the ancient Greeks.

2.2 Greek Astronomy

Intellectuals in ancient Greece were called philosophers. There were different kinds of philosophy, but the study of the world and its workings was called natural philosophy. The word *science* comes from the Greek for *natural philosophy*. Considered one of the greatest of all the natural philosophers, *Aristotle* is often revered as the world's first scientist.

Aristotle had some ideas about Earth. First, he thought that it did not move. He felt that if it did we should feel it; there would always be a wind opposite the direction of the motion, like in a ship on the ocean. He also believed that Earth was round. The introduction of the idea that Earth is spherically shaped is often attributed to Columbus during the Renaissance. However, that idea, along with many others, were things that were known during the time of classical civilization, forgotten during the Dark Ages, and rediscovered or reintroduced during the Renaissance.

Aristotle also thought that Earth was central to the *cosmos*, or as it is called today, the *universe*. Based on the observed motions of the stars, the Sun, and the Moon, discussed in Chapter 1, thinking Earth is central is a very natural idea.

For the next 500 years, different Greek astronomers studied the heavens and many contributed to this first worldview, but we owe much to the one who recorded it so it could be passed down to subsequent generations, *Claudius Ptolemy*. Ptolemy lived in

Alexandria, Egypt during the 2nd century CE. This was not Egypt of the Pharaohs, but rather Roman-dominated Egypt.

Around 150 CE Ptolemy compiled much of what was known about ancient Greek astronomy in a work called *The Almagest*, a combination Greek-Arabic word for "The Greatest." *The Almagest* contained what were indeed the greatest theories about astronomy, and perhaps even all of science, that the world had yet seen.

Figure 2.2 Aristotle and Ptolemy

2.3 The Geocentric System

Ancient Greek astronomy consisted of the geocentric explanations for the motions of the stars and the Sun. Many, including Ptolemy, just considered the ideas devices for explaining observations, and were not concerned with whether the explanations represented physical reality. Either way, the development of the explanations in the geocentric model or system may have developed as described below.

The first observations showed that the stars all seemed to be moving together in circular paths around the Earth. So a logical explanation was that they were all fixed to a gigantic sphere that rotated around an unmoving Earth once per day. This is a literal interpretation of the celestial sphere.

Further observations showed that the Sun and the Moon moved independently of the stars and therefore needed their own spheres. Both spheres had to be in front of the background stars they appeared to move through, with the Moon sphere being closer than the Sun's.

Next, several objects were noticed that looked like stars, points of light, although brighter than most, but which also moved with their own paths like the Sun and Moon. These 5 objects were referred to as the wanderers *or planetes,* the Greek word for wanderer, and the origin of the word *planet.* One sphere had to be added to the model for each planet, and they were named for the Roman gods Mercury, Venus, Mars, Jupiter, and Saturn.

Observation showed that there were clearly two types of planet. Mercury and Venus were never seen very far from the Sun and then, only in the early morning right *before* sunrise or the early evening right *after* sunset. Because of this, they were considered *inferior* or below the Sun, closer to Earth than the Sun. Mars, Jupiter, and Saturn, however, could be seen at any time of night and were sometimes even up *all* night. These planets were considered above the Sun or *superior*, farther than the Sun from Earth.

Adding spheres for the planets was not the final complication. When observed day after day, a planet's motion relative to the stars appears to be generally eastward, but at times, a planet would stop its eastward motion, move west for a while, and then resume its eastward motion. Any model attempting to explain the motions in the sky would have to account for this *retrograde motion.*

Retrograde motion was explained in the geocentric system by a planet moving in a circular path called an *epicycle*. The center of the epicycle was on another circular path called the *deferent* that centered on Earth. The two circular motions occurring simultaneously result in retrograde loops. It was also necessary to "fix" the epicycles of the inferior planets to a line between the Earth and the Sun so they would always appear near the Sun in the sky.

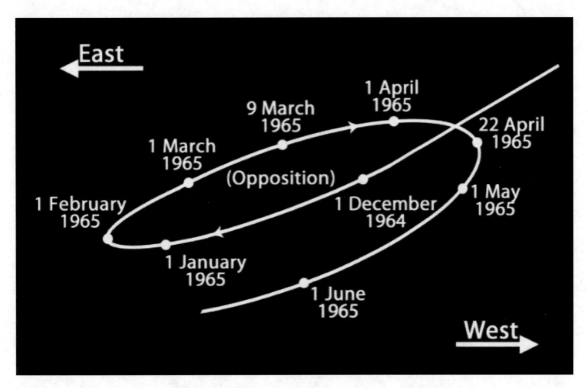

Figure 2.3 Retrograde motion of a planet.

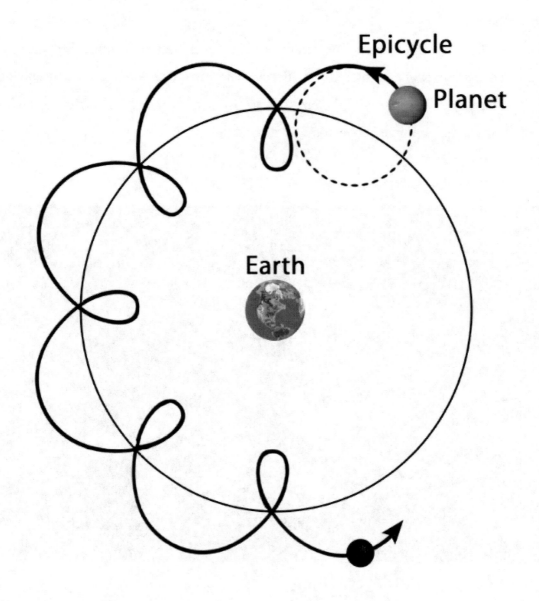

Figure 2.4 Path of a planet on an epicycle on a deferent.

The explanation of retrograde motion completed the geocentric *model*. Once a model satisfactorily explains everything that has been observed, it is called a scientific *theory*. A scientific theory is the best explanation of something based on the available data. A theory is the highest status that can be achieved in science. Theories must be tested over and over again, and there is no final test that makes a theory ultimately considered correct or makes it law. A theory can be overturned at any time by new observations, no matter how successful it has been. If new observations show that the theory is not valid, it must be either revised or discarded.

The word "theory" has a different meaning in science than in any other context. In criminal justice, a theory about a crime is a guess that must be proven before a conviction can occur. This is similar to what is called a *hypothesis* in science. In science a theory is the best explanation we have.

The term law is often incorrectly used as a colloquialism for a well-tested theory. The use of the term *law* in science is for an observed relationship. A law is *what* we observe, while a theory is *why* it occurs.

2.4 The Scientific Method

As the ancient Greek astronomers developed the geocentric system, observations were made, followed by attempts at explanations. The explanations were then tested by further observations. When the further observation revealed the current explanations inadequate, the explanations were revised. The process of explanation, observation, and revision was repeated as many times as necessary to satisfactorily explain all observations.

This process of observation, explanation, testing, and revision is called the *scientific method*. Science is *not* just a body of knowledge; it is rather the repeated process of observation, explanation, and revision by which knowledge is attained and understood. Many well-established theories have been successfully tested so many times that they may seem like a collection of facts, but to get to that point the process of science was repeatedly applied. Many less firmly established theories seem more like "works in progress." These are examples of the scientific process in action. Eventually the ideas may be widely accepted, or they may not be and will be replaced by new ideas. Only repeated application of the scientific process over time will tell.

Examination of the Geocentric or *Ptolemaic system*, as it was also known after the publication of *The Almagest*, shows all the features of a good scientific theory. The model worked, it included explanations for all observed motions, and it could be used to make accurate predictions. The explanations also had a common-sense aspect to them. The motions that were observed, a rotating sky, and revolutions of the Sun, Moon, and planets around the Earth were what appeared to be really happening. Despite the complexities of extra spheres for the planets and epicycles for their retrograde motions, this common-sense quality allowed the model to be perceived as simple, and simplicity is also a desirable quality of a scientific theory.

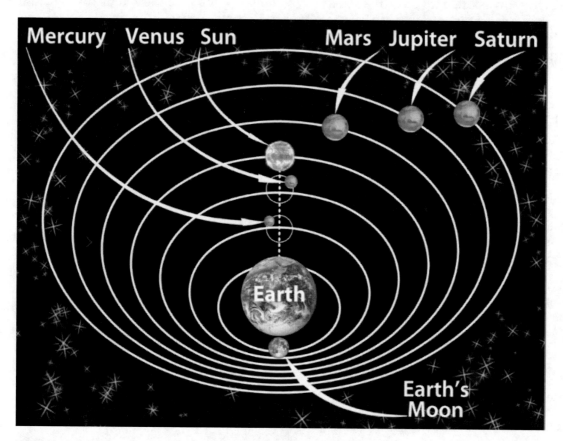

Figure 2.5 The geocentric or Earth-centered Ptolemaic system.

2.5 The Heliocentric System

Despite the success of the geocentric model, another model did exist, not only prior to the time of Ptolemy but also prior to Aristotle. *Aristarchus* of Samos proposed a heliocentric model; the Sun was central and the Earth was one of the planets in orbit. He believed this because of calculations he made that showed that the Sun was much larger than Earth, so it made more sense that the Sun would be central.

Not too much else is known about Aristarchus' ideas because his book about his work was one of many lost in the burning of the Alexandria Library. Much of the knowledge of classical civilization was kept in this great storehouse and was destroyed in a raid of conquest on Alexandria toward the end of the classical period, around 400 CE.

Ptolemy's *Almagest* was one of the few works that did survive, and Ptolemy actually mentions Aristarchus' heliocentric idea and concedes that attributing the observed motions in the sky to rotation and revolution of Earth rather than the sky and the Sun, as was discussed in Chapter 1, is a viable explanation, but too complex. He felt that since everything could be explained in terms of the motions we actually see occurring, there was no reason to say they just *appeared* to be happening because of motions of Earth, especially when there was no convincing evidence that Earth moved.

Figure 2.6 Copernicus

The heliocentric system resurfaced in the 1500s with the Polish cleric *Nicholas Copernicus*. It is not clear whether he reintroduced it when he learned of Aristarchus' ideas or if he thought of independently.

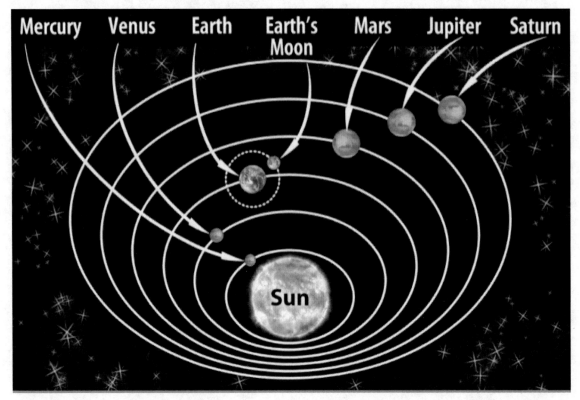

Figure 2.7 The heliocentric or Sun-centered Copernican system.

According to the Copernican system, retrograde motion occurs when one planet passes another in orbit around the Sun, each planet observing the other in retrograde motion. The outer planet will observe the inner retrograding after it passes and goes around the far side of the Sun. The inner planet observes something similar to a faster car passing a slower one on the highway. When you look in the rear-view mirror, the car you have passed will appear to be moving backward.

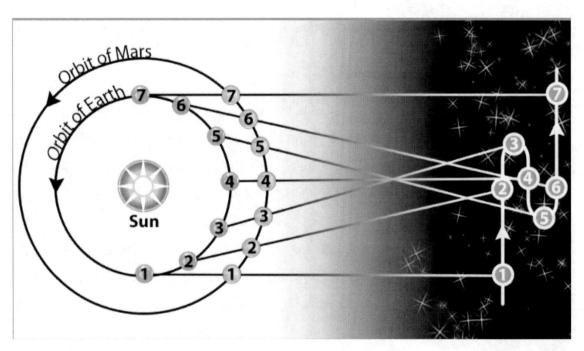

Figure 2.8 Retrograde Motion in the Copernican system.

The Copernican system seemed to work and it could be argued that the explanation for retrograde motion was simpler than epicycles, even though it still involved the Earth moving and the observed motion, like all observed motions in the heliocentric system, was considered an apparent, not actual, motion. However, when it came to making predictions of the positions of objects, the Copernican system did not seem to work as well as the Ptolemaic system.

After the end of classical civilization, most flirtations with science during the next thousand years, the *Dark Ages,* as they have been called, were dismissed by the ruling Catholic Church as mysticism or witchcraft. By Copernicus' time, officials of the church had decided that science was not going away, so it had to be controlled. The theologian St. Thomas Aquinas was a leader in this point of view. He understood the power of the scientific process, and was instrumental in getting the church to set policy on science. As a result, Ptolemy's *Almagest* was adopted as the church's doctrine on astronomy. Since, according to the theory, Earth was the center of the universe and people were dominant on Earth, the geocentric system gave people an importance in the grand scheme of the universe as in the Bible. Studying any other astronomical theory was declared scientific heresy, a capitol offense.

Being a churchman himself, Copernicus knew what could happen if he publicly championed the heliocentric system, so he only circulated his ideas among trusted friends and did not publish his work until he was on his deathbed in 1543. His book on the heliocentric system was called *De Revolutionibus*. The term revolution does not refer to the Earth revolving around the Sun, but rather a revolution or change in scientific thinking. Copernicus died believing that his work would cause the world to change its view from a geocentric to a heliocentric cosmos. He was right. The over 100-year period following his death that it took to make this transition is today referred to as the *Copernican Revolution*.

The heliocentric system did not seem to pose an immediate threat to the church-supported geocentric system, but not only the Catholic church, but also the Lutheran church, which had recently broken away from the Catholics, put *De Revolutionibus* on a list of forbidden books. There is some disagreement as to how strong Martin Luther's verbal attack of the late Copernicus actually was, but the work *was* banned causing many to become curious about the book that they were not supposed to see. By their reactions, the churches may have actually promoted the system they were trying to suppress.

By the late 1500s there were many debates about which system was better. The geocentric system had tradition and the law on its side and it actually worked better for predictions than the heliocentric system, but there was one feature of the heliocentric system that did not exist in the geocentric system, a method for determining the distances between the Sun and the planets *relative* to Earth's distance.

The actual distance between Earth and the Sun was not known in Copernicus' time; it was just referred to as 1 *Astronomical Unit* or *AU* for short. Without going into the details of the method, basically the distance from the Sun to the planets in astronomical units can be determined with a geometrical construction making use of some simple observations of the angular separation between the planets and the Sun.

No one in Copernicus' time actually knew whether or not the values were "correct." However, just the fact that they could be determined was an interesting feature of the Copernican system, a feature interesting enough to warrant further study.

Planet	Copernicus' Value (AU)	Modern Value (AU)
Mercury	.38	0.387
Venus	.72	0.723
Mars	1.52	1.524
Jupiter	5.2	5.203
Saturn	9.2	9.539

Table 2.1 Copernicus' values for the distances from the Sun to each planet compared to modern values.

The Copernican Revolution

2.6 Tycho and Kepler

One of the first astronomers to attempt to determine which system worked better by observation was the Danish nobleman *Tycho* Brahe. Tycho (history has remembered him by his first name) rented the island of Hveen from the king of Denmark and constructed one of western civilization's first observatories. Tycho had no telescopes at his observatory; his observations were strictly naked eye. He made observations for many years and kept careful track of the positions of planets, mostly Mars, as they moved through the sky. Tycho did not believe that Earth moved, and therefore felt that his observations would support the geocentric system. The reason Tycho did not believe that Earth moved was because of the absence of *stellar parallax* in his observations.

Parallax is the apparent shift in the position of an object due to a change in the point of view of the observer. To observe parallax, hold your thumb out at arm's length and, without moving it, close one eye and shake your head or keep your head still and alternately open and close each of your eyes. You will notice your thumb appearing to move even though you know that it is not. The apparent motion of your thumb is caused by parallax.

Although some thought that all stars were fixed to a giant sphere and therefore equally distant, others made the reasonable assumption that the brighter ones were closer than the dimmer ones. If the Earth was indeed in orbit around the Sun, some of the brighter stars should show a parallax shift over the six months it would take the Earth to move from one side of the Sun to the other. Tycho never observed this stellar parallax. To him, this was convincing evidence that the Earth did *not* move and was the reason for his support of the geocentric system.

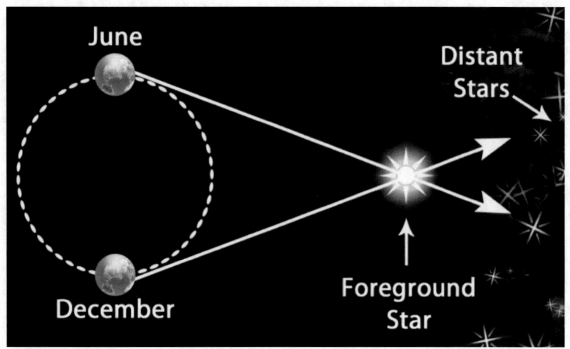

Figure 2.9 Stellar parallax due to a moving Earth.

Tycho was an example of what in science is called an experimentalist. He was the greatest observational genius of his time; gathering the best astronomical data that the world had yet seen. However, he was not a theorist. A theorist is a scientist who can take data and use it to explain what is being observed. It is possible to do both, but most scientists are better at being one or the other. Tycho developed a model that was a cross between the geocentric and heliocentric systems, with all the planets orbiting the Sun and the Sun orbiting Earth, but he was not satisfied with his system. He needed the help of a theorist.

Figure 2.10 Tycho and his observatory, Uraniburg.

Johannes Kepler, a German mathematician teaching in Graz, Austria, was that theorist. Tycho was in Austria by this time as well, working as the royal mathematician for the Archduke in Prague around 1600. Tycho had an argument with the King of Denmark and, being very arrogant, refused to back down and was kicked off his island and out of Denmark. Kepler had been working on his own version of the heliocentric system, based on geometry, when Tycho invited him to come to Prague. Kepler was reluctant at first, but had no choice when Graz was taken over by Catholics preceding the 30-Years' War after the Reformation. His school was closed and he, being a devout Lutheran, was exiled.

Kepler could not make his geometric model work, and knew Tycho had better data than he had yet seen. Unfortunately, Tycho would not give Kepler full access to the data, perhaps being paranoid that Kepler would take credit for everything that was learned from the data. Just when Kepler was ready to leave in 1601, Tycho died of an exploded bladder after drinking too much at a party he had thrown for the Archduke. Kepler inherited Tycho's job, and the data, and could finally get to work.

Figure 2.11 Kepler and his geometric model.

The Laws of Planetary Motion

Kepler worked for 8 years trying to fit Tycho's data to his geometric model. His idea was that the 5 spaces between the spheres that held up the 6 planets (including Earth) were based on nesting the Pythagorean Solids one inside another. The ancient Greek mathematician Pythagoras had discovered that there were only 5 three-dimensional shapes that had identical sides. When his model did not work, Kepler assumed it was Copernicus' calculations of the distance between the planets and the Sun, and not his model, that was the problem. He believed that Tycho's data would show that he was correct.

According to Tycho's data, the orbit of Mars was within eight angular or arc minutes (1'=1/60 of 1°) of being circular. However, the data was accurate to 1 minute, so Kepler realized that the path was actually elliptical, not circular. This was the beginning of Kepler's derivation of what would later be called the *Laws of Planetary Motion*.

Kepler derived three relationships from Tycho's data. Kepler's first law, the *Law of Elliptical Orbits,* states that a planet orbits the Sun in an elliptical path with the Sun located at one of the off-center focus points. This causes the planet's distance from the Sun to vary throughout its orbit. The point closest to the Sun is called *perihelion*. The farthest point is called *aphelion*. A line drawn from one side of the ellipse through the foci to the other side is called the major axis. Half this distance, the *semimajor axis*, is the planet's average distance from the Sun.

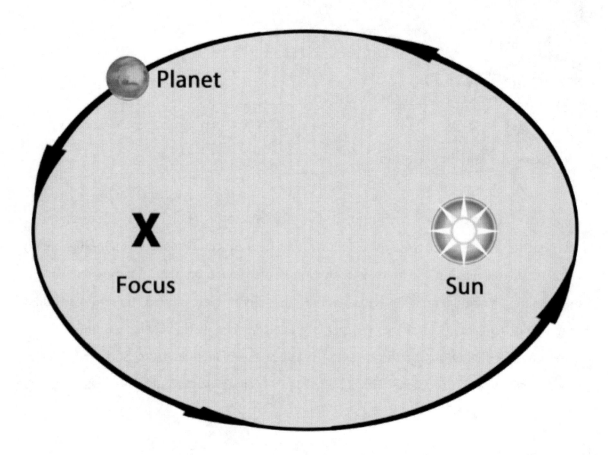

Figure 2.12 Planets orbit around the Sun in an elliptical path with the Sun located at one of the focus points.

The measurement of how far an ellipse is from being a circle is called the *eccentricity*. An ellipse with zero eccentricity is a circle. Higher eccentricity means a more elliptical orbit. Most planetary orbits have very low eccentricity. Earth's average distance from the Sun, one astronomical unit (AU), is about 150 million (150,000,000) kilometers or 93 million miles. At perihelion, in January, it is only about 1.5 million (1,500,000) miles closer than that. At aphelion, in July, it is only that much farther. One and a half million miles may sound like a lot, but it is only about 1.5 percent of the Earth's average orbital distance. Even though these eccentricities are small, they are significant. Copernicus' use of circles, and not ellipses, was the reason that when it came to predicting the positions of objects his model never worked quite as well as Ptolemy's geocentric system.

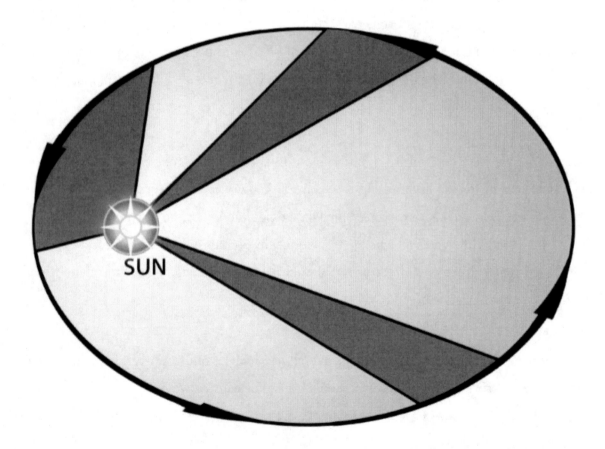

Figure 2.13 A line between a planet and the Sun will sweep out equal areas in equal amounts of time.

The *Law of Equal Areas* states that as a planet orbits the Sun, the line between the Sun and the planet sweeps out equal areas in equal amounts of time. In Figure 2.14 the area of each wedge, swept out in the same time, **t**, is the same. This also means that the planet must be moving faster, covering more distance in its orbit in the same amount of time, when it is closer to the Sun and slower, covering less distance, when farther away. This consequence led Kepler to believe that the Sun had an effect on the planet that was stronger when the planet was closer to the Sun. This is foreshadowing the idea of gravity.

The third law is called the *Harmonic Law*. Kepler believed in what he called "cosmic harmony," that the planets sang and changed pitch as the speed of their orbits varied. He felt that a simple relationship should exist between the *period*, **p**, the amount of time a planet takes to complete its orbit, and the average distance between the planet and the Sun, the semimajor axis, **a**, of the elliptical orbit. It took him 10 years after he formulated the first two laws in 1609, but he finally determined the relatively simple relationship that the square of the orbital period is equal to the cube of the average orbital distance.

Kepler's laws were derived from Tycho's observational data. Kepler had no underlying physical reason for the relationships; he did not know *why* they were true, just that the observations *showed* that they were. Since he did not know *why*, he did not have a *theory*. In science this is known as an *empirical* relationship. Kepler's laws are a perfect example of the currently accepted correct use of the term *law* in science. They are relationships based strictly on observational data.

Kepler was not pleased by what he discovered. He had set out to prove his theory based on the geometric solids, but found something else instead. However, he had the courage to accept what the data showed over what he wished were true. This is a very important quality of a good scientist.

Besides their obvious contributions to astronomy and the Copernican Revolution, Tycho and Kepler also made two very important refinements of the scientific method. Tycho was among the first to take large amounts of precise data, and Kepler was among the first to painstakingly analyze data to determine what can be learned from it. To this day, the accumulation and analysis of data are two of the most important parts of the scientific process.

2.7 Galileo and the Telescope

When Kepler recognized that as a consequence of the Law of Equal Areas, planets move faster when closer to the Sun, he thought that there must be an effect that the Sun has on the planets that varied with distance. He realized that further investigation of this was in the realm of physics. Kepler wrote to a physicist that he knew of in Italy and asked him for help in pursuing the idea. This physicist was in the process of conducting experiments that would change the world's view of physics, but he wasn't interested in Kepler's Laws. This doesn't mean he was not interested in astronomy. He was, in fact, like Kepler, an avid supporter of the Copernican system. However, he believed that astronomy should be studied in another way, with a telescope.

Galileo Galilee did not invent the telescope, but he is the first person known to use it for astronomy. In 1609, the same year that Kepler finished the first two laws of planetary motion, Galileo began making controversial observations. He discovered craters and mountains on the Moon and spots on the Sun. Although not having anything to do with whether or not the Earth orbits the Sun, these observations suggested imperfections in the "heavenly spheres." He was brought in front of the Inquisition for publicizing these observations, and was warned not to continue on his heretical course. Next, he turned his telescope to the brighter planets. He discovered four moons orbiting Jupiter, and that Venus went through phases very similar to those of our Moon.

Jupiter having moons does not challenge the Earth's central position, but it does show that not everything orbits the Earth. However, the phases of Venus being the same as the Moon's could not occur in the geocentric system.

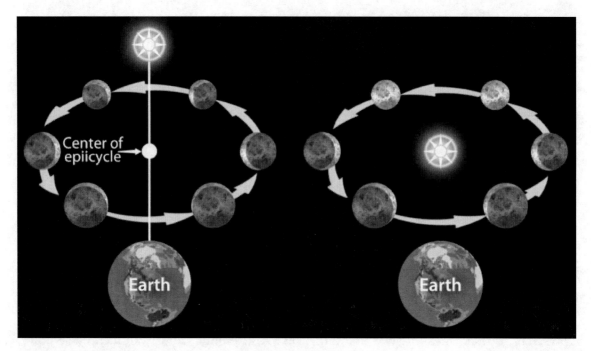

Figure 2.14 The Phases of Venus in the heliocentric (right) and geocentric systems. The phases in the heliocentric system matched what Galileo observed.

Despite the earlier warning, Galileo published his observations, publicly declaring his support of the Copernican system. He was arrested, tried, and convicted of scientific heresy. He was sentenced to be burned at the stake, but was offered the chance to have his sentence commuted to life under house arrest if he would publicly recant, or take back, his support of the Copernican system. He apparently was not prepared to become a martyr to his cause, because he did recant, and spent the rest of his life under house arrest.

It is easy to cast the church in a negative role, standing in the way of scientific progress, but it was more than religion alone that was responsible for Galileo's fate. Besides the fact that he was violating church dogma by supporting the heliocentric system, his condemnation was also partly political and personal. It was political, because he was rebelling against governmental authority, at that time the church. It was personal because in his arrogance Galileo made many enemies, including the Pope, a former friend whom he mocked and insulted in his publication, *A Dialog on Two Chief World Systems*, as representing an ignorant establishment. More recently, in 1979, Pope John Paul II began proceedings that by 1993 cleared Galileo of the charge of scientific heresy.

Figure 2.15 Galileo

2.8 Newton and Gravity

Isaac Newton was studying at Cambridge in 1662 when the Black Death broke out in London. Newton retreated to a cabin in the country provided by his uncle, who was also paying for Newton's education. It was there that he did some of his most profound thinking and produced some of his greatest work.

Figure 2.16 Newton.

Newton was the first to describe physical theories in the language of mathematics. He used mathematical equations to apply his theories and make predictions that could then be tested by observation and experiment. At the time there was no form of mathematics suited to the task, so he invented calculus, the highest form of mathematics. Tools are usually invented when the need for them arises.

Newton's theory of *Universal Gravitation* describes *gravity* as a force between masses that pulls them together. The force varies proportionally with mass, more mass means more gravity, and inversely with distance, the greater the distance between objects the weaker the gravity between them.

Newton applied his theory of gravitation to mathematically analyze the motion of a planet in orbit of the Sun and came up with equations that showed the same things that Kepler had discovered from analysis of Tycho's data. This was the end to which the entire Copernican Revolution was heading. By achieving the same results theoretically as

Kepler had through analysis of Tycho's observations, Newton proved that both were correct. There could be no more doubt that Earth orbits the Sun.

Theory and experiment giving the same results is the ultimate goal of science. Not only had Newton finished the Copernican Revolution, but he also provided the standard to which all scientific theories and experiments have been held ever since. In order to be accepted, theories and experiments must agree with one another.

Universal Gravitation was only one of many scientific contributions made by Newton. Among many other things, he invented a new type of telescope, one that uses mirrors to gather light, rather than lenses like those used by Galileo. Newton's reflector is still the original basis of many telescopes in use today.

Unlike many of the other scientists involved in the Copernican Revolution, Newton was revered in his own time. He was considered a national hero in England, eventually being knighted. Sir Isaac Newton was given a state funeral, and when he died in 1727, was buried at Westminster Abbey.

Toward the end of his life when Newton was being interviewed, a biographer suggested to Newton that he was probably the greatest scientist that had ever lived. Not being modest, he agreed, but that interview also produced one the most famous quotes in the history of science:

"If I have seen farther than others, it is because I have stood on the shoulders of giants."

Review Questions

1. What observation(s) could the ancient Greeks have made that would have been logical reasons for their belief that the Earth was spherical in shape?

2. Name two observations that the ancient Greeks could have made that would have been logical reasons for placing of the Moon's sphere closer to Earth's than the Sun's.

3. What observation was most likely the reason for the order of the planets in the geocentric system? What observation that would have been logical to try and use would have turned out NOT to work?

4. Give an example from everyday life of the application of the scientific process. It can be about anything as long as you cite an example that includes observation, an explanation followed by testing and, if necessary, revision of the explanation.

5. Today, we do think that the Earth moves. What do you think is a logical reason that Tycho failed to observe stellar parallax?

6. What were the contributions of Tycho and Kepler, specifically to astronomy, and to the scientific process in general?

7. List the telescopic observations made by Galileo. Which observation was proof of the heliocentric system?

8. Explain how Newton "finished" the work of Kepler.

9. What were the contributions of Newton, both to astronomy specifically and the scientific process in general?

10. Who were the "giants" on whose shoulders Newton stood?

Tutorial-The Phases of Venus

Use the following steps to determine the phase of Venus in each position in both the geocentric and heliocentric systems.

1-In each position in its orbit, color in the side of Venus that is not getting light, *the side facing away from the Sun.*

2-Hold the paper up perpendicular to your face (as with Lunar Phases) and look at Venus in each of the five (5) positions in its orbit from *behind Earth* in the picture.

3-In the five (5) circles along the bottom of the page, color in the appearance of Venus *as seen from Earth* in each of the five (5) corresponding positions in its orbit.

In which system   geocentric / heliocentric (circle one)   do the actual phases shown below occur?

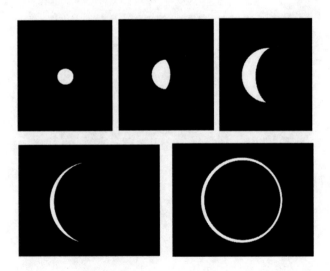

Why does the size of Venus change with each phase? Why does a full Venus appear smallest and a crescent or new Venus appear much larger?

Venus in the Geocentric System

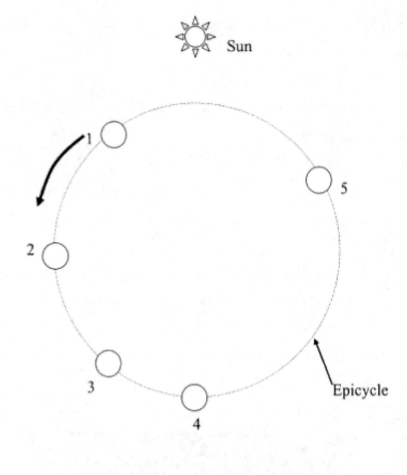

Sun

1

5

2

3

4

Epicycle

Earth

Sketch Venus's appearance as seen from Earth at the five locations shown above.

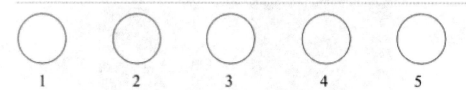

1   2   3   4   5

Venus in the Heliocentric System

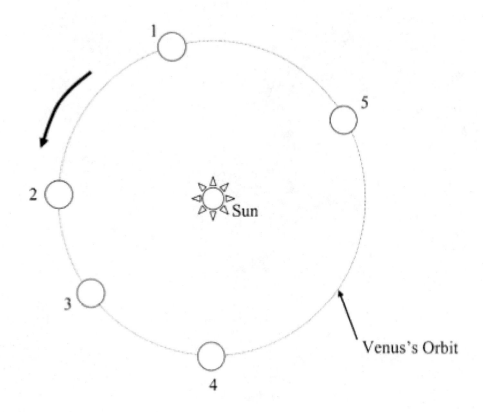

Sketch Venus's appearance as seen from Earth at the five locations shown above.

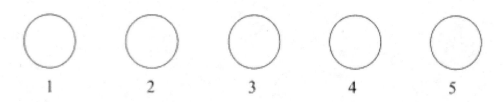

Chapter 3-Solar System Overview

Part 1-Objects in the Solar System

3.1 Introduction

Besides the Sun, the central object of our solar system, which is a star and will be discussed in Chapter 9, there are basically three types of objects in our solar system; *planets*, *moons* and *debris*. Solar system debris is the collective term used for objects that have not become part of a planet or a moon; *asteroids*, *comets*, and *meteors*. These objects will be discussed in detail in Chapter 5. Moons are objects that orbit planets, so that leaves the planets themselves to be discussed here.

3.2 Planet Types

One of the best ways to study planets is to investigate their properties and, based on these properties, compare the objects to one another. This is known as *Comparative Planetology*. The properties of planets are the quantities that we can measure, such as physical properties like size, mass, and density, or their orbital properties like distance from the Sun, orbital or revolution period, and rotational period. Table 3.1 lists the values of these and other properties for the known planets and several other objects in our solar system.

Figure 3.1 shows bar graphs or *histograms* comparing the *radii* (the *radius* is the distance from the center of a planet to its edge) or size of each of the objects listed in Table 3.1, their *mass* (of how much matter each is composed) and their *density*. Density is a combination of mass and size; it is a measure of how much mass per unit volume there is in something. Rocks and metals are objects of high density; gases, like air, are of low density, and liquids, like water, are in between.

Table 3.1-Planetary Data

	Object	Radius Earth=1	Mass Earth=1	Density Water=1	Orbital Radius AU	Orbital Period years	Rotation Period Earth=1	Number of Moons
1	Mercury	0.382	0.055	5.43	0.387	0.2409	58.6	0
2	Venus	0.949	0.815	5.25	0.723	0.6152	-243	0
3	Earth	1	1	5.52	1	1	1	1
4	Mars	0.533	0.107	3.93	1.524	1.881	1.026	2
5	Jupiter	11.19	317.9	1.33	5.203	11.86	0.41	21
6	Saturn	9.46	95.18	0.7	9.539	29.42	0.44	63
7	Uranus	3.98	14.54	1.32	19.19	84.01	-0.72	27
8	Neptune	3.81	17.13	1.64	30.06	164.8	0.67	13
9	Pluto	0.181	0.0022	2.05	39.48	248	-6.39	3
10	Eris	0.22	0.0028	2.3	67.67	557	15.8	1

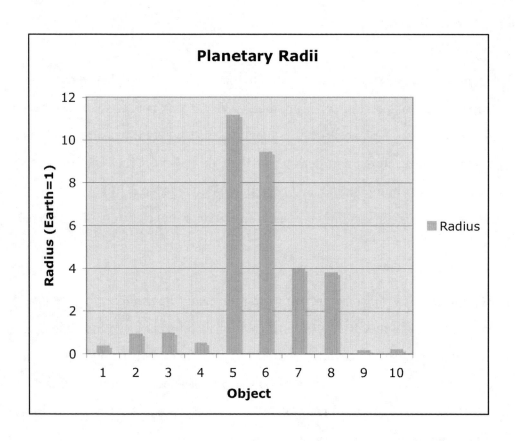

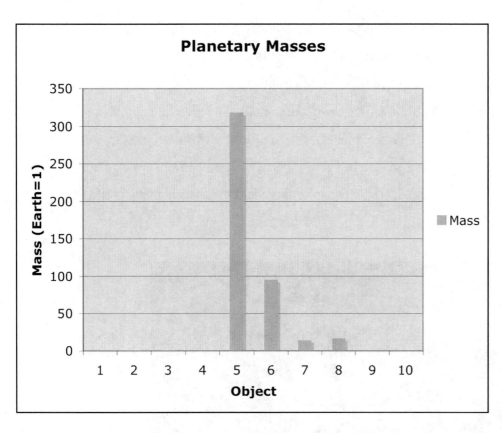

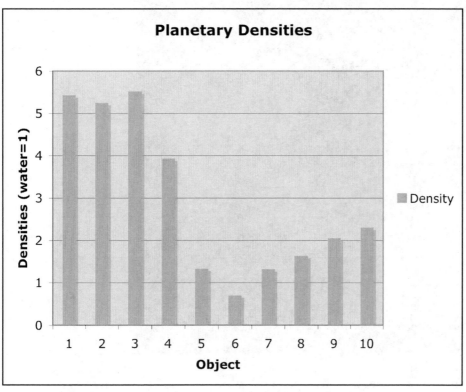

Figure 3.1 Bar graphs comparing planetary radii, masses, and densities.

Examination of the radii bar graph shows that there are different-sized planets. Planets 5 and 6 (the numbers on the bar-graphs match the numbers in Table 3.1), Jupiter and Saturn, are very large compared to 7 and 8, Uranus and Neptune, which are more medium in size, with Earth and all the others being very small. The mass bar graph shows that Jupiter is by far the most massive planet, then Saturn, with Uranus and Neptune the only other planets that even register on the graph. Perhaps at this point Jupiter, Saturn, Uranus and Neptune could be considered a group of large and massive planets, while Earth and all the others could be called small and less massive planets.

Figure 3.2 Images of our solar system's planets.

The density graph shows something different. Now Mercury, Venus, Earth, and Mars have large values or high densities, while the larger, massive planets *and* Pluto and Eris all have lower densities. The higher densities are because Mercury, Venus, Earth, and Mars are all made mostly of rocks and metals, while the lower-density objects, Jupiter, Saturn, Uranus, and Neptune, are made mostly of gases and liquids. Pluto and Eris, being so far from the Sun, are composed partly of ice.

At this point, it is possible to distinguish between two types of planets. Mercury, Venus, Earth, and Mars are all small, of lower mass and higher density, while Jupiter, Saturn, Uranus, and Neptune are all the opposite--large, higher mass, and lower density. Collectively the planets that are grouped with Earth can be called Earth-like or *Terrestrial* planets, while those grouped with Jupiter can be called Jupiter-like or *Jovian* planets. Notice that Pluto and Eris do not fit with either category.

Figure 3.3 The Planets in order of their distance from the Sun.

Looking at other data from Table 3.1, all the Terrestrial planets are closer to the Sun and therefore have faster orbital periods, while the Jovian planets are the opposite, farther from the Sun, with longer orbital periods. Rotational periods do not seem to fit the categories as well. All of the Jovian planets have rotation periods similar to each other and all the Terrestrial planets have longer periods, but, as can be seen from Table 3.1, Venus and Mercury have especially long periods. Again note Pluto and Eris not fitting in with either category; they are far from the Sun like the Jovians, but have longer rotation periods, like the Terrestrials. Also, due to their large mass and therefore greater gravitational pull, the Jovian planets all have (as also can be seen in Table 3.1) large numbers of moons and rings. Rings are large numbers of smaller particles all in similar orbits around a Jovian planet, causing them to give the appearance of a ring around the planet. Ring systems will be discussed in more detail in Chapter 7. Table 3.2 is a comparison of the properties of the Terrestrial and Jovian planets

Table 3.2 Properties of Terrestrial and Jovian Planets

	Terrestrial Planets	**Jovian Planets**
Members	Mercury, Venus, Earth, Mars	Jupiter, Saturn, Uranus, Neptune
Size	Smaller	Larger
Mass	Low mass	Great mass
Density	High	Low
Composition	Rock and Metal	Gas and Liquid
Distance	Close to Sun	Far from Sun
Rotation	Slower	Faster
Moons	Few or none	Many
Rings	No	Yes

3.3 The Kuiper Belt

As observed several times, Pluto and Eris do not fit into either of major planet categories and in fact, they could be classified together as very small, low mass icy-rocky objects (thus their medium density) that are very far from the Sun. These are precisely the characteristics of the objects in what is known as the Kuiper Belt.

First proposed by Gerard Kuiper in 1951, many small icy objects, which have also been called "Trans-Neptunian" objects and also "Ice Dwarfs," have now been observed beyond the orbit of Neptune. There are thousands of Kuiper-Belt objects known to exist, including several discovered more recently that rival the size of Pluto, such as Eris, which is actually larger than Pluto.

In the summer of 2006, Pluto lost its status as one of the solar system's planets. The International Astronomical Union (IAU), a group of astronomers from throughout the world that meets every other year and makes such decisions, reclassified Pluto, along with Ceres, the largest member of the inner-solar system asteroid-belt located between Mars and Jupiter, and several other objects large enough to be spherical, as "Dwarf-Planets." The asteroid belt, Pluto, and the rest of the Kuiper-Belt objects will be discussed in more detail in Chapter 5.

Part 2-The Formation of the Solar System

3.4 The Solar Nebula

Our sun was formed by a gravitational collapse within a gigantic cloud of mostly hydrogen gas and dust in the otherwise nearly empty "*interstellar*" space between the stars in our galaxy. The leftover material surrounding the not-yet shining *protosun* was called the *solar nebula*. Eventually, the protosun accumulated enough material from the nebula to become massive enough to put sufficient pressure on its core to raise the core temperatures high enough for nuclear fusion to occur. This process provided the energy necessary for the sun to give off light and heat, to shine, and thus become a star. The process of star formation and nuclear fusion will be discussed in more detail in Chapter 10.

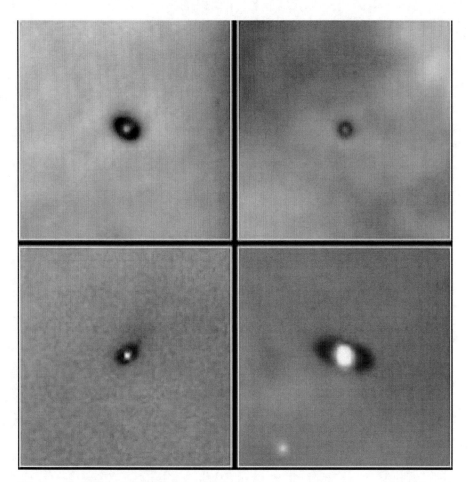

Figure 3.4 Solar Nebulae

3.5 The Rock-Metal Condensation Line

The leftovers of the solar nebula were the material from which the planets of our solar system would form. Initially, temperatures were so hot that most of the solar nebula remained gaseous, but as the young sun cooled, temperatures reached a point where rocks and metals could begin to condense out of the nebula. Too close to the sun, the temperatures never cooled enough for this to happen and no planets could form. However, beyond about 0.3 AU, which is known as the *rock-metal condensation line*, the solid objects could begin gravitationally pulling together, first forming small rocky-metal objects called *planetisimals* and then larger *protoplanets*.

	Metals	**Rock**	**Hydrogen Compounds**	**Gases**
Examples	Iron, Nickel, Aluminum	Various Minerals	Water, Methane, Ammonia	Hydrogen, Helium
Condensation Temperatures	1,000-1,600 K	500-1,300 k	< 150 K	DO NOT condense in Nebula
Relative Abundance	0.2%	0.4%	1.4%	98%

Table 3.4 Condensation Temperatures of materials in the solar nebula

3.6 Formation of the Terrestrial Planets

Within about 5 AU of the sun, temperatures remained high enough that no other materials could condense out of the nebula and, due to the higher temperatures, the gases were very fast-moving. This left the rocky-metal protoplanets not massive enough to gravitationally capture appreciable amounts of these gases. The protoplanets continued to accumulate more of the rock and metal in their orbits, and eventually became what are now known as the small, low-mass, high-density (rock-metal) Terrestrial, or Earth-like, planets found close to the Sun.

3.7 The Frost Line and the Jovian Planets

Beyond 5 AU, temperatures cooled enough for water, methane, and ammonia to condense from the solar nebula and form layers of ice on the rocky-metal objects. This is known as the *frost line*. The cooler temperatures in this region of the nebula, out further from the Sun, slowed the motions of the gases, making them easier for planets to "catch." This factor, and the now greater mass of these objects from the ice they collected, allowed them to gravitationally collect large amounts of these gases and grow to tremendous sizes, much more massive than their cousins nearer to the sun. They became what are now known as the Jupiter-like, or large, massive, low-density (gas and liquid) Jovian Planets that are found farther from sun.

The pressure from the large mass of gas above the icy layers likely warmed and melted the ice, leaving the basic structure of a Jovian planet, which is a Terrestrial-planet sized rocky-metal core, surrounded by a large liquid ocean below a huge, thick atmosphere of gases, mostly hydrogen and helium. The formation of the three-layered Jovian planets was a three-step process, while the Terrestrial planets were basically formed in only one step, so the Jovian planets are considered more evolved than the Terrestrial planets.

3.8 The Leftovers-Solar System Debris

Some of the planetisimals, and even protoplanets, did not become part of a Terrestrial or Jovian planet. Some were gravitationally captured, mostly by the more massive Jovian planets, and became *moons*. Other small rocky objects of the inner solar system are now called *asteroids*. Many of the asteroids are concentrated in a "belt" between the orbits of Mars and Jupiter. The material in this belt was never able to pull together and form a planet due to the gravitational influences of Jupiter. Mars' two small moons were likely captured from this asteroid belt. Small rocky objects of the cold outer solar system were covered by condensing ice, and are now known as *comets*. A large group of comet-like objects, called the Kuiper Belt, lies beyond the orbit of Neptune. A few of Neptune's moons may have been captured from this population. Neptune's orbit is crossed by the orbit of the most well-known member of the Kuiper Belt, the *"dwarf-planet"* Pluto. Asteroids comets and the Kuiper Belt will be discussed in more detail in Chapter 5.

During the formation of the solar system, when there were more objects that had not yet become parts of planetary systems, many collisions occurred. Earth's moon is believed to have been formed by a collision with a large object. A collision is also believed to be the reason that Uranus' rotational axis lies nearly in the plane of its orbit rather than more "upright" relative to it, like the other planets. When an object is falling toward an impact with Earth and gives off a bright flash of light due to friction with the gases in the atmosphere, it is called a *meteor*. The holes the collisions leave are called *impact-craters*. There are many impact-craters on the surfaces of the Terrestrial planets and their moons and on Jovian moons from collisions. As collisions occur, over time, the number of objects "available" for further collisions becomes less and less. Most impact-craters, like we see on our Moon, were formed long ago, but there are still occasional large-impacts, like the Tunguska event on Earth just over a century ago or the collision of a comet with Jupiter in 1994. Impacts will also be discussed in Chapter 5.

Review Questions

1. Write a definition of each type of solar system object; *Planet, Moon, Asteroid, Comet,* and *Meteor*.

2. Name the two types of planets found in our solar system.

3. List the planets that are members of each group.

4. List the properties that define each group of planets.

5. What *one* word could be used to describe how the properties of the planets in one group compare to the properties of the planets in the other group?

6. Give an example of a solar system object that does not fit into either planet group. Explain why it does not fit in.

7. As the solar nebula cooled, about how far from the sun would be the *closest* distance that any materials could condense?

8. What type of materials could condense inside (closer to the sun than) the rock-metal condensation line? What type of planets form inside this line?

9. As the solar nebula cooled, parts of it cooling to as low as 500 K, which type (s) of materials condensed (became solid) out of the solar nebula first?

10. About how far from the sun did temperatures cool down as low as 150 K or less, the frost line?

11. What materials could then condense (become solid) on the already formed *protoplanets* beyond the frost line, creating a second layer of material on these objects? What *common* name do we give to these materials when they condense on something (remember- they are <u>beyond</u> the *<u>frost</u> line*)?

12. Where relative to the sun, did the larger objects form? Where did the smaller object form? Where could *no* objects form?

13. Describe the smaller objects that formed. Of what materials are they mostly composed? Where did they form, relative to the sun and to the larger objects? In how many layers (or steps) did they form? What type of planet that you are familiar with are these?

14. Which materials *will not* condense (will not become solid) anywhere in the solar nebula? Why won't they? Which planetary objects, the larger or smaller ones, were able to collect large amounts of the remaining uncondensed gases from the solar nebula? Give two reasons that this was the case. HINT--Keep in mind that temperature is a measure of the energy of molecular motion, so molecules in warmer regions are moving much faster that those in cooler regions.

15. Describe the larger objects that formed. Where did they form relative to the sun and to the smaller objects? In how many layers (or steps) did they form? What type of planet that you are familiar with are these?

16. Which type of planet is more evolved (has gone through more steps in its formation)?

17. What is the single most important factor in determining what kind of planet will form at a given location? What controls this factor?

18. Many smaller objects that condensed from the solar nebula are "leftovers," that did not become part of a planet. Of what would small objects that formed closer to the sun be made? What do we call them? Of what would small objects that formed farther from the sun largely be made? What do we call them?

19. How do you think the numbers of collisions that occur or the *rate of cratering* in the solar system would change over time? Explain your answer.

20. What might we call an object that does not impact, but rather is captured into the orbit of a larger object like a planet?

Tutorial--Comparative Planetology

1. Plot bar-graphs comparing each of the following categories of data for all of the planets:

    Radius, Mass, Density, Distance from the Sun, Orbital Period, Rotational Period, Number of Moons

    Each group will be assigned ONE bar graph to plot and put on the board.

Planetary Data

	Object	Radius Earth=1	Mass Earth=1	Density Water=1	Orbital Radius AU	Orbital Period years	Rotation Period Earth=1	Number of Moons
1	Mercury	0.382	0.055	5.43	0.387	0.2409	58.6	0
2	Venus	0.949	0.815	5.25	0.723	0.6152	-243	0
3	Earth	1	1	5.52	1	1	1	1
4	Mars	0.533	0.107	3.93	1.524	1.881	1.026	2
5	Jupiter	11.19	317.9	1.33	5.203	11.86	0.41	21
6	Saturn	9.46	95.18	0.7	9.539	29.42	0.44	63
7	Uranus	3.98	14.54	1.32	19.19	84.01	-0.72	27
8	Neptune	3.81	17.13	1.64	30.06	164.8	0.67	13
9	Pluto	0.181	0.0022	2.05	39.48	248	-6.39	3
10	Eris	0.22	0.0028	2.3	67.67	557	15.8	1

2. Examine the bar graph comparing the **Radii** of the planets; which planets seem large?

    Which planets seem small?

3. Examine the bar graph comparing the **Mass** of the planets; which planets are more massive?

Which planets are less massive?

4. Examine the bar graph comparing the **Density** of the planets; which planets are more dense?

Which planets are less dense?

What does density tell you about a planet?

5. Based on the comparisons you have made, have any planets been grouped together every time?

How many groups are there?

Which planets are in which groups?

6. Examine the bar graph comparing the number of moons orbiting each planet. Which planet group's members have many moons?

Which planet group's members have few (or no) moons?

On what does the number of moons orbiting a planet likely depend?

7. Examine the bar graphs comparing the distance of the planets from the Sun.

Which planet group is closer to the Sun?

Which planet group is farther from the sun?

8. Examine the bar graph comparing the rotational periods of the planets; which planet group rotates faster?

Which group rotates slower?

What do you think the negative-signs mean?

9. List the members of each of your planet groups.

    List the properties from the bar graphs that the planets in each of your groups have in common.

    In general, how do the properties that you listed differ when compared between the different planet groups?

10. Is (are) there an (any) object(s) that *do not* seem to fit into a group?

    Have you heard about a recent decision made about this object?

    Did this exercise help clarify the decision for you?

    Do you agree with the decision? Why or why not?

Chapter 4 - Extrasolar Planets

4.1 Introduction

According to the theory of planetary formation discussed in the last chapter, it should be likely that many stars have planets However, since planets are so much smaller than stars and shine only due to light reflected from them, visual detection of planets, even those orbiting the closest stars, is virtually impossible. In the past, astronomers have claimed to have found evidence of a planet orbiting a distant star, but further observation would usually show that this was not the case.

4.2 Detecting Extrasolar Planets

This changed in 1995 when astronomers used an indirect method of detection to find evidence of a planet orbiting the star 51-Pegasi. The method makes use of the fact that, in reality, one object does not orbit another, but two objects orbit the center of mass between them. The center of mass of a system is closer to the more massive object. It will be as many times closer as the number of times more massive that object is than the other. For example, the Sun is about one thousand (1000) times as massive as Jupiter, so both objects orbit a point that is one-one thousandth (1/1000) the way from the Sun to Jupiter, a point one thousand times closer to the Sun. Since Jupiter is about five times as far from the Sun as Earth, it is about five hundred million (500, 000, 000) miles from the Sun, and one-one thousandth of that distance is about five-hundred thousand (500, 000) miles.

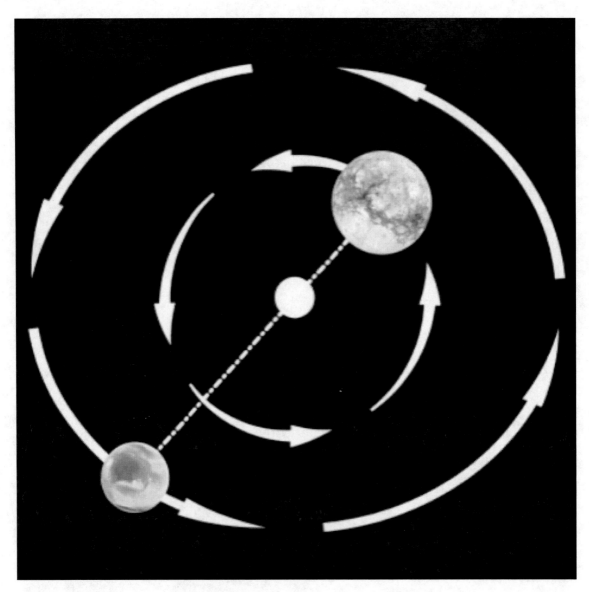

Figure 4.1 Two objects orbiting the center of mass of their system

4.3 The Doppler Detection Method

In the case of any star, and even a very large planet, the center of mass will be so much closer to the star that the star will move in an orbit much smaller than the planet's orbit. However, the orbits will have the same period (they will take the same amount of time). This motion is detectable through variations in the star's light caused by the Doppler-effect, a shift in the wavelength of the star's light caused by the motion of the star.

As the star orbits the center of mass, if the star is moving toward an observer, it appears to catch up with its light waves, compressing or shortening them, and a shift toward the shorter- wavelength, blue end of the visible spectrum will occur. This is often called a blueshift. If the star is moving away from an observer, it appears to leave its waves behind, lengthening them and a shift toward the longer, red end of the spectrum occurs. This called a redshift.

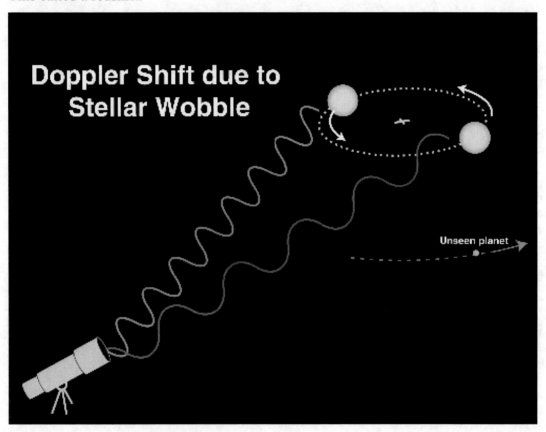

Figure 4.2 Observed redshifts and blueshifts in the light from a star as it moves away from and then towards the observer.

The Doppler shifts will alternate from a maximum blueshift, to a maximum redshift and back to the maximum blueshift in a time equal to the period of the star's orbit, which is also equal to the orbital period of the planet. Knowing the orbital period, Kepler's third law can then be used to determine the planet's orbital distance.

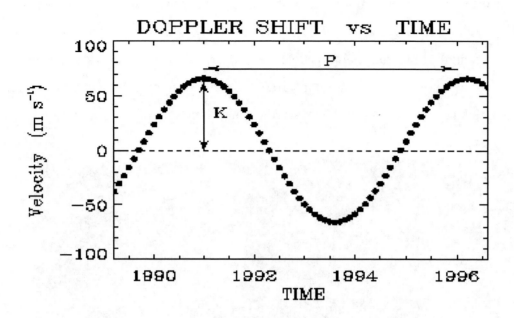

Figure 4.3 One cycle of the changing Doppler-shifts of the light from a star

The maximum amount of redshift or blueshift can be used to determine speed of the star's motion. Knowing this speed allows the distance the star is from the center of mass to be determined. Finally, using the mass of the star (usually already known from its brightness--this will be discussed in Chapter 9) and the planet's orbital distance allows us to determine the mass of the planet. This is actually only a lower limit for the planet's mass, since we have no way of knowing if we are observing the distant planetary system exactly edge on, in which case our mass would be correct, or at an angle, in which case we would not be able to see the entire shift in the star's light. This would cause us to underestimate the mass.

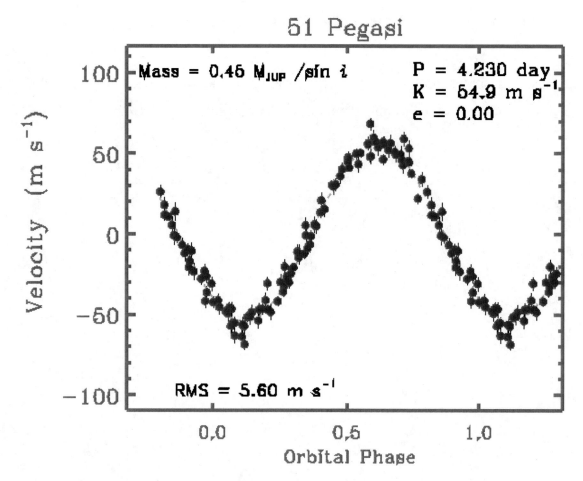

Figure 4.4 Alternating blueshifts and redshifts of the light from the star 51-Pegasi. The period of the unseen planet and the orbital velocity of the star can be used to determine the orbital distance and mass of the planet.

4.4 Orbital Distance and Mass of Planets

The closer a planet is to its star, the more often it orbits the star, so the more rapidly the waveform of the alternating Doppler-shifts will repeat, as seen in Figure 4.5.

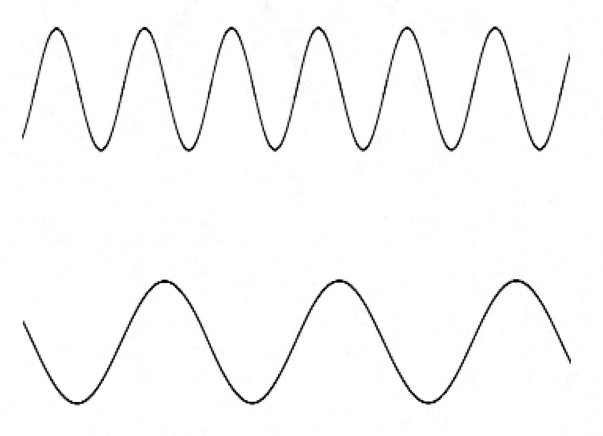

Figure 4.5 The planet represented by the upper graph is closer to its star than the planet represented by the lower one.

A closer planet will also exert more gravitational pull on its star, causing more wobble. This effect is even more pronounced the more massive the planet. This will cause a planet's waveform to vary more in the up-and-down direction as seen in Figure 4.6

120

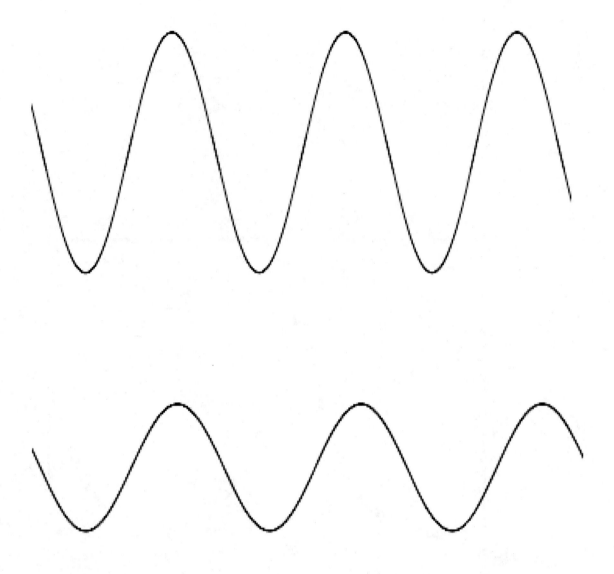

Figure 4.6 The planet represented by the upper graph is more massive than the planet represented by the lower one.

4.5 Eccentric Orbits

The planet orbiting the star 51-Pegasi, Figure 4.4, is in a perfectly circular orbit. The eccentricity of the orbit is zero. If a planet's orbit is more elliptical, the waveform of the star's varying Doppler-shifts will reflect that by appearing more unusual, as seen in Figures 4.7 and 4.8.

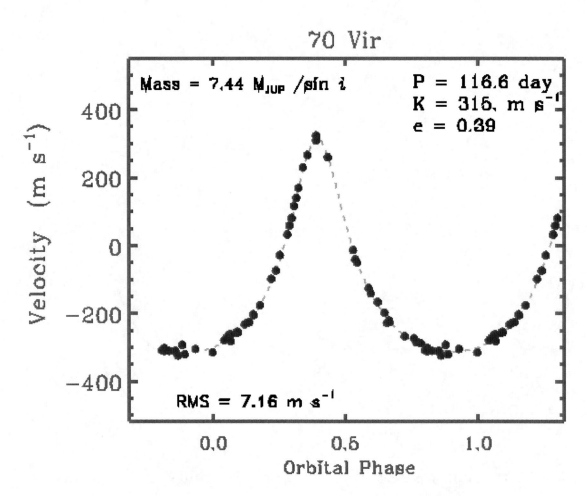

Figure 4.7 The planet represented by this graphs is in an eccentric orbit.

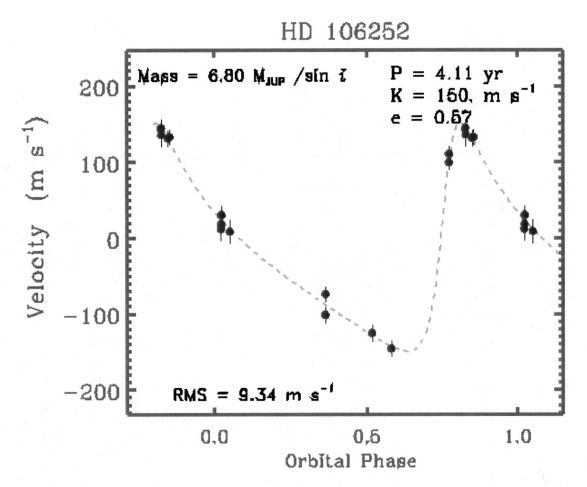

Figure 4.8 The planet represented by this graph is in an even more eccentric orbit than the one in Fig. 4.7.

4.6 Multiple Planet Systems

The waveform of the repeating Doppler-shifts will also show if there is more than one planet in orbit of a star, by appearing complex, showing more than one repetition pattern, as in Figure 4.9. The plot for the star Upsilon Andromeda, shown in Figure 4.10, shows that there are two planets, a more massive planet farther from the star, that is completing about two orbits in the time shown, and a less massive planet orbiting about five times as fast. Note that there are five smaller repetitions "riding" on each repetition of the longer wave.

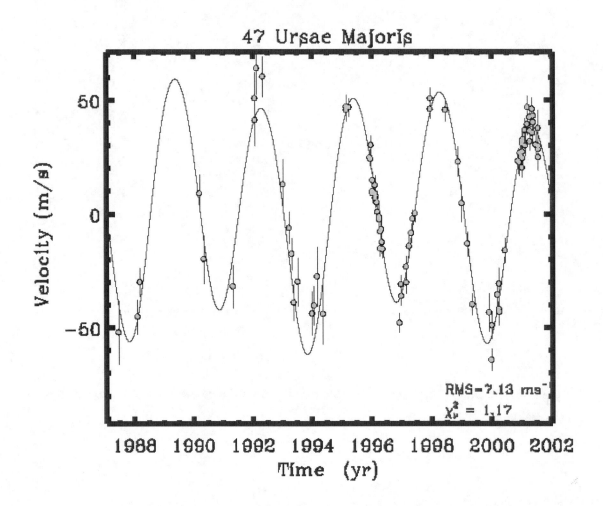

Figure 4.9 Shifts in the light from 47-Ursae Majoris. The complex form of the wave indicates the presence of two planets.

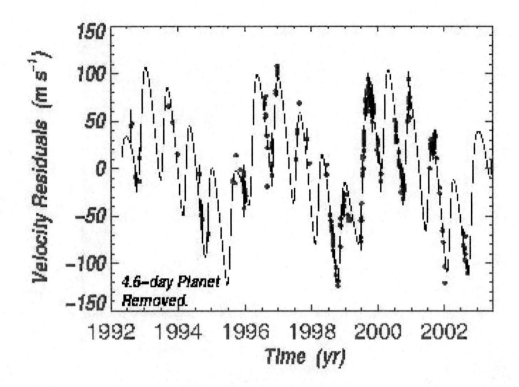

Figure 4.10 Shifts in the light from Upsilon Andromeda. The complex form of the wave is caused by the presence of planets c and d in Figure 4.11.

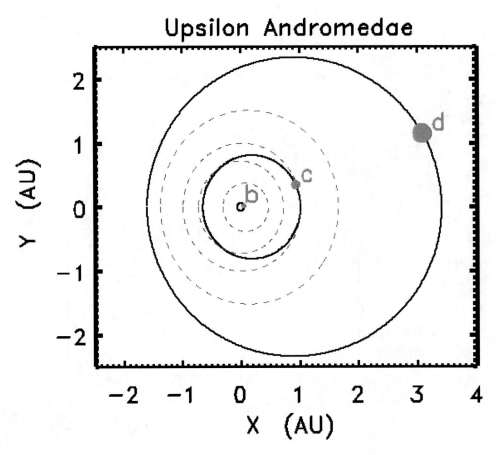

Figure 4.11 The effects of planets c and d cause the complex form of the wave seen in Figure 4.10.

4.7 Detection of Earth-like Planets

The first planets detected were more massive than Jupiter and in orbits very close to their stars, in most cases much closer than would be expected for planets of that size. This is not surprising because the detection method favors more massive planets in closer orbits. The very massive planets cause more noticeable shifts in their star's light, which will be repeated rapidly due to a short orbital period. However, more recently, planets of masses comparable to Jupiter and Saturn have been found in orbits similar to those of Jupiter and Saturn, with no other planets yet detected closer to the star. This suggests that there may be undetected smaller planets, making the systems similar to our own solar system. Even more recently, planets similar in mass to Uranus and Neptune, and even smaller, have been found. Some astronomers feel that detection of smaller still Earth-sized planets is inevitable and will happen very soon.

Figure 4.12 Artist's conception of an extrasolar planet in orbit of a Sun-like star.

Review Questions

1. Describe the Doppler Detection Method for finding extra solar planets.

2. What information can be determined about a planet from its star's changing Doppler-shift graph? Which is determined directly from the graph?

3. How will the waveform of the changing Doppler-shifts differ for two planets that are different distances from their stars?

4. How will the waveform of the changing Doppler-shifts differ for two planets that are of different mass?

5. How will the waveform of the changing Doppler-shifts show that a planet is in an eccentric orbit?

6. How will the waveform of the changing Doppler-shifts show that multiple planets are in orbit of a star?

7. Why were the first extra-solar planets discovered massive stars in orbits close to their stars?

8. Have solar systems similar to our own been detected? Have planets similar to Earth been found?

Tutorial--Extra Solar Planets

When one object orbits another, the less massive object does not actually orbit the more massive one; they both orbit the center of mass between them. This is a point that is as many times closer to the more massive object as the amount of times more massive the object is. For instance, our Sun is 1000 times more massive than Jupiter, so our Sun and Jupiter both orbit a point between them that is 1000 times closer to the Sun.

If a planet is massive enough it will cause its star to move in an orbit large enough that the motion can be observed from Earth with the Doppler effect.

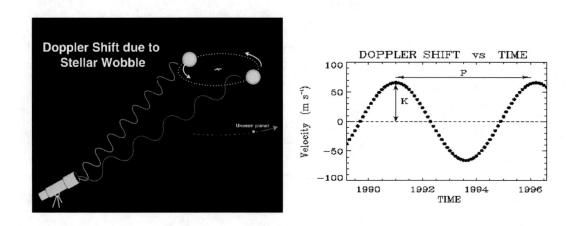

As the star orbits the center of mass between the large planet and itself, a blueshift in its light will be noticed when the star is moving toward Earth and a redshift when it is moving away. The Doppler shifts will alternate, from a maximum blueshift to a maximum redshift and back to the maximum blueshift in a time equal to the stars orbit, which is *equal to the orbital period of the planet*.

Once the orbital period of the planet is known, the planet's *orbital distance* can be immediately determined from Kepler's third law; then, the *mass* of the planet can be calculated from Newton's theory of gravitation.

Using this **Doppler Detection Method**, we can determine the *orbital period*, *orbital distance* and *mass* of planets in orbit of distant stars--planets that we otherwise cannot even see!

Part 1

Data determined from the Doppler-shifts caused by planets orbiting the three stars HD 46375, HD 16141, and HD 195019 is recorded in the table below.

Star	Mass (Jupiters)	Orbital period (days)	Orbital Distance r (AU)	Maximum Doppler-shift K (m/s)
HD 46375	0.25	3	0.04	34.5
HD 16141	0.25	76	0.35	11.3
HD 195019	3.6	18.2	0.14	271

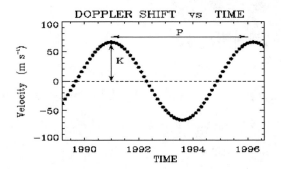

The horizontal variations (back and forth) on the graph measures *time*, so the horizontal variations on a graph are most likely more affected by the planet's (circle one);

mass   distance from the star

Looking at the data, the amount of Doppler-shift (labeled K on the data table and graph) caused by the planets (the vertical variation, up and down on the graphs) seems to be *most* affected by

mass   distance from the star

Now based on the answers you just gave and the values on the table:

Label each of the three graphs below with the name of the star from the table that is most likely to represent the Doppler-shift variations caused by its planet.

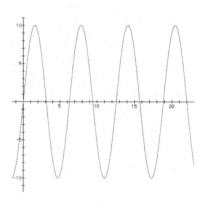

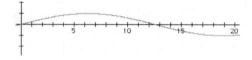

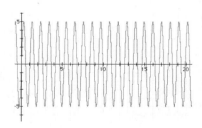

Based on your choices above:

Stars that show larger Doppler-shifts (K-value) (up and down on the graph) probably have planets that are (circle all that you think apply):

More massive

Less massive

In closer obits

In farther orbits

Stars with a more rapid repetition in the variations of their Doppler-shifts (back and forth on the graph) probably have planets that are (circle all that you think apply):

More massive

Less massive

In closer orbits

In farther orbits

Now, based on what you have learned:

Draw the Doppler-shift graphs caused by each of the planets described below (ignore the numbers on the axes):

A more massive planet in a farther orbit

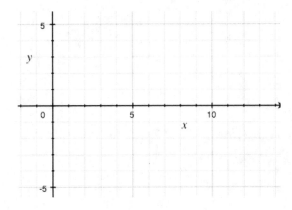

A more massive planet in a closer orbit

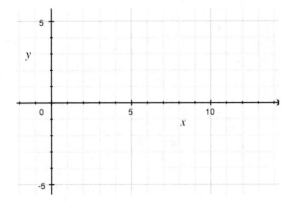

A less massive (lighter) planet in a farther orbit

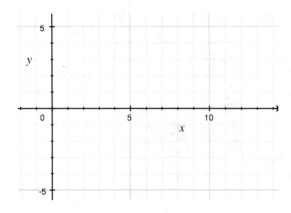

A less massive planet in a closer orbit

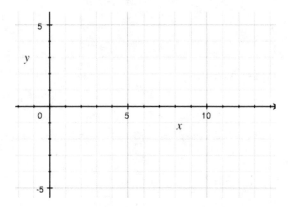

Part 2

The eccentricity of an orbit is a measure of how elliptical or how far it is from being circular. More circular orbits have low eccentricity orbit (close to 0) and more elliptical orbits have higher (0.2 or greater) eccentricity.

In the space below, draw a star and the path of a planet orbiting the star in a *low* eccentricity orbit.

In the space below, draw a star and the path of a planet orbiting the star in a high eccentricity orbit.

Now examine the Doppler-shift graphs below and note the waveforms and the orbital eccentricities (e)

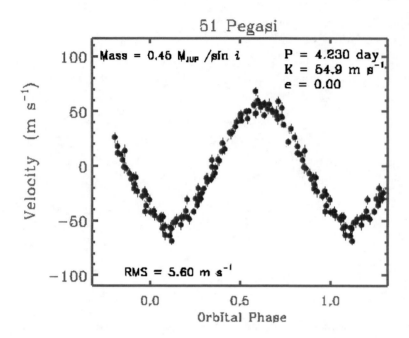

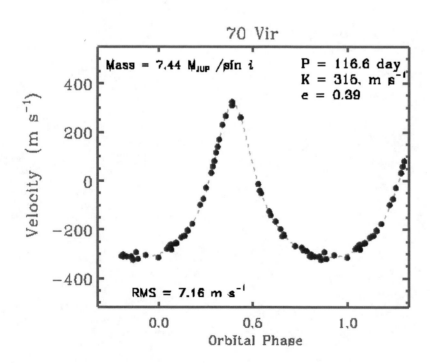

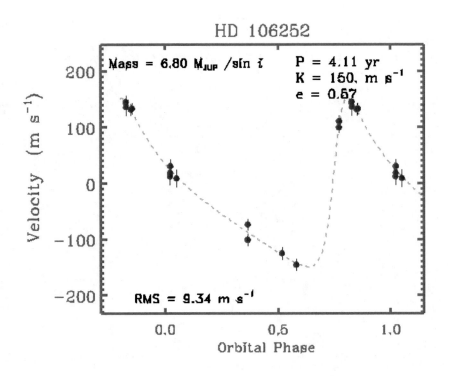

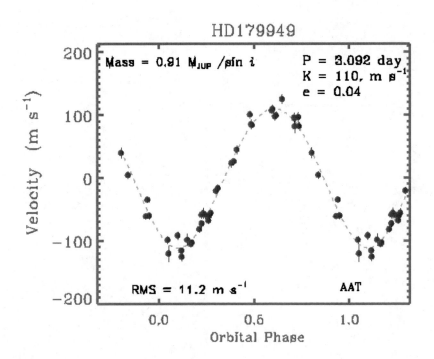

What difference did you notice in the waveforms of the above Doppler-shifts plots of the low (close to 0) and high (0.2 or greater) eccentricity orbits?

Part 3

Below are several Doppler-shift graphs from stars that have multiple planets in their systems.

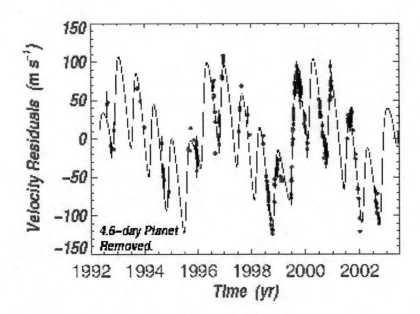

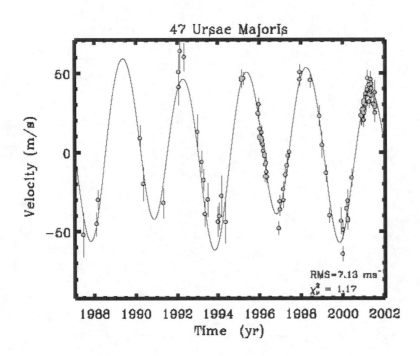

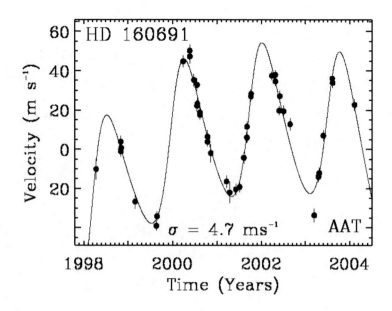

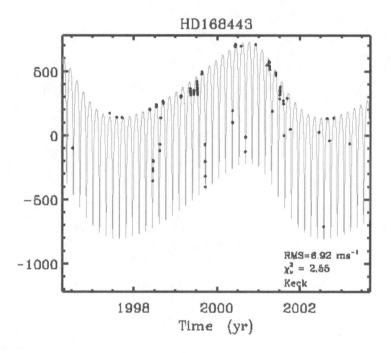

How do these plots seem to differ from those you have seen for stars with only single planets in orbit?

Single planets will result in Doppler-shift variations that repeat in the form of a simple waves, but when more than one planet is present, the combination of multiple Doppler-shifts of different amount and period creates a more complicated or compound waveform.

For instance, in the graphs below, the one on the left is for two individual planets; the one on the right is for their combination.

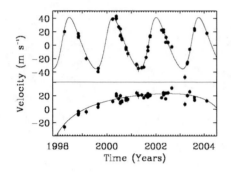
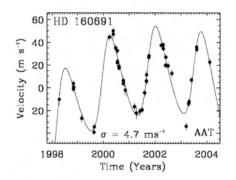

Below are Doppler-shift graphs for two individual planets of a multiple system.

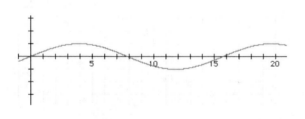
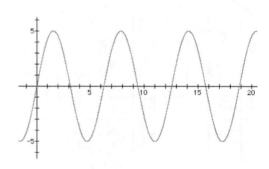

Which planet is farther from the star?   left / right (circle one)

Which planet has a greater mass?   left / right (circle one)

Extrasolar Planet Questions

Label each description with the letter that matches the plot that it most likely represents

_____A massive planet in a close orbit

_____A massive planet in a far orbit

_____A lighter planet in a close orbit

_____A lighter planet in a far orbit

A

B

C

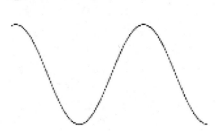

D

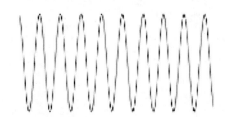

Choose which graph below represents:

_____ a planet in an eccentric orbit

_____ a multiple planet system

_____ a planet in a circular orbit

E

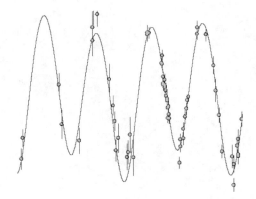

F

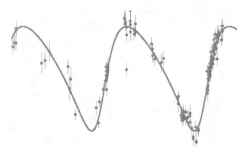

G

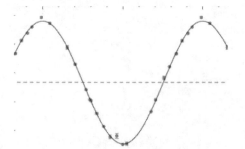

Chapter 5 - Solar System Debris

5.1 Introduction

Solar System Debris is the collective term for any object that has not yet become part of a planet or moon. The different types of objects considered solar system debris are asteroids, comets, and meteors. The objects of the Kuiper Belt are also debris and have features in common with both asteroids and comets.

5.2 Asteroids

In 1801, Giuseppe Piazzi, an Italian monk, discovered what he believed to be a "missing planet." *Ceres*, as it would eventually be named, orbited the Sun at 2.8 AU, precisely in the position predicted for a planet between Mars and Jupiter by the Titus-Bode law, (as will be discussed in Chapter 7). The unusual thing about Ceres was that it was much dimmer, not visible without a telescope. That meant it was much smaller than the other known planets.

Soon, several similar objects, which would be named *Vesta*, *Pallas*, and *Juno*, were discovered in orbits similar to *Ceres*. The group was then referred to as the *minor planets*. By the end of the 1800s, several hundred small objects were discovered in orbits between Mars and Jupiter and now we now know that *Ceres*, at about 600 miles across, is the largest member of an *asteroid belt* that may have as many as 100, 000 members.

The name *asteroid* actually means star-like. It is used because asteroids are so small that when viewed through a telescope they appear as points of light, just like stars. The only way to distinguish an asteroid from the stars in the field of view is that, if observed over time, it will appear to *move* relative to the star field due to its orbit around the Sun, as shown in Figure 5.1. This is how most asteroids are discovered.

Figure 5.1 A photographic trail of an asteroid moving through a star-field.

Asteroids are largely just chunks of rock. The asteroid belt is reminiscent of the debris from which we think planets formed, as was discussed in Chapter 3. This brings up the interesting question of why the material in the asteroid belt never formed a planet.

The answer seems to lie in the position of the asteroid belt relative to the giant planet Jupiter. Gravitational effects exerted by Jupiter on the asteroid belt have prevented the material from gravitationally pulling together and forming a planet.

The Trojan Asteroids

First, Jupiter steals mass from the asteroid belt. As seen in Figure 5.2, there are two collections of asteroids, called the Trojan Asteroids, actually in Jupiter's orbit. They are approximately one-sixth of the orbit in front of and behind Jupiter in its orbit, so one group is always about 2 years ahead of Jupiter and the other about 2 years behind Jupiter in its almost 12-year orbit around the Sun. This position is a gravitationally stable point in any two-body system, in this case the Sun and Jupiter, known as a *Lagrange* point. These are locations that material, caused to drift from the asteroid belt by gravitational attraction from Jupiter, is likely to settle. Losing material to Jupiter's gravitational pull decreases the overall mass of the asteroid belt and also the collective gravitational pull with which the objects attract one another, making formation of a planet by the material less likely.

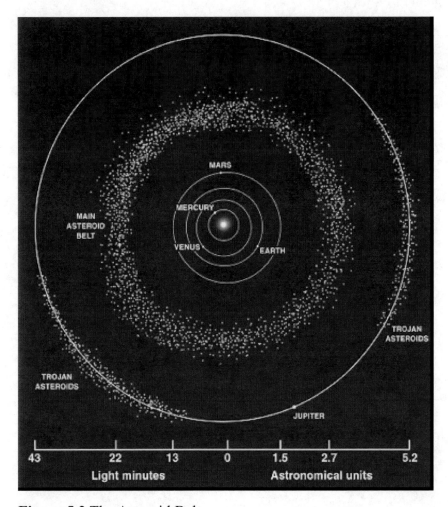

Figure 5.2 The Asteroid Belt.

The Kirkwood Gaps

There is also evidence that Jupiter's gravitational pull stirs up the asteroid belt. No asteroids are found in orbits within the asteroid belt that are distances from the Sun that would have periods that are whole number fractions of Jupiter's. These empty orbits are called the Kirkwood gaps, named after the astronomer who discovered them. For instance, Jupiter's orbital period is, again, about 12 years, so orbits that would take about 1/6, 1/4, 1/3, 1/2, 2/3, and ¾ of 12 years, or about 2, 3, 4, 8 and 9 years are locations of Kirkwood Gaps, orbits in which no asteroids are found. Asteroids that were once in these positions were subject to regular tugs from Jupiter at the same points in their orbits and eventually caused the asteroid to shift out of that orbit. Jupiter's gravitational pull creating gaps in the asteroid belt also made it more difficult for the objects to gravitationally pull together to form a planet.

Figure 5.3 George Kirkwood

A common myth about the asteroid belt, created by science fiction films and video games, is that it is crowded, so crowded that spacecraft flying through the asteroid belt run the risk of being smashed up by collisions with numerous objects through which they are trying to maneuver. By solar system standards, the asteroid belt *is* crowded, but by human standards it is not. In the scale model partially developed in the introduction, asteroids would be grains of sand or specks of dust separated by a human arm span. In reality, they are objects at most several hundred miles across, separated by millions of miles. Of the many robot space explorers that have crossed the asteroid belt en route to the outer planets, none have been in collisions, and those that had encounters with objects were by design.

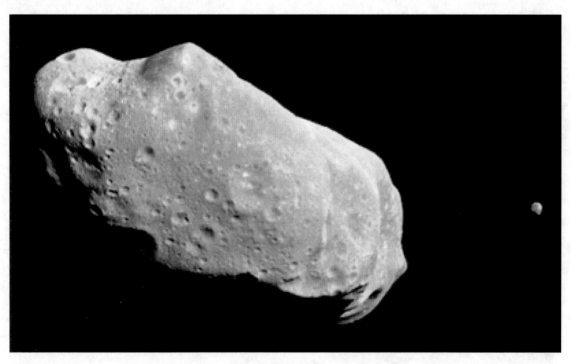

Figure 5.4 Asteroids *Ida* and *Dactyl* imaged by the *Galileo* spacecraft.

5.3 Pluto and The Kuiper Belt

At the beginning of the twentieth century, a search for a "Planet-X" based on small irregularities or gravitational perturbations observed in Neptune's orbit had begun. Perturbations in Uranus' orbit had previously led to the discovery of Neptune, so this had become the preferred method for discovering planets. Percival Lowell, a well-to-do businessman who had built an observatory near Flagstaff, Arizona, took the lead in the search for what he thought would be another Jovian planet, but he died without success in 1916.

In 1928, straight off his family's farm in Kansas, 18-year-old Clyde Tombaugh asked for a job at the Lowell Observatory. He was initially hired as a maintenance worker, but his proficiency with telescopes eventually got him a job as a full-time staff member. He reopened the search for Planet-X, using the observatory's new photographic telescope. Tombaugh could compare photographs of regions of the sky taken on consecutive nights to look for any object that appeared to be moving in front of the fixed background of stars. On February 18, 1930, after 10 months of searching, Tombaugh found the elusive object. He wanted to name it Lowell, but keeping with tradition, it was called *Pluto*, the first two letters being the initials of the man who began the search.

Figure 5.5 Lowell and Tombaugh

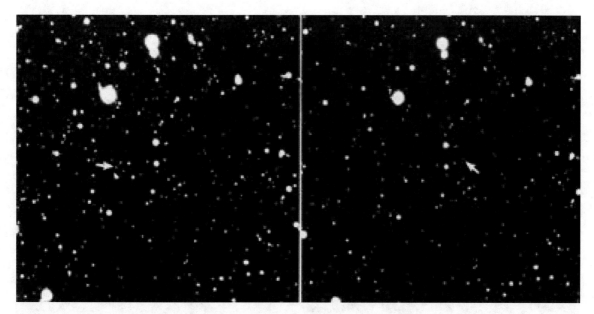

Figure 5.6 Photographs in which Tombaugh identified Pluto

Pluto was not at all what was expected. It was much too small to cause perturbations in Neptune's orbit. The perturbation calculations were later discovered to be in error due to uncertainties in the measurements. Pluto's orbit actually crosses Neptune's. This caused some speculation that Pluto was once a moon of Neptune that somehow escaped. A moon escaping its planet is physically unlikely. What is more likely is that Pluto, and its moon *Charon*, discovered by James Christy in 1978, are both members, along with Pluto's two more recently discovered smaller moons, of a population of outer solar system objects known as the *Kuiper Belt*.

As first mentioned in Chapter 3, the Kuiper Belt is a collection of many small icy objects beyond the orbit of Neptune. Neptune may have captured its moons from the Kuiper Belt in a manner similar to how Mars' moons were captured from the asteroid belt between Mars and Jupiter. Also as mentioned in Chapter 3, there are now known to be thousands of objects in the Kuiper Belt, including more recently discovered ones similar in size to, or larger than, Pluto.

Sedna
800-1100 miles
in diameter

Quaoar
[800 miles]

Pluto
[1400 miles]

Moon
[2100 miles]

Earth
[8000 miles]

Figure 5.7 The larger Kuiper-Belt objects compared in size to Earth and Earth's Moon.

It is now understood that Pluto, being among the largest and closest, was just the first Kuiper-belt object to be discovered. This is why its classification was recently changed from being one of the solar system's planets. This does not make Pluto any less interesting or less important. The change in Pluto's classification is in fact an excellent example of the process of science at work. It is an example of how knowledge from new observations and discoveries can cause scientific theories, or in this case, classification, to change.

Figure 5.8 Gerhard Kuiper

There are as of yet no really good images of Pluto. Figure 5.9 is a computer-enhanced image taken by the Hubble space telescope, and Figure 5.10 is an artist's conception of what Pluto and its moon Charon may look like up close. This should change when the *New Horizons* spacecraft, Figure 5.11, currently en route to Pluto and the Kuiper Belt, arrives at its destination in 2015 after a 10-year journey from Earth.

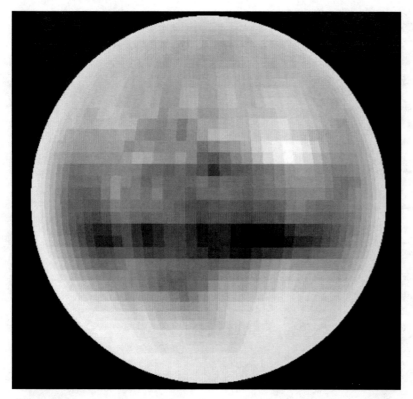

Figure 5.9 Computer-enhanced image of Pluto.

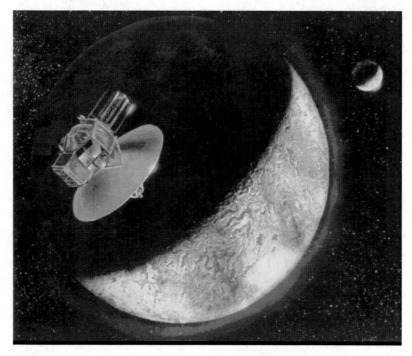

Figure 5.10 Artist's conception of Pluto and Charon.

Figure 5.11 The New Horizons spacecraft at NASA prior to launch.

5.4 Comets

Figure 5.12 is *NOT* a still image of an object in rapid motion toward the bottom-left of the picture's frame. *Comets* are not the same thing as meteors. *Meteors*, or their misnomer, *shooting stars*, are objects falling through our atmosphere and burning up as they head toward the ground. They will be discussed in the next section. Comets are actually small asteroid-size chunks of rock and ice in orbit around the Sun. When a comet like Comet Hale-Bopp is visible in the sky, as it was in 1997, its motion is more similar to that of a planet; it appears to move slowly with the rest of the sky each day due to the Earth's rotation, and over the course of days, weeks, and months, it gradually changes position relative to other objects in the sky. This should make sense, because, like a planet, a comet is an object in orbit around the Sun.

Figure 5.12 Comet Hale-Bopp

Again, comets are chunks of rock and ice, most of which originate from the far outer reaches of the solar system, even beyond the Kuiper belt, from what is known as the *Oort Comet Cloud*. They venture into the inner solar system in extremely eccentric orbits, and only when they get near the hot sun does the heat of the sun begin to vaporize the ice, and the small, asteroid-sized nucleus of the comet becomes surrounded by an envelope of gas. This gaseous envelope is called the *coma* or head of the comet, and can expand to the size of a Terrestrial planet. Material blown off the comet's nucleus by the Sun's rays forms the tails. Both the gas and dust tails are shown in Figure 5.12. Gases from the evaporated ice form the gas tail. The dust tail is formed by material dislodged from the rocky portion of the nucleus after the ices evaporate. A comet's tail can grow to be as much as an astronomical unit in length. Through most of its very long and eccentric orbit, a comet is simply an unremarkable asteroid-sized chunk of rock and ice, often referred to as a "dirty snowball." Only when close to the Sun does the comet form a head and tail and put on this comet "show."

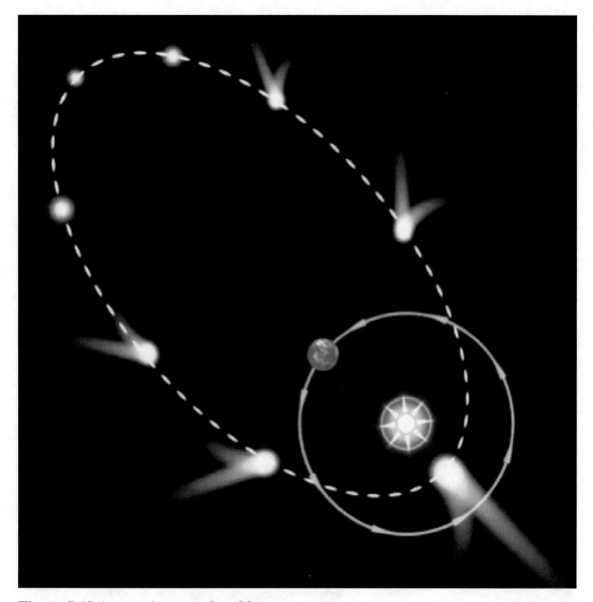

Figure 5.13 A comet's eccentric orbit.

Figure 5.13 shows a comet in its eccentric orbit around the Sun. Notice that when it is far away, the comet consists only of the nucleus, and only when it gets close to the Sun do the coma (head) and tails form. Note that *the tail always faces away from the sun*. This should make sense, since as stated above, the tails are material being thrown off the comet's nucleus by the heat of the Sun. The Sun's rays emanate from the Sun, so the comet's tail, caused by the rays, should *always face away from the Sun* and be *longer when closer to* the Sun and *shorter when farther* away, and not exist at all when even farther away from the Sun. The circular orbit shown in Figure 5.12 is Earth's. Note that when the comet is near the Sun is also when it is near Earth, so that when its head and tail are largest, when it is brightest, is also when it is closet to Earth and can be readily seen.

Generally, most comets are too dim to be seen without a telescope and most of those that are bright are in such long eccentric orbits that they come into view only once in thousands of years or more. Occasionally, however, one of these *long-period* comets will have a gravitational encounter with one of the large planets, such as Jupiter or Saturn. This cause the comet's orbit will shift and it will become a denizen of the inner solar system, completing its orbit in a much shorter amount of time and being repeatedly visible from Earth. The most famous of these *short-period* comets is of course Comet Halley, named after Edmund Halley. When looking over historical records of a bright comet appearing once every approximately 76 years, he became the first to suggest that the comet was an object in a 76-year orbit around the Sun. Since it had last been seen in 1682, he predicted its return in 1758. He did not live to see it, but the comet did indeed return as he had predicted and has borne his name ever since. Since that time, comets have been named after their discoverers.

Figure 5.14 Edmund Halley

Prior to Halley's time, comets were thought of as bad omens, predicting a loss in battle or the death of a king. Even the 1910 apparition of Comet Halley caused widespread concern when it was made known that Earth would pass through the comet's tail, in which the presence of cyanogen-gas (the gaseous form of the poison cyanide) made from the combination of the nitrogen and carbon freed from the vaporized methane and ammonia ices, had been detected. People threw end of the world parties. Two entrepreneurs even made some money selling comet pills, until they were arrested for fraud. In reality, when Earth passes through a comet tail, most people would not even know, because the gases in the tail are so diffuse, being spread out over the immense length of the tail. Recall that all the material in a comet begins packed into the size of an asteroid and when heated by the Sun expands to form the much larger coma and tail. Thus the densities are very low.

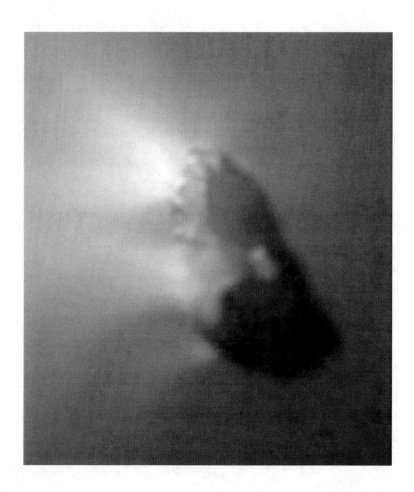

Figure 5.15 Image of the nucleus of Comet Halley taken in 1986 by the *Giotto* spacecraft.

Comet Halley returned in 1986 and will be back again in 2062. 1986 was the fist time that humankind had the technology to send a spacecraft to meet it. One of the things that the *Giotto* spacecraft learned was that Comet Halley lost less than 1 percent of its mass during its 1986 trip around the Sun, so it is still good for quite a few more return trips. However, all comets will eventually make a last trip around the sun, using up the last of the ices that it has to spare, and "burn out" or "die." The inner solar system populations of objects called the *Apollo* and *Amore* asteroids, in eccentric orbits that cross Earth and Mars' orbits respectively, are thought to once have been comets.

5.5 Meteors

Meteors, meteoroids, and meteorites

An object is called a *meteor* only during the time it is actually falling toward an impact with another body. If that body is Earth, the meteor will be burning up in the oxygen in Earth's atmosphere and appear as a light streaking through the sky. Often, as mentioned above, it will be mistakenly referred to as a "*shooting-star,*" because it really can look like a star falling out of the sky, but a meteor is actually a rock that is falling from space toward another object. Objects in space that have the potential to become meteors are called *meteoroids* and if an impacting object does not completely burn up during its fall, what is left of the object once on the ground is called a *meteorite.*

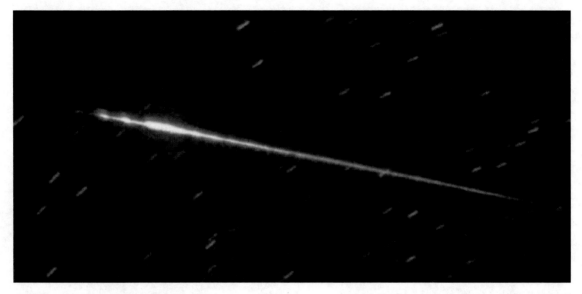

Figure 5.16 A falling meteor.

Meteorites

If a falling meteor is witnessed by someone, it is called a *fall*, and an especially bright fall is referred to as a *fireball*. A recovered meteorite is called a *find*. Most meteorites are called *stones* because they are similar to Earth rocks. Stones come from the outer crusts of asteroids and are freed during collisions. However, since stones are similar to Earth rocks, they are difficult to distinguish and can go unnoticed. Thus most finds are actually *irons* that come from the inner cores of asteroids and are more rare, because they are only freed from asteroids in larger collisions. There are also *stone-iron* meteorites that are a mixture of the two.

Figure 5.17 Meteorites

Meteor Showers

Most meteorites come from asteroids, but another source of meteoroids are comets. Comets leave a trail of tiny particles along the portion of their orbits near the Sun where they form their head and tail. If the comet's orbit crosses Earth's orbit, when Earth enters the swarm of meteoroids, there will be a *meteor shower*. Since the intersections with the comet orbits are in specific places in Earth's orbit, meteor showers occur at predictable times of year. A meteor shower is named after the constellation that Earth is moving toward in its orbit when the shower occurs. This is because the meteors will appear to come from this constellation when they fall. Since the meteoroids left over from comets are very tiny, most of them burn up before ever reaching the ground. A particularly intense meteor shower that can occur when the source-comet is nearby is called a *meteor storm*.

Figure 5.18 A meteor shower.

5.6 Impacts

If a meteor survives to reach the surface of the Earth, the resulting impact will leave a *crater*. Objects without protective atmospheres, like Earth's Moon or the planet Mercury, are covered with many impact craters, not only because of their lack of atmospheric protection, but also because nothing erases the craters after the impacts. Earth's atmosphere causes erosion, mostly from water and wind, weather that can wear away craters. The reworking of Earth's surface through geological activity, such as plate tectonics and volcanism, also often destroys the evidence of past impacts.

The larger the meteor, the larger and deeper the crater will be. Meteor Crater in Arizona, shown in Figure 5.19, is Earth's largest well-preserved impact crater. It is about the size of a small city and the impacting body is believed to have been the size of a small building. Larger impacts are more rare than smaller ones simply because it take more material to make a larger object, so there are more smaller, potentially impacting bodies. The risk of a large impact has also decreased over time, since the formation of the solar system, as more and more objects have become part of the planets and moons that they impact.

Figure 5.19 Meteor Crater in Arizona.

However, as shown by Meteor Crater in Arizona, large impacts can and do happen. In 1908 in a remote area of Siberia a huge explosion known as the Tunguska Event or Siberian Explosion, occurred that was heard as far away as Moscow, creating shockwaves in London. Trees in the forest were leveled and burned, radiating away from a central point for miles. The biggest mystery was that there was no crater, suggesting that the impacting body could have been an icy piece of a comet that vaporized during the explosion.

Figure 5.20 Trees burned and felled by the Tunguska Event in 1908.

The current theories about the extinction of the dinosaurs and the formation of Earth's Moon both involve large impacts. Sixty-five million years ago, an impact occurred that was so large that it threw enough debris into the atmosphere to shield Earth's surface from much of the incoming sunlight. Evidence that this can happen comes, on a smaller scale, from periods of cooler weather that often occur after massive volcanic eruptions spewing dust into the atmosphere that is then carried all over the world by air.

Many creatures would have been killed during the massive impact and the debris stayed in the atmosphere for a time long enough to kill a majority of the plants.

After the plants died, giant vegetarian dinosaurs that ate tons of plants a day could not find enough food and died. Then, consequently, there was not enough food for the carnivorous dinosaurs that fed on them. The survivors were the small mammals that could take shelter and forage for the smaller amounts of food they needed. There is evidence of the remains of a large crater off the Yucatan Peninsula in Mexico that contains unusually large amounts of the element *iridium* in a geologic-layer of sediments that dated to be from 65-million years ago. Iridium is an element that is rare on Earth, but more abundant in some meteorites.

Figure 5.21 Could a meteor impact 65-million years ago have caused the extinction of the dinosaurs?

Billions of years ago, an even larger impact may have formed Earth's moon. Rocks from the Moon brought back by the astronauts of the Apollo mission of the late 1960s and early 1970s, show that, compared to Earth rocks, Moon rocks are deficient in volatile elements, materials that would vaporize if temperatures were too high. This suggests that if a large enough body to throw material from Earth into orbit did indeed impact Earth, that volatile materials from both Earth and the object would have been vaporized in the explosion and the debris left in orbit to gravitationally pull together and form the orbiting body would have less of these materials.

Figure 5.22 The *Large Impact Theory* is currently the leading theory about Lunar Formation.

More recently, in 1994, 21 pieces of the fragmented Comet Shoemaker-Levy 9 smashed into Jupiter, resulting in huge explosions and leaving noticeable scars in the cloud tops that lasted for days, and even weeks, after the impacts occurred.

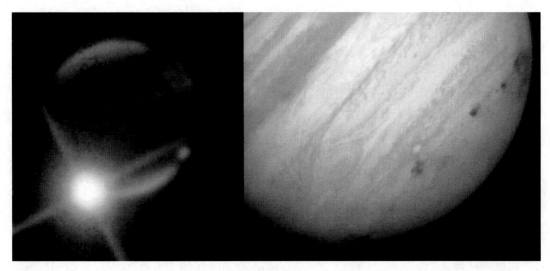

Figure 5.23 Impact of a fragment of Comet Shoemaker-Levy 9 with Jupiter and disturbances in Jupiter's cloud tops after the impacts.

Will Earth experience a major or even catastrophic impact in our lifetimes? It is really a matter of probabilities. Impacts of tiny micrometeorites occur constantly, while larger impacts are more rare. An impact the size of the Tunguska event is likely to happen about once per century, or less, so Earth may be due, but even then, the chances of an object hitting land are only about one in three or four, and the chances of hitting a densely populated area even smaller. Of course, a large impact in the ocean could trigger devastating Tsunamis. Globally catastrophic impacts, such as the one that killed the dinosaurs, are only likely once in a hundred million years.

Large objects passing close to Earth have been detected. There has even been the occasional prediction of a "doomsday" impact that has always, upon closer inspection of the object's orbit, turned out to be a false alarm. There has also been speculation about whether or not an impact could be prevented by somehow diverting the path of an object heading toward Earth, but no definitive answer as to whether or not this would be possible.

Review Questions

1. How are asteroids discovered?

2. What is the theory about why there is a belt of asteroids between 2 AU and 5 AU instead of a planet? What evidence is there for this theory?

3. How large are the largest asteroids?

4. How crowded is the asteroid belt? Do spacecraft have trouble traveling through it?

5. What is the Kuiper Belt? Where is it located? Describe the objects found there. What object is its best-known member?

6. What is the difference between a comet and a meteor? What is a "shooting star"?

7. What are the two main reasons for a comet's interesting behavior?

8. How do the coma (head) and tail of a comet form?

9. Explain how and why a comet eventually "dies."

10. Distinguish between meteors, meteoroids, and meteorites.

11. Where do most meteorites come from?

12. What are the two basic types of meteorites? What is the reason for the difference between them?

13. Explain why meteor showers occur.

14. How do we think Earth's Moon was formed?

15. Why does the Moon have so many more impact craters than Earth?

Tutorial-Comets

Comets are asteroid-sized chunks of rock and ice that come from the far outer solar system to the inner solar system in extremely eccentric orbits. For much of their orbit, they remain as these small rocky/icy comet *nuclei*, but when they get to the inner solar system, close to the sun, where temperatures are higher, they become very interesting.

The ice begins to vaporize and forms an envelope of gas around the nucleus. This is called the *coma* (or head of the comet). *The closer the comet gets to the sun, the larger the coma will be!*

Material, both gas from the coma and dust from the rocky portion of the nucleus, begins to stream away from the nucleus, forming both a gas and a dust *tail* on the comet. *Since the tails are caused to form by the sun's rays, they will always point in the direction opposite the sun!*

1-**Figure 1** shows the portion of a comet's highly eccentric orbit that is close to the sun. At each numbered position of the comet's *nucleus* draw the comet's *coma* (head) and *tail*. *Make sure that your drawing clearly shows any differences between the <u>size of the coma</u> and <u>length of the tail</u> and the <u>direction the tail is pointing</u>.*

2-List the position numbers in **Figure 1** in order from the smallest to the largest size of the *coma* (head).

3-List the position numbers in order form shortest to the longest length of the *tail*.

4- For each numbered position in **Figure 1,** choose which arrow in **Figure 2** best represents which way in space the comet's tail will be pointing.

Position 1	A	B	C	D	E
Position 2	A	B	C	D	E
Position 3	A	B	C	D	E
Position 4	A	B	C	D	E
Position 5	A	B	C	D	E

Figure 1

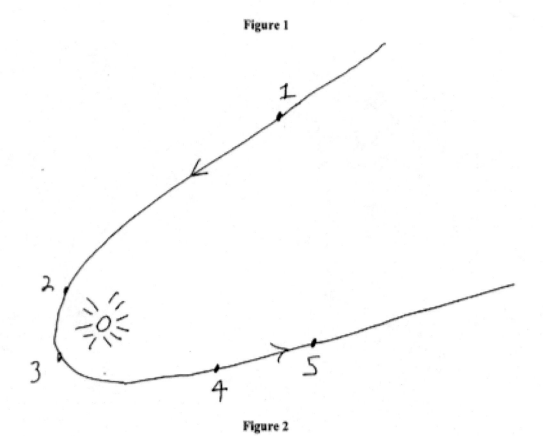

Figure 2

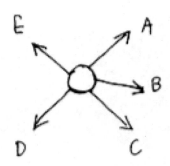

Chapter 6 - The Terrestrial Planets

6.1 Introduction

Analysis of planetary data has shown that there are two major types of planet in our solar system, the large gas-giant or *Jovian* planets that form in the cold outer-solar system and the smaller, rocky and metallic *Terrestrial* planets, named after our Earth, found in the warmer inner solar system.

The characteristics Mercury, Venus, and Mars have in common that put them into a category with Earth are that, relative to Jupiter, Saturn, Uranus, and Neptune (the *Jovians*), they are all small, of low mass, high density (composed primarily of rock and metals) and have few or no moons and no rings. They also have longer rotational periods and, since they are closer to the Sun, they have faster orbital periods.

Despite what they have in common, there is much diversity among the Terrestrial planets. Our Earth's surface is nearly three-fourths covered with oceans that interact with an oxygen-nitrogen atmosphere to moderate temperatures and create active weather systems, resulting in much reworking of the planet's surface. This is known as erosion. The solid landmasses and ocean floors are geologically active, and the whole planet is teeming with both animal and plant life. Though of similar size and mass, Venus is shrouded in a permanent cloud cover beneath which lies a barren, desolate landscape, an acid-laden poisonous atmosphere, oven-like temperatures, and incredibly high atmospheric pressures. Mercury appears very similar to Earth's moon; they are both geologically dead (or nearly so) rocks covered with impact craters due to a lack of a atmospheric protection, and minimal, if any, reworking of their surfaces from either geologic activity or atmospheric erosion. Mars is somewhat larger than Mercury, but small enough that it can only retain a thin atmosphere which, combined with its distance from the Sun, leaves it very cold. All of its once-running water is frozen, and its internal heat is spent, no longer able to drive the once-thriving geologic activity. Despite its current condition, Mars is by far the most Earth-like of the other Terrestrial worlds, which inevitably prompts us to ask if it is possible that Mars has ever had life or maybe even currently does support life.

From their initial formation out of the solar nebula to their current states, each Terrestrial planet has its own unique history. A story of how, despite their many similarities, slight differences in a few key factors, amplified over the last few billion years, have made them into the unique individual worlds we see today, is a fascinating history.

Figure 6.1 The Terrestrial planets, Mercury, Venus, Earth, and Mars.

6.2 Factors That Control Planetary Surface Development

The two basic factors that control almost everything that eventually happens on a terrestrial planet's surface after it forms are its *size* and its *distance from the sun*.

Size and Mass

The size and mass of a Terrestrial planet will determine much about the planet's eventual surface conditions. Recall from Chapter 3 that planets form from material gravitationally pulling together. The energy released from the collisions that occurred in this process heated the planets into molten states from which they have been cooling ever since, the outer layers cooling off before the interiors. The larger and more massive a planet, the longer it will take to cool down. The heat released from this cooling is the energy that fuels geologic activity like volcanism and plate tectonics. If a planet is too small there is not enough internal heat to drive much if any geological activity. If a planet is larger, activity may last for a while, but will eventually stop. On an even larger planet, geologic activity can last for a very long time. The amount, type, and duration of geologic activity that occurs play a very important role in shaping Terrestrial planetary surfaces.

Mass will also determine whether or not a planet has enough gravitational pull to retain an atmosphere. When planets cool from their molten state, they release gases. If a planet is not massive enough, most of the gases will escape into space. More massive planets will retain some gases and have a thin atmosphere. The most massive planets retain thicker atmospheres. Earth's atmosphere protects our planet's surface from both meteor impacts and harmful radiation from the sun, as well as providing insulation and air to breathe. All of these functions make the atmosphere of a Terrestrial planet a very important part of a planet's surface conditions and their development over time.

Distance from the Sun and Temperature

The distance from the sun directly affects the surface temperature of a planet. The closer the planet is to the Sun, the more energy it receives and the higher its initial surface temperature will become. The surface temperature, in turn, has profound effects on the development of the atmosphere. This includes which gases, in what percentages, will ultimately compose the atmosphere, and how much erosion, or reworking of the planet surface, largely with wind and water, will occur.

6.3 Processes That Shape a Planetary Surface

The main processes that affect planetary surface conditions are; *impact cratering*, from meteors that fall from space, *geological activity* (mainly volcanism and plate tectonics) and *erosion*, the reworking of the planet surface largely through the agents, wind and water.

Cratering

Impact *cratering* is the result of the bombardment of a planet surface by meteors. Impacting meteors will leave craters that reflect the size of the meteor and the speed and angle of impact. In the early history of the solar system, there were many more objects in orbit of the sun that had yet to become part of larger bodies, so the rate of cratering was very high. Over time this rate decreased dramatically and leveled off to its much lower current rate. For example, looking at the surface of Earth's moon, one might think that it is constantly bombarded, but the vast majority of the impacts occurred in the distant past. In the entire recorded history of astronomy, an impact on the moon has been observed only once.

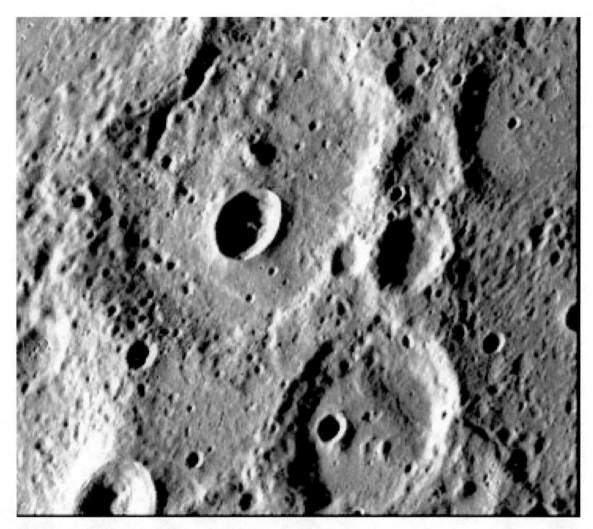

Figure 6.2 Impact Craters on the surface of Earth's Moon.

The reason that the craters that were formed on the moon so long ago are still so well preserved is that due to its smaller size, the moon could not sustain enough geological activity to rearrange its surface or retain enough of an atmosphere to protect it from impacting meteors by burning them up or to erode the craters with water or wind.

Geologic Activity

The two main types of geological activity that affect a planetary surface are *volcanism* and *tectonics*.

Volcanism

Volcanism is the expulsion of material from the interior of a planet to its surface. A volcanic eruption is the most dramatic example of volcanism, where molten rock, magma, and gases from beneath the surface are ejected to the surface. Another example of volcanism is a geyser, hot liquid being expelled from a planet's interior.

Figure 6.3 A volcanic eruption on Earth

Tectonics

Tectonics is the shifting of sections of the outermost layer of a planet, the crust. A hard-boiled egg is a decent example of the structure of a terrestrial planet, the yolk being the central core, the white being the middle, mantle, and the shell being the outer crust. The shell of a boiled egg can be cracked without being removed from the white; the different sections of the cracked shell then represent the different plates into which the crust is divided. Earth's crust is divided into about 20 plates. Tectonics is the motion of these plates. A short-range effect of tectonics is an earthquake, shockwaves that occur along the boundaries between plates, or faults, during motion of the plates. A longer-range effect is continental drift. Many of Earth's continents look like they are pieces of a puzzle because they were once part of a single super-continent that was broken up by tectonics.

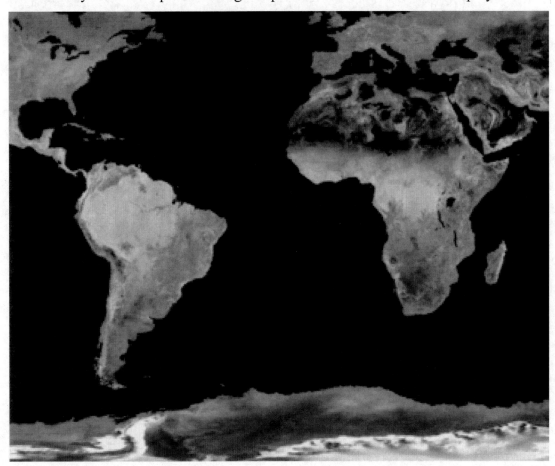

Figure 6.4 South American and Africa look like pieces of a puzzle that were separated by plate tectonics.

Mountains

Mountain building can be a result of volcanism or tectonics. Repeated volcanic eruptions in the same place can literally build mountains. The Hawaiian Islands are the tops of the tallest volcanic mountains on Earth. Mountains can also be built when tectonic plates overlap or push into one another and drive crustal material upward. Earth's highest mountain range, the Himalayas, was built by the collision of the Indian plate with the Eurasian plate.

Erosion

Erosion is the reworking of a planet's surface, usually by the agents, wind and water. To have either wind or water, it is necessary to retain an atmosphere; so smaller terrestrial bodies like Mercury and Earth's moon show very little evidence of erosion. Earth, on the other hand, has abundant liquid water and a very active lower atmosphere. Over time, evidence of past events, like impact craters and geological activity, are literally worn away.

Venus is hotter than Earth, too hot for water to be liquid, so there is not as much erosion. Mars' water is mostly frozen, but erosion does occur there in the form violent wind-driven dust storms.

The processes of cratering, volcanism, tectonics, and erosion, occurring in varying degrees depending on the size and surface temperature of each Terrestrial planet, have transformed their surfaces in different ways, creating the unique individual worlds we observe today.

6.4 Mercury and Earth's Moon

Mercury and Earth's moon are the smallest Terrestrial objects. The surfaces of both bodies are very similar, covered almost completely by impact craters. All the Terrestrial planets were subject to intense bombardment in their early history, but only Mercury and Earth's moon show the evidence so clearly today. This is precisely because of their smaller size. Neither body is large enough to drive or sustain much geologic activity or retain an atmosphere. So there was no atmospheric protection from impact cratering and neither planet's surface was reworked by geologic activity or erosion.

Figure 6.5 Due to the absence erosion on the surface of the Moon, over 40 years after it was made; an *Apollo* Astronaut's footprint is probably still there.

The fact that Mercury and Earth's moon are so similar in appearance shows that for small objects, objects not massive enough for geologic activity or to retain an atmosphere; *size* is a much *more important* factor in affecting surface conditions *than* surface *temperature*. Mercury is much closer to the sun than Earth's moon and therefore has a much higher surface temperature, yet their surfaces appear much the same. Since their surfaces appear so similar and the factor they have in common is similar size and not temperature, size must be the factor that is responsible for their surface conditions.

Due to their lack of atmospheres, both Mercury and Earth's moon experience wide variations in day and night temperatures. Atmospheres act as insulation, keeping a planet from getting too hot during the day and too cold at night. Being so close to the sun, it is no surprise that Mercury is very hot during the day, as high as about 350°C or 660° F, but at night it cools down by over 500°C, 900°F, to almost -150°C or -300°F. Earth's moon, being further from the sun, is cooler overall, its temperatures varying over a range of almost 280°C, about 500°F, from over almost 100°C, 200°F, during the day to -185°C, almost -300°F, at night.

Both worlds also have extremely long days to heat up and nights to cool off. Mercury orbits the sun in about 88 Earth-days, but takes about 59 Earth-days to rotate. The combination of these two motions causes the day on Mercury, the amount of time between two passages of the sun over the meridian to be about 2 Mercury years (about 178 Earth-days). This means that at any given location on Mercury, the sun is up for a whole Mercury year and then down for a whole year. The situation on Earth's moon is similar, but on a shorter time scale. The moon rotates in the same amount of time it takes to orbit Earth, just over 27 Earth-days, so at any given location on the moon, the Sun is up, then down, for about 2 weeks at a time.

Figure 6.6 Mercury and Earth's moon. Can you tell which is which?

6.5 Planetary Geology

Earth

Earth, Venus, and Mars are all massive enough to have had the internal heat necessary to drive geological activity. Earth is still geologically active. Volcanic eruptions and tectonic shifting are occurring regularly, constantly rearranging the planet's surface.

Venus

Venus is similar to Earth in size and mass, so it should be or have been nearly as geologically active as Earth. However, this is more difficult to determine, since Venus is completely covered with clouds all the time. Radar images taken by the *Magellan* spacecraft show evidence of volcanic features and impact craters but no tectonics. Since the cloud cover makes it impossible to continually observe its surface, it is difficult to tell for sure if Venus is currently geologically active. Being slightly smaller than Earth, Venus' internal heat may no longer be sufficient for geologic activity to occur. A possible reason for no evidence of tectonics having ever occurred on Venus is that the intense heat may have made the crust more pliable and less brittle than Earth's crust so that it did not break into individual plates. An analogy for this is candle wax. When warm, it is pliable and easily bent, but when cool, it is brittle and easily broken.

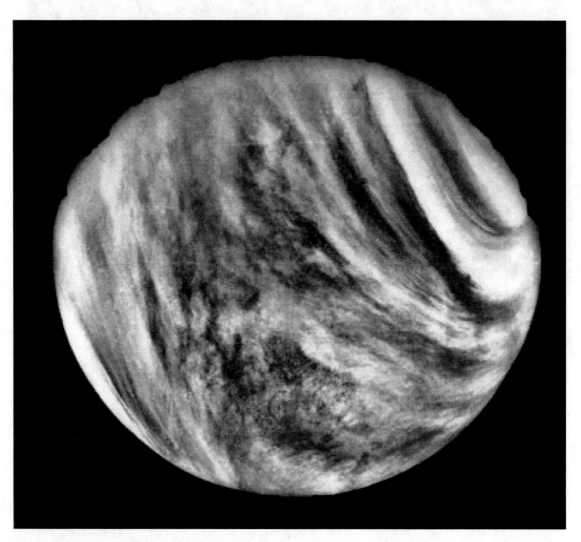

Figure 6.7 The surface of Venus is always completely covered by clouds.

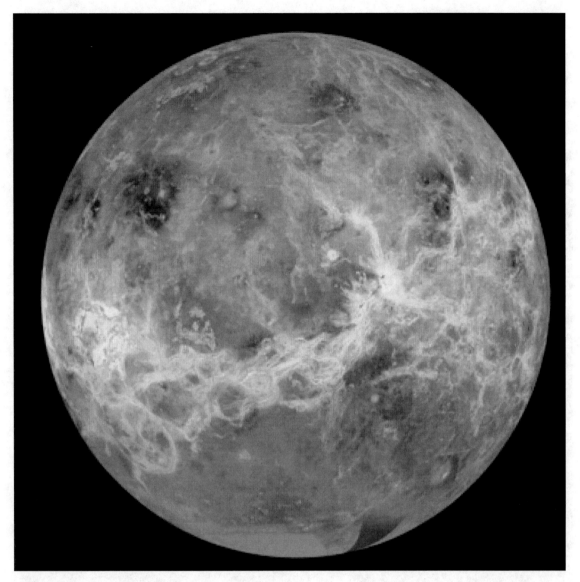

Figure 6.8 Computer-enhanced radar image of the usually hidden surface of Venus.

Mars

Mars is smaller than Earth or Venus, so it has not been geologically active for a long time. However, there is evidence that both volcanism and tectonics occurred in grand fashion there in the past. There are giant volcanic mountains including Mount Olympus (*Olympus Mons* in Latin), which is as large as the entire state of Arizona and three times as tall as Mount Everest. An eruption must have been a sight to behold. Mars also has a grand canyon. Earth's Grand Canyon in Arizona was carved out of the landscape by water erosion, the flow of the Colorado River. Mars' grand canyon, called the Valley of the *Mariner* (*Valles Marinaris* in Latin), named after the spacecraft that took the first close look at it, is a *rift valley*, a gigantic gap along a fault, the boundary between two tectonic plates that have moved apart. It is as long as the entire United Sates and much deeper than Earth's Grand Canyon.

Figure 6.9 Volcanoes (ovals on far left) and a rift valley (center) on the surface of Mars.

6.6 Planetary Atmospheres

Volcanic Degassing

After rock and metal first condensed out of the solar nebula, gravitation between the objects began to pull them together to form larger bodies, which then also began gravitationally pulling together. The collisions between these larger objects generated much energy and heated the forming planets until their material became molten. As they eventually cooled, they released the gases that became the initial atmospheres of the Terrestrial planets. This process, called volcanic degassing, can be observed when lava from volcanic eruptions on Earth cools. The gases released are *water vapor, carbon dioxide,* and *nitrogen.*

Smaller Bodies

Mercury and Earth's moon are too small and therefore not massive enough to retain the gases, so the gases escaped to space leaving these objects without atmospheric protection from meteor impacts or erosion to erase the craters, and thus showing the evidence of this ancient bombardment that we see today.

Larger Bodies

Earth, Venus and Mars are large enough that they did have the gravitational pull necessary to retain their initial atmospheres. The atmospheres they have today have been shaped by chains of events that were begun by their initial surface temperatures, which were set by their differing distances from the sun.

Earth

Earth's surface temperatures cooled so that most of the water-vapor condensed into liquid water filling up the lower elevation basins and creating the oceans that cover almost three-fourths of the planet surface today. Liquid water absorbs carbon dioxide, so much of the carbon dioxide was also taken out of the atmosphere, leaving nitrogen as the most abundant gas. Today, Earth's atmosphere is about 78 percent nitrogen and 21 percent oxygen, with the other 1 percent being traces of other gases, including what was left of the water vapor and carbon dioxide.

An important question about Earth's atmosphere is; where did the oxygen come from? Earth's atmospheric oxygen is unique among Terrestrial planet atmospheres. The answer is that the abundance of liquid water made Earth a hospitable environment for life to develop, specifically plants. In their respiratory process, photosynthesis, plants absorb sunlight, take in carbon dioxide, and expel oxygen. This even further reduced the atmospheric concentration of carbon dioxide and introduced the oxygen necessary for the development of animal life, including eventually, human beings.

Figure 6.10 Earth's surface is mostly covered by water. Rainforests, green color in central Africa, are the only evidence of life that is visible from space.

The Greenhouse effect

The greenhouse effect is the process by which a planet heats its atmosphere. Because of its high temperature, the Sun emits high-energy shortwave-radiation that easily penetrates the atmosphere and is absorbed by a planet. Being at a much lower temperature, planets reemit much lower-energy, long-wave radiation, some of which is then absorbed by atmospheric gases. The absorbing gases are known as the "greenhouse gases," water vapor and carbon dioxide being chief among them. A good example of the greenhouse effect is what happens in a car parked outside on a hot day. Energy from the very high temperature sun easily passes through the windows, but after it is absorbed and reemitted by the lower temperature interior of the car, much of it cannot escape and the temperature in the interior of the car gets much higher.

Greenhouse-effect heating on Earth is only moderate. This is because most of the initial atmospheric water vapor on Earth cooled and condensed to liquid. The liquid water in turn absorbed much of the initial carbon dioxide, and gave rise to plants that removed even more carbon dioxide from of the atmosphere through photosynthesis.

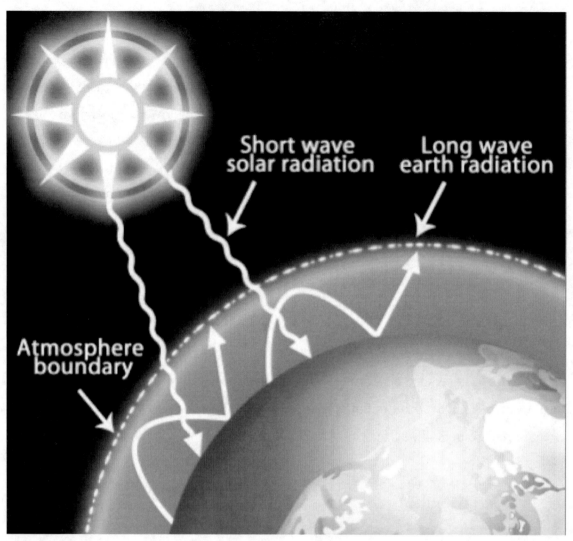

Figure 6.11 The greenhouse effect. Short-wave energy from the hot Sun easily penetrates the atmosphere, then is absorbed and remitted as long wave energy by the cooler Earth. Much of this long-wave energy is then trapped in the atmosphere.

Venus

On Venus, surface temperatures never cooled enough for water-vapor to condense, so it did not absorb the carbon-dioxide and the two greenhouse gases trapped tremendous amounts of heat, resulting in a runaway greenhouse effect that left Venus the way we find it today. The atmosphere is mostly carbon dioxide and the atmospheric pressure, the weight of the atmospheric gases pushing down on the planet surface, is over 90 times higher than that on Earth. Venus's atmosphere is so thick because of the fact that little or none of the original carbon dioxide was removed like happened on Earth. Friction with this incredibly thick atmosphere is believed to be what slowed the rotation rate of Venus down and actually reversed it to a slow rotation in a direction opposite most other planets. Venus takes 243 Earth-days to rotate, while only 224 days to orbit the sun.

Temperatures are nearly 500°C or about 900 °F, which is hotter than Mercury, day or night. Droplets of sulfuric acid condense out of the atmosphere, much the way water does on Earth. The dew on Venus is acid. Water vapor is a much lighter gas than carbon dioxide, so most of the original water vapor rose as the heavier carbon dioxide sank to the surface. Much of the water vapor escaped to space and some of it condensed into the thick cloud cover we always see around Venus.

Although scientists had theorized about the hostile surface conditions on Venus, the conditions were not actually verified by observation until 1975 when a robot spacecraft, *Venera* (Russian for Venus) actually landed on the surface. The first two *Veneras* crash-landed on the surface, but the third and fourth attempts finally made successful landings. They only operated for less than an hour, but in that time they photographed a desolate and barren landscape through a hazy atmosphere and took readings that verified the high temperatures, immense pressures and acidic-corrosion to which their predecessors fell, and to which they would soon fall victim.

Figure 6.12 *Venera* spacecraft image of the surface of Venus.

Too Hot, Too Cold, Just Right

Venus is an example of how an atmosphere can end up if it is subject to too much greenhouse effect. This suggests that it could be perhaps used as an example of the dangers of *global warming*. Global warming is an enhancement of the greenhouse effect that is occurring on Earth due to extra carbon dioxide being emitted into the atmosphere through pollution. Although scientific studies overwhelmingly show that global warming is a real environmental problem that human beings need to deal with, Venus is not its "poster-child." Being similar to Earth in mass and size and proximity to the Sun, Venus had the potential to develop surface conditions much like those on Earth, but being just a little closer to the Sun, and not cooling off enough for its water vapor to condense into liquid, began a chain of events that resulted in the conditions we find on Venus today.

Mars

If Venus is an example of what too much greenhouse effect can do, Mars provides an example of conditions when there is too little greenhouse warming. Being farther from the sun than Earth, most of the water vapor ended up frozen into ice. Being much smaller than Earth or Venus, Mars could not gravitationally retain nearly as thick an atmosphere as either of its Terrestrial cousins. Today we find Mars with a mostly carbon dioxide atmosphere that is as much thinner than Earth's as Venus' is thicker. The combination of being farther from the Sun than Earth and, therefore, getting less energy to start with and very little greenhouse warming occurring in the thin air, leaves the warmest places on Mars even at their warmest times of year, very cold.

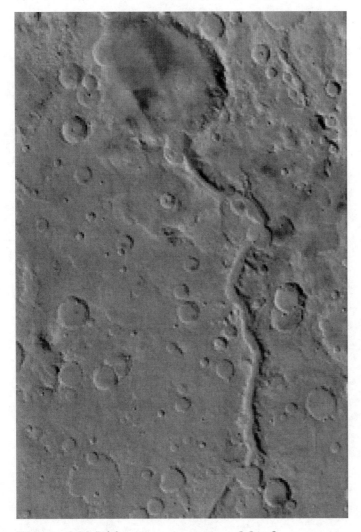

Figure 6.13 Did water once run on Mars?

Although most of the water is currently frozen, there is evidence that liquid water once ran on Mars. Water-erosion exists in the form of now dried-up riverbeds. This suggests that in its past Mars had warmer temperatures. That, along with the fact that there once was active geology, means that past conditions on Mars were more Earth-like. This brings up the question, "Has there ever been, or even is there now, life on Mars?"

Life on Mars?

Mars has been visited by more spacecraft from Earth than any other object in the solar system. None of these spacecraft, including several that landed on the Martian surface, have found any direct visual evidence of plant or animal life and tests run on the Martian soil found evidence of chemical reactions, but not biological activity. A meteorite discovered in Antarctica, of a type know by its chemical composition to have originated on Mars, has been found to contain a microscopic structure that resembles fossilized bacteria, but there is debate about whether it is indeed organic in origin and if so, is it indeed from Mars or did it contaminate the meteorite after the meteorite landed on Earth. This meteorite, known as ALH-84001, will be discussed in more detail in Chapter 13.

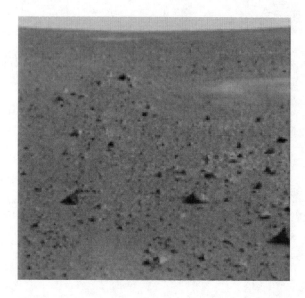

Figure 6.14 The surface of Mars.

Review Questions

1. What are the four processes that shape Terrestrial planet surfaces?

2. What are the two main factors that control how a Terrestrial planet's surface will evolve?

3. Which factor controls whether or not a planet will have an atmosphere and how thick it will be?

4. Which factor controls whether or not a planet will have geological activity and how long it will last?

5. Since the surface of Mercury and Earth's moon are so similar, which factor was likely most important in shaping their surfaces and why?

6. What properties do Venus and Earth have in common? What ONE initial difference is ultimately responsible for how vastly different conditions on the two planets are now, and what caused this difference?

7. Name TWO reasons that it is so cold on Mars.

8. Why is Mars no longer geologically active?

9. What gas, abundant in Earth's atmosphere, is unique to Earth, and what was the source of this gas?

10. Explain the differences among the greenhouse effects on Venus, Earth, and Mars and the reasons for the differences.

Tutorial-Terrestrial Planet Surfaces

Fill out the table below by classifying the **Size** of each Terrestrial planet as either *Large*, *Medium*, or *Small*; and **Temperature** as either *hot*, *medium*, or *cold*. Base your temperature estimate on the planet's distance from the Sun.

Object	Size	Temperature
Mercury		
Venus		
Earth		
Earth's Moon		
Mars		

Based on your entries in the above table, fill out the **geologic activity** you would expect to find on each planet as either *Current*, *Past*, or *None* recalling that the larger a planet is, the more internal heating it has to drive geologic activity and atmospheric **pressure** as *Thick*, *Thin*, or *none* recalling that more massive planets have more gravitational pull with which to retain an atmosphere, and phase of any **water** as *vapor*, *liquid*, or *ice*.

Object	Geology	Atmosphere	Water
Mercury			
Venus			
Earth			
Earth's Moon			
Mars			

Based on your entries in *both* tables, put a check mark in the column for each process that you think will have affected each planet's surface.

Object	Impact Cratering	Geology (tectonics and/or volcanism)	Erosion (from wind & water)
Mercury			
Venus			
Earth			
Earth's Moon			
Mars			

Now, *based on the table you just filled out*, describe the atmospheric and surface condition of each planet and whether or not they seem accurate from what you read in the chapter. Earth has been done for you as an example.

Object	Temperatures	Atmospheric Pressure	Geological Activity	Sate of Water	Visible Craters	Accurate?
Mercury						
Venus						
Earth	Moderate	High	Active Volcanoes & Tectonics	Oceans	Very few	yes
Earth's Moon						
Mars						

Based on what you have learned about the factors that control the processes that affect planetary surfaces, predict the likely surface conditions of each type of object in the table below.

Object	Size	Distance from Sun	Atmosphere	Geology	Surface Conditions
Asteroid	Very small	Far			
Jovian Moon	small	Very Far			

Chapter 7 - The Jovian Planets, Their Moons and Ring Systems

7.1 Introduction

The Jovian or Jupiter-like planets, Jupiter, Saturn, Neptune, and Uranus, are all very large, massive, of low density, made mostly of gases and liquids, far from the Sun and therefore with longer orbital periods. They also all have faster rotations (all less than a day). Being of high mass and therefore having greater gravitational pull, they all have many moons and ring systems.

Figure 7.1 The Jovian Planets

7.2 Tidal Forces and Ring Systems

Ring Systems

Ring systems are composed of trillions of tiny rocky and icy particles in similar orbits around a planet. From a distance they may look like a solid ring. Saturn has the most extensive ring system and was once thought to be the only planet with rings, but rings are now known to be a characteristic of Jovian Planets.

The Roche Limit

Rings could be considered analogous to the asteroid belt, planetary material in orbit of the Sun that never gravitationally pulled together. However, rings are small particles in orbit of a planet, but the particles are believed to have once been part of moons, *not* material that never formed a moon. The reason for this is that rings are always found within a distance from a planet called the Roche limit. Inside the Roche limit, tidal forces from a Jovian planet are too strong for the mutual gravitation of the ring particles to pull together and form a moon. French astronomer Edouard Roche first calculated this distance, about 2.5 times the radius of a Jovian planet.

Figure 7.2 Saturn's rings are just inside the Roche limit.

Tidal Forces

Tidal forces are the same forces that cause the ocean tides on Earth. Tides are caused by the *difference* in gravitational pull from the Moon, and the Sun, from one side of Earth to the other. The side of Earth facing the Moon or Sun will be pulled with greater force than the opposite side. This *differential gravitation* causes a tidal bulge. Since water is a very fluid substance, Earth's oceans will be deeper along the line of the tidal bulge, high tide.

The excess water for high tide comes from the surface locations perpendicular to the bulge, which are therefore at low tide. Since Earth rotates once per day, there are about six hours between a high and low tide and about twelve hours between two high or two low tides.

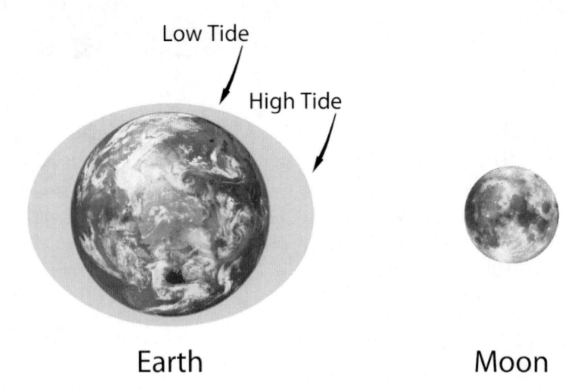

Figure 7.3 Differential gravitational pull on Earth from the Moon creating a tidal bulge.

Even though the Sun is much more massive than the Moon, the Moon is much closer, so the difference in the gravitational pull from one side of Earth to the other from the Moon is more than from the Sun. Therefore, the position of the Moon determines the locations of high and low tides and the position of the Sun will determine whether it is spring or neap tide. Spring tide occurs when all three objects are along a straight line, during full or new moon, causing higher high tides and lower low tides, the greatest difference between high and low tide. Neap tide is when the Sun and Moon are at right angles to each other, at the quarter phases, causing lower high tides and higher low tides, the smallest difference between high and low tides. Since it takes about a week to go from full or new moon to a quarter phase, there is about a week between spring and neap tide.

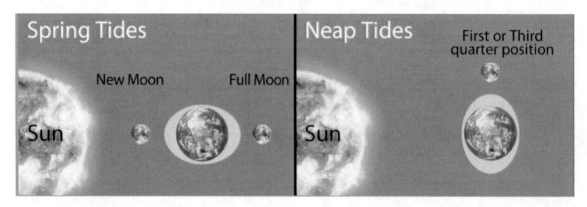

Figure 7.4 Spring and Neap Tides on Earth.

Inside the Roche limit, or closer than 2.5 times the radius of the planet, there are ring particles in orbit. Outside the Roche limit, further than that distance, is where the moons are found. Rings are believed to be materials released during collisions between the numerous moons in the Jovian systems and also material from moons that, due to shifts in their orbit caused by the gravitational pull of other moons, crossed inside the Roche limit and were literally crushed into ring-rubble.

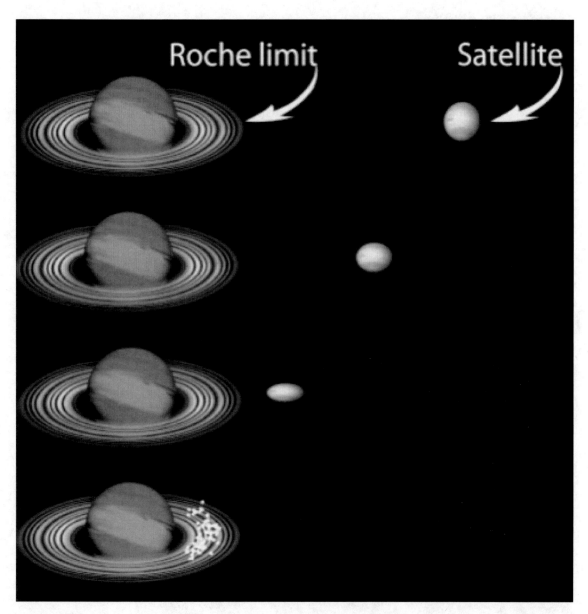

Figure 7.5 Tidal forces will tear moons into ring material if they cross the Roche limit.

Shepherd Moons

Individual rings are maintained by the presence of tiny moons (or large ring particles) found within a Jovian planet's Roche limit that orbit on the inside and outside edges of a ring. The moon on the inside of the ring orbits faster than the ring particles and tugs them forward; the moon on the outside orbits slower and pulls them backward. The combined effect keeps the particles in the ring shape. Without shepherd moons, all the ring particles would spread out evenly between the planet and its Roche limit.

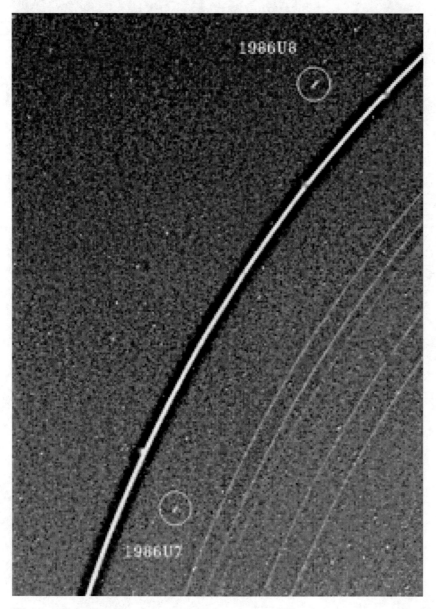

Figure 7.6 Shepherd moons in the rings of Uranus.

7.3 The Discoveries of Uranus and Neptune

Astronomers have known the five planets visible to the unaided eye, Mercury, Venus, Mars, Jupiter, and Saturn, since ancient times. It was not until after the invention of the telescope that new ones that could not be seen with the unaided eye were discovered. In the late 1700s, German Astronomer Johann Titus devised a numerical formula that matched the distance of each of the known planets from the Sun relative to Earth's distance fairly well. Starting with a series of numbers beginning first with 0, then 3, and then doubling 3 and each number after that, then adding 4 to that number, and finally dividing by 10, gives the values shown in the table in Table 7.1. The idea was publicized by the then director of the Berlin Observatory, Johann Bode, and thus is called the *Titus-Bode Law*. Interestingly enough, 2.8 AU, where there was no known planet, was a location where many, including Kepler, thought there probably was a planet that had not yet been discovered.

A Series of Numbers	Add 4	Divide by 10	Known Distance (in AU)	Planet
0	4	0.4	0.38	Mercury
3	7	0.7	0.72	Venus
6	10	1.0	1.0	Earth
12	16	1.6	1.52	Mars
24	28	2.8		
48	52	5.2	5.2	Jupiter
96	100	10.0	9.5	Saturn

Table 7.1 The Titus-Bode Law

Uranus

Using the Titus-Bode law to calculate the position of the "next" planet after Saturn gives 19.6 AU. Several astronomers had searched the sky for a planet at this position, but nobody found anything until 1781. William Herschel was born in Germany but was living in England. A musician by day and an amateur astronomer at night, he built a large reflecting telescope. He was actually more interested in studying stars, and in fact would eventually be known as the father of stellar astronomy. Over the course of observing the same part of the sky on several nights, he noticed an object that was not a point of light, but a disk that, over several observations, appeared to be moving in front of the fixed background stars. This relative motion is the telltale sign of a planetary object. He had dismissed the object as a comet, but closer investigation showed that the object was in an orbit that was too circular for a comet. Comet orbits are very eccentric ellipses. The discovery was at first resisted by professional astronomers, probably due to jealousy over an amateur making a discovery that they had not, but the quality of Herschel's telescope, and thus the validity of his observations, could not be denied. Soon he was credited with the first discovery of a planet since ancient times, and before long received a royal appointment as a full-time astronomer. His sister Caroline, who started as his assistant, became a successful astronomer in her own right and received an appointment as well.

Figure 7.7 Herschel

The discovery created an interesting problem that no one ever had before: what to name a new planet? Some wanted to name it after the discoverer. Herschel himself wanted to name it after his sponsor, the King of England. Whether Herschel and George would have been good names for a planet could be debated. However, it was decided that the ancient tradition of naming planets after mythological characters should be continued and the new planet was named Uranus.

Neptune

Uranus turned out to be 19.2 AU from the Sun, matching the Titus-Bode law equally as well as the other planets. At this distance, it orbits the Sun once every 84 years, which coincidentally, was also how long William Herschel lived. This discovery excited astronomers about using the Titus-Bode law to find planets. This excitement intensified in 1801 when Giuseppe Piazzi discovered *Ceres*, the largest member of the asteroid belt at 2.8 AU, precisely the position of the "missing planet." The next predicted position was 38.8 AU. However, by the mid-1800s, astronomers had another method to use when searching for planets.

Irregularities in the orbit of Uranus, first detected in 1821, suggested that there was another sizable object beyond Uranus exerting a gravitational influence. In 1844 a young English mathematician, John Couch Adams, used these perturbations to predict the position with a size similar to Uranus at about 30 AU. Now he needed time on a good telescope to search for it. He tried to convince British Astronomer Royal, George Airy, to get him time on a large telescope for the search, but Airy was difficult to contact and skeptical of Adams' idea, and did not help him.

Urbain Leverrier, a young French mathematician, had made similar predictions and had similar frustrations in getting telescope time. So he went to Germany in 1846 and asked Johann Galle, director of the Berlin Observatory, to take up the search. Galle found the object on the very first night.

It is not hard to imagine Adams' frustration when Leverrier and Galle published the results and were credited with the discovery of Neptune. Much controversy, intensified by the nationalistic rivalry between England and France, followed. Having published their results first, Leverrier and Galle rightfully got credit from the scientific community for the discovery of Neptune, but clearly history has also remembered Adams.

Historical records show that both Uranus and Neptune had been observed several times before their credited discoverers found them. Most notably, Neptune was observed by Galileo, but he either did not recognize the object for what it was or he was concentrating more on other things he was observing and never took the time to investigate it further.

7.4 Jupiter and Its Moons

Jupiter is by far the solar systems largest and most massive planet. It is twice as massive as all the other planets combined and more than 10 times the diameter (distance across) of Earth. Jupiter's gravitational pull is so strong that you would weigh 2.5 times as much there as you do on Earth. But, as with all the giant planets, it is only solid at core. The composition of its atmosphere is more similar to the Sun's than Earth's, being made almost entirely of hydrogen and helium gas. When you look at Jupiter you are seeing the tops of the clouds. The lighter-colored bands are called zones and are warmer gases, rising, while the darker-colored belts are cooler, sinking gases. This vertical atmospheric motion, similar to that in Earth's atmosphere, is called *convection*. The oval-shaped features are storms. The largest, the Great Red Spot, was discovered over 300 years ago. Astronomers have no idea how long it has been going on and it shows no signs of slowing down or stopping. As large and powerful as hurricanes are on Earth, this hurricane on Jupiter is three times the size of the entire Earth.

Figure 7.8 Jupiter: note the belts, zones, and oval storms. including the Great Red Spot.

At last count Jupiter has over 60 moons. The four largest, *Ganymede, Europa, Callisto* and *Io,* were all discovered by Galileo about 400 years ago and are still collectively referred to as the *Galilean Satellites. Ganymede*, the largest moon in the entire solar system, is larger than Mercury; *Callisto* is almost as large and nearly completely covered by craters. *Europa* is similar in size to Earth's moon and covered with ice. Astronomers have speculated that underneath the ice, it may be warm enough for there to be liquid water, an ocean. If verified, this would be the first ocean anywhere in the solar system besides Earth. This brings about speculation of *Europa* being one of the solar system's more promising environments for life to develop. Io, a little larger than *Europa*, is closest to Jupiter, close enough that tidal forces from Jupiter to nearly rip *Io* apart. Normally any object the size of *Io* would not be large enough to have enough internal heating to fuel volcanism, but the repeated flexing and squeezing from the tides cause its interior to heat up and become molten. Eruptions on Io were the first volcanic activity seen anywhere in the solar system other than Earth.

Figure 7.9 Montage of Jupiter's Red Spot with (from the bottom up) heavily cratered *Callisto*, large *Ganymede*, icy *Europa,* and volcanic *Io.*

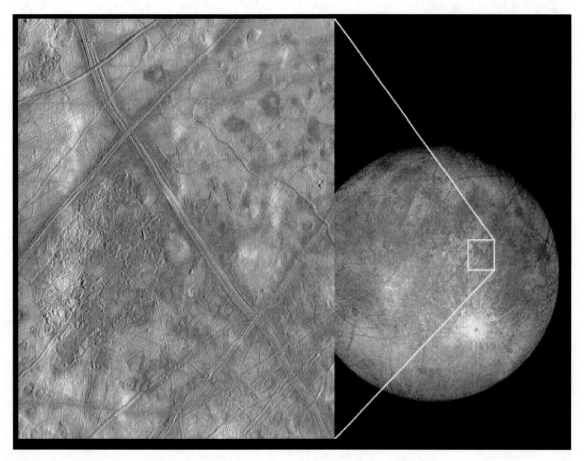

Figure 7.10 A close up of a portion of *Europa*'s ice-covered surface.

Figure 7.11 A volcanic eruption on *Io*.

7.5 Saturn

Saturn is like a smaller Jupiter in many ways. It has many similar features, but being almost twice as far from the Sun, getting only about a fourth as much solar energy, it is much colder there and, being smaller, its atmosphere is much less active. Together, the combination of gases and other material that make up Saturn are less dense than water. If you could find a body of water big enough to put it in, Saturn would float.

Saturn's largest Moon, *Titan,* has the most substantial atmosphere of any moon in the solar system. Like Jupiter's larger moons, *Titan* is similar in size to Mercury, so it should not have enough gravitational strength to retain an atmosphere, but being 10 times as far from the Sun as Earth, and therefore receiving one-hundredth as much solar energy, it is very cold there, so the gases are not as active and are easier to retain. The composition of *Titan*'s atmosphere suggests that there could be chemistry going on there similar to that

216

on Earth when life was first forming. However, the same cold temperatures that allow the atmosphere to be retained make it unlikely that life actually did develop. In 2005 the *Cassini* spacecraft successfully deployed the *Huygens* probe that actually landed on the surface of *Titan*.

Figure 7.12 *Cassini* image of *Titan*.

Figure 7.13 *Huygens* probe image of *Titan*'s surface

One of Saturn's smaller moons, *Mimas*, has a crater so large that it is likely that if the impacting body had been any bigger, *Mimas* would have been smashed to bits. This crater represents evidence of the solar system's more violent past. This past likely played a very important role in conditions at the solar system's next planet, Uranus.

Figure 7.14 *Mimas* and her gigantic impact crater.

7.6 Uranus, Neptune and Their Moons

Uranus and Neptune are considerably smaller than Jupiter and Saturn, each only being about 15 times as massive as Earth and about 4 times the diameter. Their compositions, like their larger siblings, are mostly hydrogen and helium, but they have more atmospheric methane, and this is responsible for their bluish color. Because it is so cold at nearly 20 AU, or 20 times as far from the Sun as Earth, Uranus has a very calm atmosphere with almost no surface features. Temperatures are as low as -200°C, -350°F. Being farther from the Sun where it is even colder, a calm atmosphere could also be expected to be the case on Neptune. However, because there is little or no friction at Neptune's frigid temperatures, winds can blow at faster speeds than anywhere else in the solar system. Neptune also had a large storm system, dubbed the Great Dark Spot (see Fig. 7.15), in a similar position in its atmosphere as Jupiter's Great Red Spot. But the feature, first seen by the *Voyager* Spacecraft in 1989, was not as long-lasting as Jupiter's Red Spot, and Hubble Space Telescope images showed that it was no longer there just a few years later,

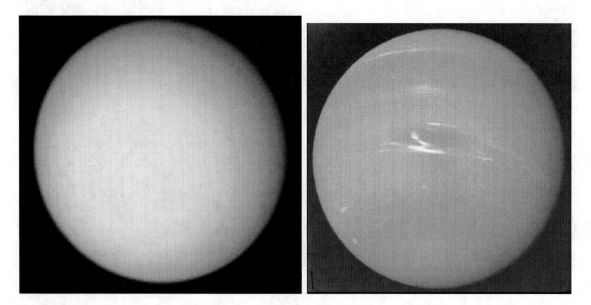

Figure 7.15 Uranus and Neptune

The most unusual feature of Uranus and its moons is that the entire system, relative to the other planets in the solar system, is on its side. Uranus' rotational axis lies nearly on the line between the planet and the Sun, while most other planets' axis are almost perpendicular to that line. Earth's axial-tilt, the cause of the seasons, is 23 ½°, about one-fourth of the way from being straight up and down relative to the line between it and the Sun. Evidence for the reason for Uranus' extreme axial-tilt is found in the moons of Uranus. They show scars of early solar system violence, from the time when the rate of bombardment was much higher than now, when there were larger quantities of material that had not yet become part of planets or moons, impacting other objects. In some cases, as with Uranus' small moon, Miranda, they literally look as if they had been smashed into pieces and just barely pulled back together by gravitational forces. Perhaps at one time, Uranus's system was oriented similar to the solar system's other planets but was knocked on it side in a collision during this early epoch of bombardment. Uranus's moons were likely also impacted, but even more damage could have been caused by collisions with one another because of the shifts in their orbits caused by Uranus tilting over. Eventually the moons would settle into the orbits around Uranus that we observe today, but still bearing the scars of their violent past.

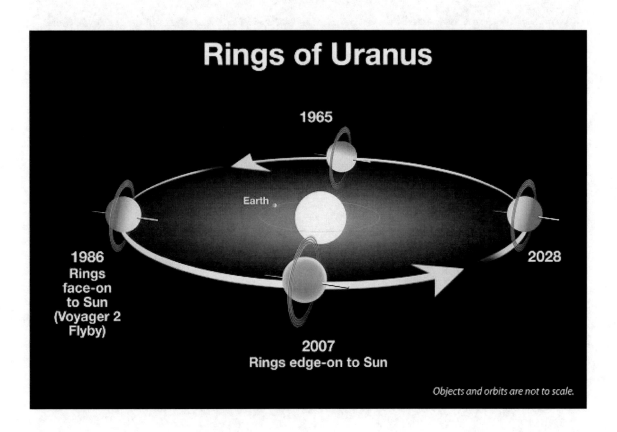

Figure 7.16 The tilt of Uranus' rotational axis is nearly in the plane of its orbit around the Sun.

Figure 7.17 Montage of Uranus and is Moons. Notice the cracks and fissures on the two in the foreground, *Ariel* (closest) and *Miranda*.

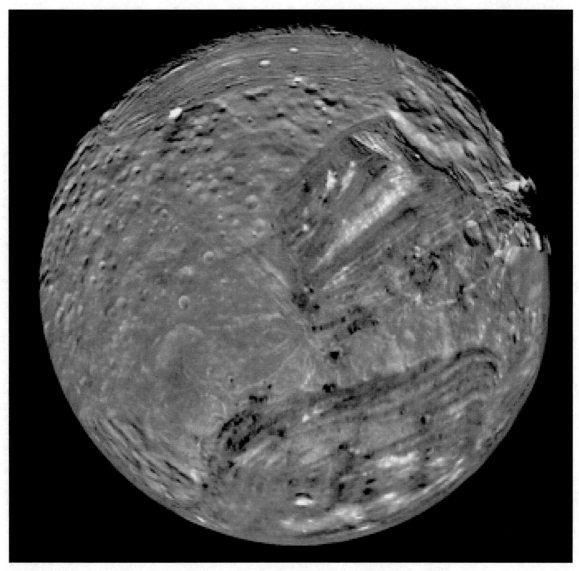

Figure 7. 18 A close-up of Uranus' moon *Miranda*.

The *Voyager* spacecraft also observed nitrogen geysers on Neptune's largest Moon, *Triton*. This was only the second time that active geology had been observed anywhere in the solar system besides Earth.

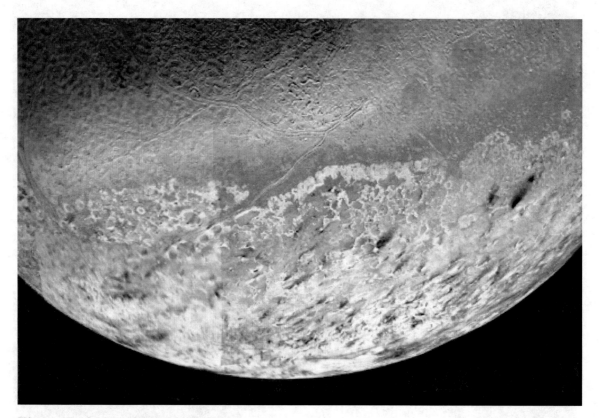

Figure 7.19 Neptune's moon *Triton*.

Review Questions

1. How do we think planetary ring systems were formed?

2. What is the Roche limit?

3. What are tidal forces? Why are they important in Jovian planet systems?

4. What are Shepherd moons? What do they do?

5. Explain how the positions of both Uranus and Neptune were predicted prior to their discoveries. Which prediction was more scientifically accurate?

6. Of what two gases are the atmospheres of Jovian planets mostly composed?

7. What is Jupiter's Great Red Spot?

8. Explain why Jupiter's moon Io is volcanic?

9. What is unusual about Jupiter's moon Europa?

10. Explain how Saturn's moon Titan is able to retain an atmosphere.

11. What do Europa of Jupiter and Titan of Saturn have in common?

12. What do Io of Jupiter and Triton of Neptune have in common?

13. About how large are the largest Jovian satellites?

14. What causes the bluish color of Uranus and Neptune?

15. What is the theory for why Uranus's entire system is on its side? What evidence is there for this?

16. What was the Great Dark Spot?

Tutorial--*Jovian* Planets Worksheet

Match each planet with its feature:

Jupiter   On its side

Saturn   Fastest Wind

Uranus   Great Dark Spot

Neptune   Great Red Spot

Match each moon of Jupiter with its feature:

Ganymede   Volcanic

Callisto   Ice-covered

Europa   Largest

Io   Most craters

Name the planet to which each moon belongs, then match it with its feature:

Titan   _____   Geysers

Mimas   _____   Destroyed and reassembled

Miranda   _____   Atmosphere

Triton   _____   Huge crater

What are the Great Red Spot and the Great Dark Spot?

What are Shepherd Moons? What do they do?

Despite the fact that, based on the causes of geological and atmospheric conditions on terrestrial planets, it would be expected that Jovian moons are too small (the largest are about the size of Mercury and Earth's moon and most are smaller), and therefore not massive enough to provide the necessary internal heat for geological activity or to have the gravity to retain an atmosphere, Jovian moons with geologic activity and atmospheres have been discovered.

1-What is the explanation for the observed occurrence of volcanic eruptions on Jupiter's moon *Io,* despite the fact that it is barely bigger than Earth's moon?

2- What is a possible explanation for the presence of an atmosphere around Saturn's moon *Titan,* despite the fact it is barely bigger than Mercury?

Hint-Think of the other factor besides size that you learned can affect conditions on a planet.

3-Do the above explanations suggest that geological activity and the presence of an atmosphere would be common on Jovian moons or are these objects exceptions?

Chapter 8 - Light, Telescopes, & Spectra

8.1 Introduction

Light is very important in astronomy because almost everything that astronomers study is too far away to touch. So any information comes from various forms of light. Therefore, it is necessary for astronomers to know as much as possible about light, so they can understand everything that it can tell them about the objects it came from.

8.2 The Speed and Nature of Light

In the late 1800s, physicist James Clerk Maxwell combined the basic ideas that describe the nature of electricity and magnetism and discovered *electromagnetic waves*. The speed of such waves can be calculated from the basic constants of electricity and magnetism and is equal to about c=300,000,000 m/s (c=3 x 10^8 m/s in scientific notation), the speed of light. The symbol "c" is simply an abbreviation or shorthand that physicists and astronomers use for the speed of light.

Figure 8. 1 Maxwell

Heinrich Hertz verified the existence of electromagnetic waves experimentally by producing them with the vibrations of an electrified antenna. Because of his contribution, the unit for the frequency of waves is called the *Hertz*.

Figure 8.2 Hertz

Later, physicist Alfred Michelson experimentally obtained the same result as Maxwell's theoretical speed for these electromagnetic waves. Michelson was the last in a line of scientists, beginning with Galileo, who had attempted to measure the speed of light, but Michelson's experiments were the most precise and the first that could be compared with theoretical predictions.

Figure 8.3 Michelson

8.3 Electromagnetic Waves

The colors of the visible spectrum of light--red, orange, yellow, green, blue and violet--known collectively as *visible* light, are actually only one kind of light. Light includes the entire electromagnetic spectrum shown in Figure 8.4. Light is a type of electromagnetic wave, and all electromagnetic waves are light.

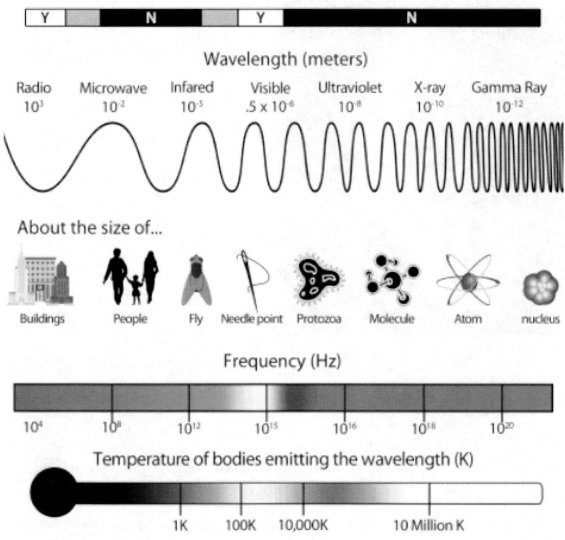

Figure 8.4 The Electromagnetic Spectrum

The only differences between one type of electromagnetic wave and another, or one color of visible light and another, are the wavelength and frequency. Wavelength is literally the physical length of one cycle of a wave. Frequency is a time measurement, the measure of how frequently a wave repeats its cycle. Longer waves take a longer time to repeat their cycle, so they have lower frequencies. Shorter waves can repeat their cycles more rapidly, so they have higher frequencies. Red light has a longer wavelength and lower frequency than violet light, on the other end of the visible spectrum, which has a shorter wavelength and higher frequency. The color of a light wave that we *see* with our detectors, our eyes, is controlled by the light's wavelength.

Visible light is about in the middle of the entire electromagnetic spectrum. Ultraviolet means "above violet" and has a higher frequency and therefore shorter wavelength than visible light. Infrared means "below red" and has a lower frequency and therefore longer wavelength than visible light. Waves with higher frequencies and shorter wavelengths than visible light and ultraviolet are X-rays and gamma rays. Waves with lower frequencies and longer wavelengths than visible light and infrared are microwaves and radio waves.

The one thing all electromagnetic waves, all light, have in common is traveling at the same speed, the speed of light. From short wavelength, high frequency gamma rays to visible light to long wavelength, low frequency radio waves; all travel at c=300,000 km/s. This is equivalent to c=186,000 miles/sec. A light wave could orbit the Earth about seven times in one second, travel the quarter of a million miles to the moon and back in about two and a half seconds, and light from the Sun, 93 million miles away, travels to Earth in eight minutes.

This includes radio waves. It is a common myth that since we *hear* radio, radio waves travel at the speed of sound, about a million times slower than light. Amplitude and frequency modulation (AM and FM) are used to allow our ears to hear what is being broadcast by radio waves, but the waves themselves actually travel at the speed of light.

Astronomers have telescopes that can collect every type of electromagnetic wave in the spectrum, so they can study as many objects in as many different ways as possible.

8.4 Telescopes

Our atmosphere absorbs the majority of all electromagnetic waves except for visible light and radio waves. Consequently, all telescopes, other than those that collect visible light (known as *optical* telescopes) and radio telescopes must be put on satellites in orbit of Earth. Being in space, like the famous *Hubble Space Telescope*, is actually the best option for any telescope; this way, the effects of our turbulent atmosphere that cause stars to appear to *twinkle*, weather, and urban light pollution can be all be avoided. However, this is very expensive, so there are also many telescopes on Earth's surface.

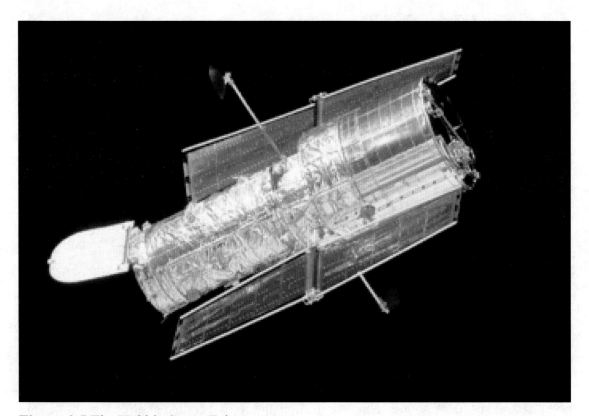

Figure 8.5 The Hubble Space Telescope

Seeing

The optimum location for an Earth-bound telescope is one with favorable conditions for its use. Astronomers call this good *seeing*. Locations with more stable atmospheric conditions are desirable. These are usually drier locations, because moist air tends to rise, causing atmospheric turbulence, then clouds and precipitation. Remote locations, away from city lights are also desirable because light pollution can render even the most powerful telescopes useless. A nearly ideal location for an Earth-bound telescope is a desert mountain, a desert because of the dry, stable air and a mountain because air is thinner at higher altitudes. Because gravity holds atmospheric gases to Earth, air is thicker or more dense near the ground, and thinner, less dense, higher up. Thinner air will disrupt light collected by the telescopes less than thicker air. It is a common myth that telescopes are put on mountains so they can be closer to space, but most objects being observed are literally billions and trillions of miles away and being a few thousand feet closer does not make any difference.

Figure 8.6 Telescopes atop Kitt Peak National Observatory in the desert south of Tucson, Arizona.

Optical Telescopes

There are two basic types of optical telescopes, the *refractor* and the *reflector*. The basic design of a refractor, the type first used by Galileo, is two lenses on either end of a hollow tube (see Figure 8.8). Refraction is a change in the direction of a light wave caused by a change of speed that occurs when light travels from one substance to another. The lenses are glass, ground into a convex shape (thicker at the center and thinner at the edges) that will concentrate or *focus* the light at a certain point. The lens used to collect the light, the lens pointed at the object being viewed, is called the *objective*. The lens the observer looks into is called the *eyepiece*. The eyepiece is basically a magnifying glass used to make the image larger, but if an image is magnified too much it will be blurry. The power of a telescope is not in its magnification, but rather in how much light it can gather. The more light that can be gathered from an object, the more the image can be magnified and still be seen clearly. A powerful telescope is one with a large objective lens. The larger the diameter of the objective lens, the more light the telescope can gather.

Figure 8.7 Forty-inch (just over a meter) refracting telescope at Yerkes Observatory in Wisconsin.

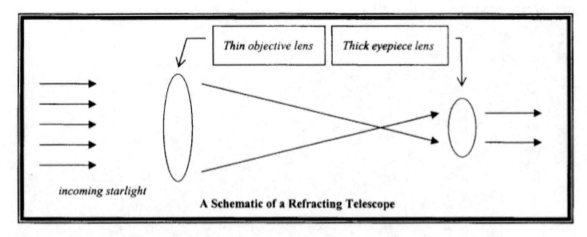

Figure 8.8 Diagram of a refractor.

A reflecting telescope, originally invented by Newton, uses a concave (curved inward) mirror and an objective to gather and focus light. Unlike a refractor, where the objective is at the end of the tube facing the object, in a reflector the light must travel all the way down the tube before hitting the objective mirror. This mirror then reflects the light back to a flat mirror that reflects it to an eyepiece lens off to the side, a *Newtonian* focus (as seen in Figure 8.9), or to a convex mirror that reflects the light to an eyepiece in a hole in the center of the original objective mirror. The latter (seen in Figure 8.11) is called a *Cassegrain* focus.

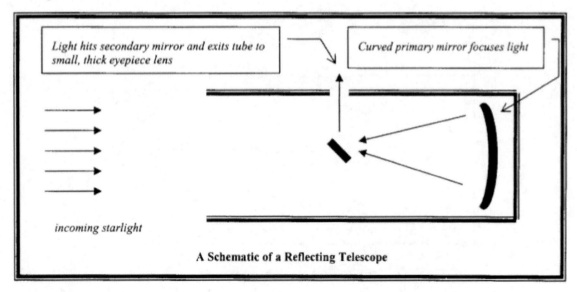

Figure 8.9 Diagram of a Newtonian reflector

Figure 8.10 Two hundred-inch (just under 5 meters) Hale reflecting telescope at Mt. Palomar in California.

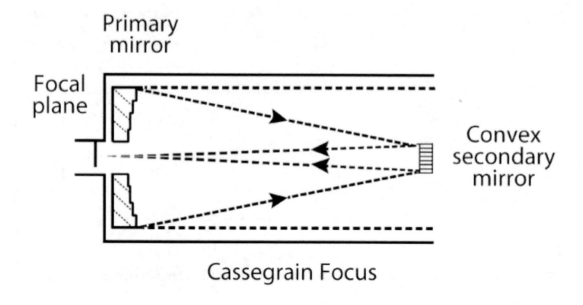

Figure 8.11 Diagram of a reflector with a *Cassegrain* focus.

Light only reflects from one side of a mirror, so the other side can be supported and thus the mirror can be very large, up to 4 or 5 meters across before becoming distorted by its own weight and thus distorting images. Since light must travel through both sides of a lens, a lens cannot be supported as well as a mirror and a lens greater than about 1 meter across will become distorted under its own weight and no longer useful for telescopes. This means that larger, more powerful telescopes are normally reflectors.

Computer control allows modern telescopes to consist of many smaller mirrors being used together to make larger and larger telescopes capable of gathering more and more light; these can even be adjusted for atmospheric conditions. This technology is known as *adaptive optics*.

8.5 Spectra

In order to study light in even more detail and learn more about its sources, astronomers use a device known as a spectrometer to separate light into components of different wavelength. This is probably most familiar as visible white-light being passed through a prism and separated into the colors of the visible spectrum. The device that separates the light in a spectrometer is a piece of glass with many lines etched into it very close together called a *diffraction grating*. Diffraction is the bending of light rays caused when they encounter an obstacle. The lines in a grating are so close together that they provide obstacles for the light waves. Different wavelengths are diffracted by different amounts, and the light gets separated into its spectrum.

Temperature

One of the first things astronomers can learn from a spectrum is the temperature of the object that it came from. The higher the frequency of an electromagnetic wave, the more rapidly it repeats its cycle, the more energetic it is and, therefore, the more energetic its source. Temperature is actually a measurement of energy. When the temperature in a room is higher, the air molecules are moving faster and are more energetic. When a room is cooler, they are slower and less energetic. Therefore, objects that give off high-frequency gamma-rays or X-rays are very hot, and objects that give off low-frequency radio waves are very cold. Stars that give off mostly red light are cooler, while stars that give off mostly blue light are hotter. Yellow stars are in between. Stars that give off most of the visible spectrum in about the same amounts will appear white. These stars are hotter than yellow stars, but actually are cooler than blue stars. Stars that appear blue give off most of their light at invisible ultraviolet wavelengths, but give off more blue light than any other visible color.

The reason for being careful to say a star that gives off mostly red or mostly yellow light is that stars actually give off many wavelengths of light, but the wavelengths and therefore the colors that we see are those which they give off the most. It can be seen in Figure 8.12 that the spectrum of a star will peak at a specific wavelength and this determines the color the star will appear to be and will tell astronomers its exact temperature.

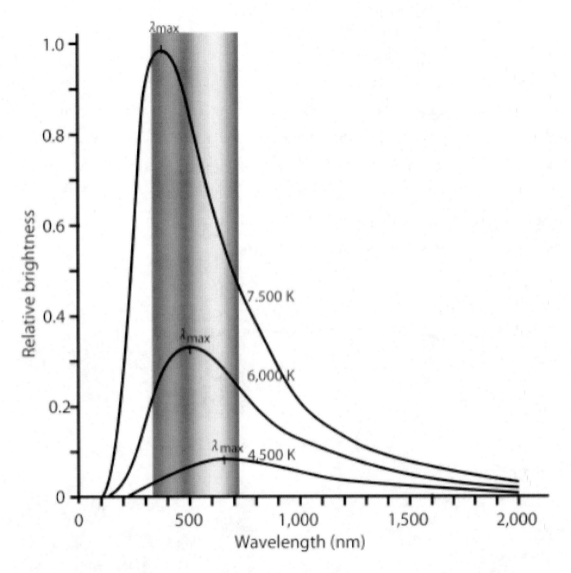

Figure 8.12 Spectra for a blue, yellow, and red star.

Composition

Another important property that a star's spectrum can tell astronomers is its composition. There are three kinds of spectra as shown in Figure. 8.13. A *continuous* spectrum comes from a heated solid, like a light-bulb filament, or a gas under very high pressure, like the core of a star. A *bright-line* or *emission* spectrum comes from a hot gas and a *dark-line* or *absorption* spectrum is what astronomers see when they observe stars.

It is not hard to see in Figure 8.13 that subtracting the bright-line spectrum from the continuous spectrum will leave the dark-line spectrum. This is exactly what happens in stars. If light could come to us directly from the core of a star, since the gas in the core is under tremendous pressure from the mass of the star's outer layers, we would see a continuous spectrum. If we could look only at the light from the star's outer layers that are heated by the energy from the star's interior, we would see an emission spectrum. But what we see is what remains after light from the core of the star has passed through the star's outer layers, an absorption spectrum.

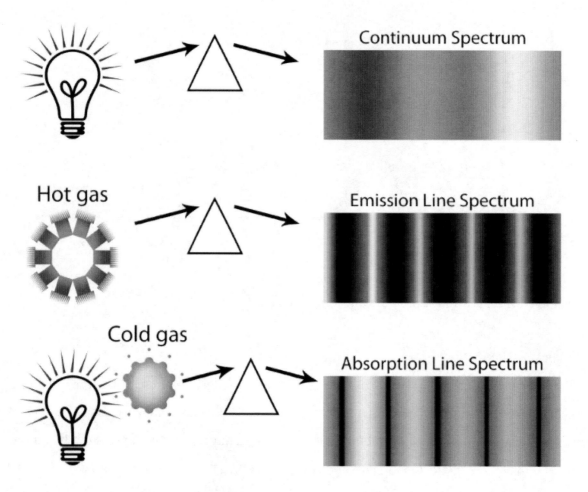

Figure 8.13 The three types of Spectra.

The reason that these spectra tell us the composition of stars is that the emission spectrum of a particular gas is like a fingerprint or DNA pattern. No two gases have the same spectrum. Danish physicist Niels Bohr determined that the spectrum of a gas depends on the structure of the atoms of that make up the gas.

Figure 8.14 Bohr

When an atom absorbs energy it will give back or emit the energy in the form of particles of light called photons. The exact amounts of energy, and therefore the frequencies and wavelengths of the photons the atoms will emit, is dependent on the structure of the individual atoms. Atoms will absorb the same amounts of energy they emit, so when energy comes from the core of a star, it is absorbed in the outer layers and what is left for astronomers to see is an absorption spectrum. The wavelengths of the spectral lines that are absorbed can be matched with the bright lines of different emission spectra, to determine the exact composition of a star. Stars, as it turns out, are made mostly of hydrogen and helium with smaller amounts of many other types of gases.

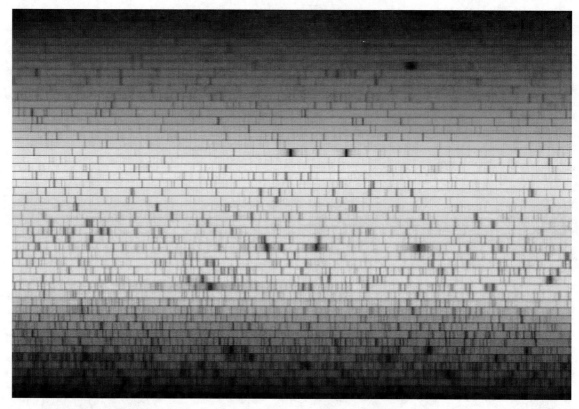

Figure 8.15 The Sun's absorption spectrum

Fortunately for astronomers, it was discovered by Annie Jump Cannon of the then Harvard College Observatory that there are only seven basic types of stellar spectra. Examples of each are shown in Figure 8.16. There are numbered sub-types of each spectral type. The letters, O B A F G K M are in order of *decreasing* temperature. A simple way to remember this is "B" for blue then recalling the star colors in order of decreasing temperature. B-type stars are very hot blue stars. A-type stars are hot and white. G-types are cooler yellow stars like our Sun, and M-type stars are the coolest, red stars. Larger, slightly warmer reddish-orange stars are K-type.

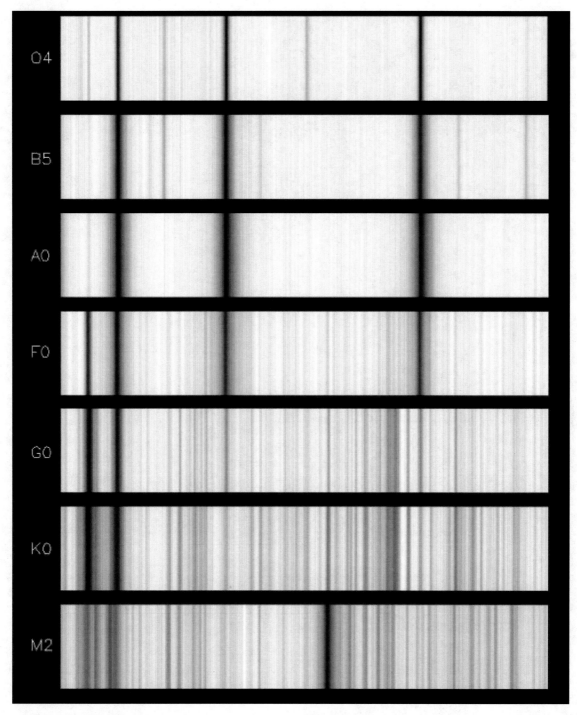

Figure 8.16 Stellar Spectra

Review Questions

1. On what does the color of light depend?

2. What is the longest wavelength type of electromagnetic wave? What is the highest frequency type of electromagnetic wave? What type of electromagnetic waves comes from the highest temperature sources? What type comes from the lowest temperature sources? What type of electromagnetic waves travels the fastest?

3. List the four most common colors of stars in order from hottest to coolest.

4. Which is more energetic, a red or a violet photon?

5. Which types of electromagnetic waves penetrate our atmosphere best?

6. What are the factors involved in good *seeing* for a telescope?

7. Why are telescopes often put on mountains? What is the advantage of putting an optical telescope in orbit? Why do some telescope <u>have</u> to be put in orbit?

8. Explain what is meant by the "size" of a telescope.

9. What two things can be learned by examining the spectrum of a star?

10. How is the temperature of a star determined?

11. Which kind of spectrum is observed to come from stars? Explain how this type of spectrum is created.

12. List the spectral-types of the four most common colors of stars in order of increasing temperature.

Tutorial--Classification of Stellar Spectra

The spectrum of each of the stars shown below is labeled on the right with its *spectral type*.

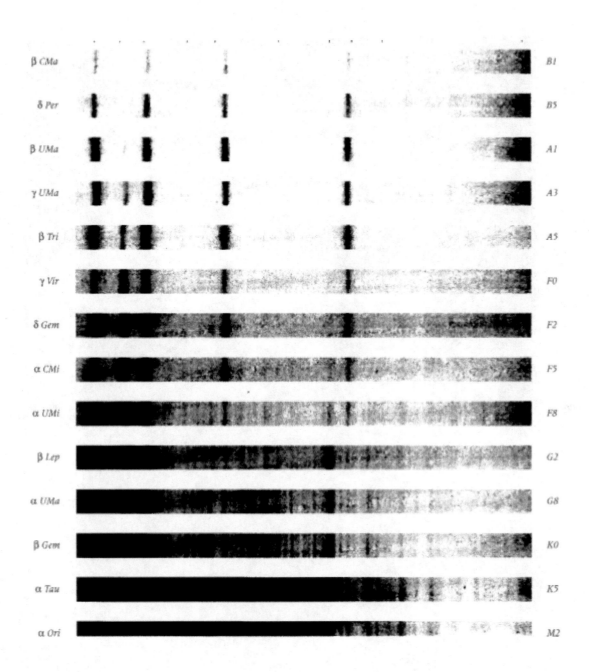

Use these spectra as a key to determine to type of each spectrum shown on the next page.

Use the spectra on the previous page as a key to determine the type of each spectrum shown below. Label the letter of each star's *spectral type* on its right.

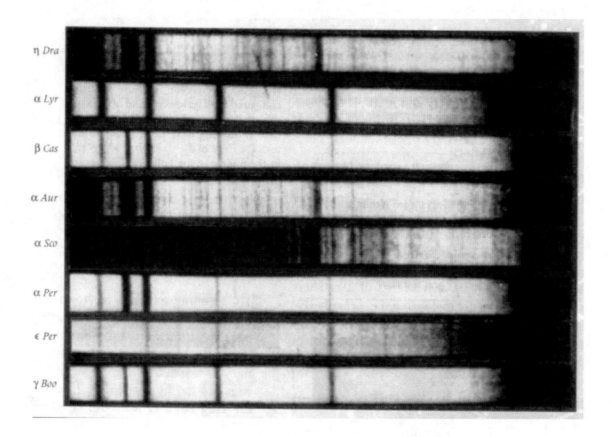

η *Dra*

α *Lyr*

β *Cas*

α *Aur*

α *Sco*

α *Per*

ε *Per*

γ *Boo*

Chapter - 9 Properties of Stars

9.1 Introduction

How spectra are used to determine the temperature and composition of stars was the subject of the last chapter. This chapter will discuss how other important properties such as brightness and mass are determined.

9.2 Brightness

One of the first things someone may notice about a star-filled sky is that many of the stars appear to be brighter or dimmer than others. The term that astronomers use for brightness is *magnitude*. The ancient Greek astronomer Hipparchus devised what is known as the magnitude scale. He simply called the brightest stars first-magnitude and rated stars all the way down to the dimmest at sixth-magnitude.

The modern version of this magnitude scale includes objects that were unknown to the Greeks because they did not have telescopes. Objects that cannot be seen with the unaided eye will have magnitude numbers greater than six. The modern scale also includes objects brighter than stars, planets, the Moon, and the Sun. Since the brightest stars are already labeled as first-magnitude, this will involve using zero and negative numbers on the scale. This can become confusing, but very simply, the smaller the object's magnitude number, the brighter the object. The brightest object in our sky, the Sun, has a magnitude of about -26, the full-moon is about -12, Venus about -4, most visible starts 1 through 6, and dimmer stars and other objects too dim to be seen without a telescope have magnitude numbers greater than 6.

The scale just described is a scale of *apparent magnitude*--how bright the objects *look*. It says nothing about how bright the objects really are. To know how bright stars really are, their *absolute magnitude*, it is necessary to determine how far away they are, their distance from Earth. It is possible that stars could look bright because they are close or because they really are bright, or look dim because they are far away or because they really are dim. Once their distance is determined, astronomers can compare the brightness as if they were all at the same distance and then know which stars really are brighter or dimmer.

9.3 Distance

As discussed in Chapter 2, as Earth orbits the Sun, closer stars should show an apparent shift in their position relative to more distant background stars due to the changing position of Earth. This apparent shift is known as *stellar parallax*. See Figure 9.1. A star at a distance **d** from the Sun will show an apparent shift of angle **p**. The further away the star is, the larger **d** is, the less parallax there is and the smaller **p** will be. Since the distance between Earth and the Sun, an AU, is known, measuring the parallax angle allows astronomers to calculate **d**.

Stars turned out be so far away, even the closest stars are over 20 trillion miles away that a new unit of measurement had to be invented. This is similar to solar system distances. Astronomers discuss these distances in AU rather than kilometers or miles because the numbers in these units are so big. Recall that 1 AU=150 million kilometers =93 million miles. When it comes to the distance between stars, even the AU is small, so astronomers defined a new distance unit. The unit is called the *parallax-second*; a star that has a parallax angle of precisely p=1" (one angular minute 1'= 1/60 of a degree and one angular second 1"= 1/60 of an angular minute) is exactly one parallax-second or *parsec,* for short, away. A parsec turns about to be about 20 trillion miles and the closest stars to the Sun, those of the alpha-Centauri system (a trinary system-three stars together in one solar system), are even farther away than that; they have a parallax angle of less than one angular second.

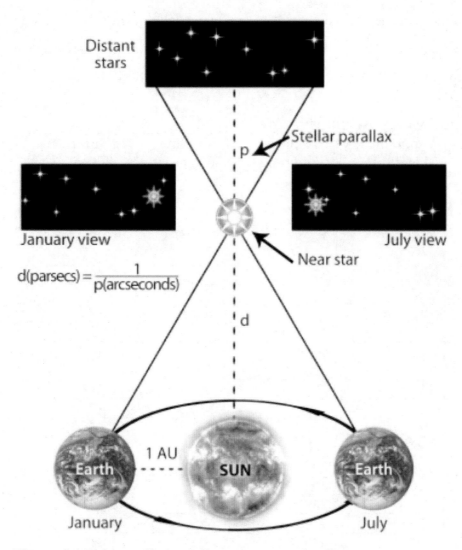

Figure 9.1 Using *stellar parallax* to measure the distance to a star.

Once the distance to a star has been determined, astronomers can calculate what the magnitude of the star would be if it were 10 parsecs away; that is termed its *absolute magnitude*. Since absolute magnitudes are determined for all stars this way, it is a scale that tells astronomers which stars really are brighter and dimmer than others. Next, from absolute magnitude, the *luminosity* of a star can be determined. The luminosity is a measurement of the amount of energy actually given off by the star. Tables 9.1 and 9.2 are lists of the *Brightest Stars* and *Nearest Stars* and include their apparent and absolute magnitudes as well as their distances and spectral types.

Table 9.1 The Twenty Brightest Stars

Star	Apparent Magnitude	Distance (light-years)	Absolute Magnitude	Spectral Type
Sirius	-1.44	9	1.5	A1
Canopus	-0.62	310	-5.4	F0
Arcturus	-0.05	37	-0.6	K2
Rigel Kentaurus	-0.01	4	4.2	G2
Vega	0.03	25	0.6	A0
Capella	0.08	42	-0.8	G8
Rigel	0.18	800	-6.6	B8
Procyon	0.40	11	2.8	F5
Achernar	0.45	144	-2.9	B3
Betelgeuse	0.45	520	-5.0	M2
Hadar	0.58	500	-5.5	B1
Altair	0.76	17	2.1	A7
Aldebaran	0.87	65	-0.8	K5
Spica	0.98	260	-3.6	B1
Antares	1.06	600	-5.8	M1
Pollux	1.16	34	1.1	K0
Formalhaut	1.17	25	1.6	A3
Deneb	1.25	1500	-7.5	A2
Acrux	1.25	320	-4.0	B1
Mimosa	1.25	352	-4.0	B1

Table 9.2 The Twenty Nearest Stars

Star	Distance (light-years)	Apparent Magnitude	Absolute Magnitude	Spectral Type
Proxima	4.2	11	15.5	M6
a Centauri A	4.4	-0.01	4.3	G2
a Centauri B	4.4	1.35	5.7	K0
Barnard's Star	5.9	9.5	13.2	M4
Wolf 359	7.8	13.5	16.6	M6
Lalande 21185	8.3	7.5	10.5	M2
Sirius A	8.6	-1.44	1.5	A1
Sirius B	8.6	8.44	11.3	A0 (WD)
Luyten 726 A	8.7	12.6	15.4	M6
Luyten 726 B	8.7	13	15.8	M6
Ross 154	9.7	10.1	13.3	M3
Ross 248	10.3	12.3	14.8	M4
ε Eridani	10.5	3.7	6.2	K2
Lacaille 9352	10.7	7.35	9.8	M2
Ross 128	10.9	11.12	13.5	M4
Luyten 789	11.2	12.52	14.6	M5
61 Cygni A	11.4	5.2	7.5	K5
Procyon A	11.4	0.4	2.7	F5
Procyon B	11.4	10.7	13	A0 (WD)
61 Cygni B	11.4	6.1	8.3	K7

Light Years and Look-Back Time

The distances in each table are not given in parsecs but rather in *light-years*. A light-year is the *distance* that light at c=186,000 miles per second can travel in one year, about 6 trillion miles. Note that a light-year is a measurement of distance and *not* time A light-year is a smaller distance than a parsec. There are about 3.3 light-years in a parsec, so measuring distances in light-years is more precise than in parsecs. Light-years also tell you the *look-back time* of an object. Since light takes time to travel the immense distances through space, objects are never seen as they are; they are seen as they were when the light left them. Look-back time will always be equal to the number of years that something is light-years away. The star Vega in Table 9.1 is about 25 light-years away, so it always seen as it looked, 25 years ago. Look-back time does not matter much for closer objects, since most stars probably do not change much even in hundreds or over a thousand years. However, for more distant objects, like the faraway galaxies that will be discussed in Chapters 11 and 12, look-back times are so great that these objects probably no longer look as they appear, if they are even still there at all.

9.4 The Hertzsprung-Russel Diagram

The temperature and luminosity of a star are two important intrinsic properties of a star that can be determined by astronomers. The temperature comes from the star's spectrum and the luminosity from its absolute magnitude, which came in turn from the star's apparent magnitude and the distance to the star. Plots or graphs of these two properties were first made by the Danish astronomer Ejnar Hertzsprung and an American, Henry Norris Russell. In honor of both of the founders, such a graph is now called an *HR-diagram*.

Figure 9.2 Hertzsprung and Russell

Figure 9.3 is an HR-diagram. Absolute Magnitude and Luminosity are plotted vertically (up and down) while temperature and spectral class are plotted horizontally (back and forth). Brighter stars are plotted higher on the graph than dimmer stars, but unlike most graphs you may have seen, higher temperatures are plotted to the left and lower temperatures to the right.

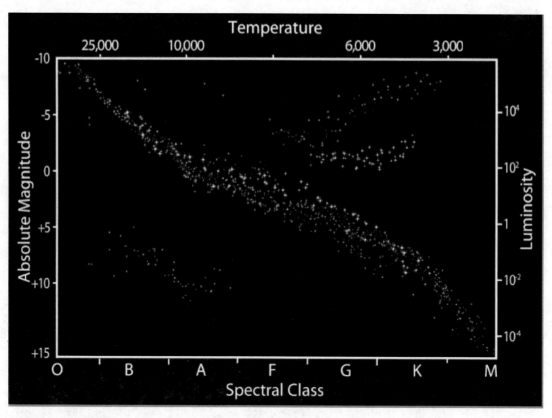

Figure 9.3 The Hertzsprung-Russell (HR) Diagram

The first thing that can be learned by plotting stars on an HR diagram is that there are different kinds of stars. Stars on the lower left are dim, because they are lower, but hot because they are on the left. Stars on the lower right are also dim, but cooler because they are on the right. Stars on the upper right are bright but cool and those on the upper left are bright and hot.

Different types of stars are named based on their positions on the HR diagram. Since the temperature of a star controls its color, most stars are, in order of decreasing temperature, either blue, white, yellow, or red. Since the larger a star is, the more surface area it will have to give off energy, dimmer stars are generally smaller, and brighter stars larger. Stars along the bottom of the diagram are called dwarfs. Those along the top are called giants or supergiants. The diagonal line that goes from the upper left, where the hot and bright stars are, to the lower right, where the dim and cool ones are, is called the *main sequence*. It can been seen in Figure 9.3 that most stars lie along the main sequence.

Star types are named with their color first and size second. As can be seen in Figure 9.3, the hot, dim stars on the lower left are called *white dwarfs*. The giants and supergiants shown in the upper right are called *red giants* or *red supergiants*. Main-sequence stars can also be named more specifically. The cool, dim stars on the lower right are called *red dwarfs* and on the other end of the main sequence, the hot, bright stars on the upper-left are called *blue giants*. Our Sun is a G-type star with an absolute magnitude of about +4.4, so it is near the middle of the main sequence in Figure 9.3 and is often called yellow, a medium-sized star.

Any star that is in the same position to the left or right on the HR Diagram has the same temperature and therefore the same color. Any star that is in the same position up and down has the same luminosity or brightness, but as shown in Figure 9.4 not the same size. The stars to the right tend to be larger than those to the left. The reason for this is not hard to understand. A blue giant is hotter than a red giant but if both are at the same height on the diagram they have equal brightness. In order to be as bright, to give off as much energy, a cooler red giant *has to be bigger* than the *hotter* blue giant. This works for dwarf stars too. If a white dwarf and red dwarf are at the same height on the diagram they have the same brightness. The white dwarf *can be smaller* and be as bright as red dwarf because it is *hotter*. Or the cooler red dwarf has to be bigger than the white dwarf to give off as much energy and be as bright.

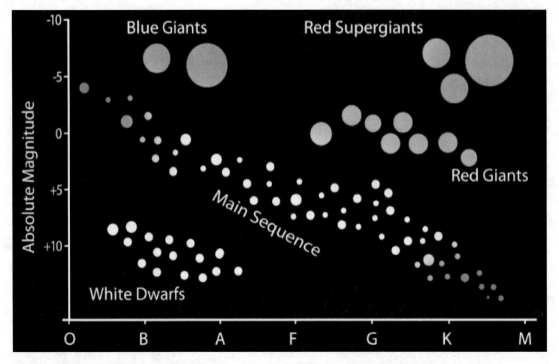

Figure 9.4 HR diagram showing the sizes of different stars.

9. 5 Stellar Masses

How hot and bright a star will be when it first begins to shine and first appears on the HR diagram, changes in temperature and brightness that will occur during its evolution causing it to change position on the diagram, and ultimately how long the star will last are all dependent on the *mass* of a star. Therefore, being able to determine the mass of stars is very important to astronomers.

The majority of stars in our galaxy are not alone. Most stars are found in groups of two or more. The situation of two stars in orbit of one another is called a *binary* system. Most stars are members of binary systems. To the unaided-eye they may look like a single star, but when viewed through a telescope two often appear. This is called an *optical binary*. It is also possible that the stars are so far away that they will still appear as one, but as they orbit one another, the apparent brightness of the system will change as the stars block out part of each other's light. This is known as an *eclipsing binary*. A *spectroscopic binary*, as the name suggests, can only be detected by viewing the stars' spectrum.

Binaries should not be confused with double stars. Two stars can appear to be in the same place in the sky from the point of view of Earth because they lie along the same line of sight. This is a double star. The way to tell a double and a binary apart is that the stars in the binary system will be about the same distance away, whereas the two stars in the double will be at different distances from the observer and could actually be very far from one another.

Using the same techniques astronomers use to determine the mass of extrasolar planets, if the orbital period, the amount of time the two stars take to orbit one another, of a binary can be determined, then so can the masses of the stars. This makes finding and observing binary systems very important for astronomers.

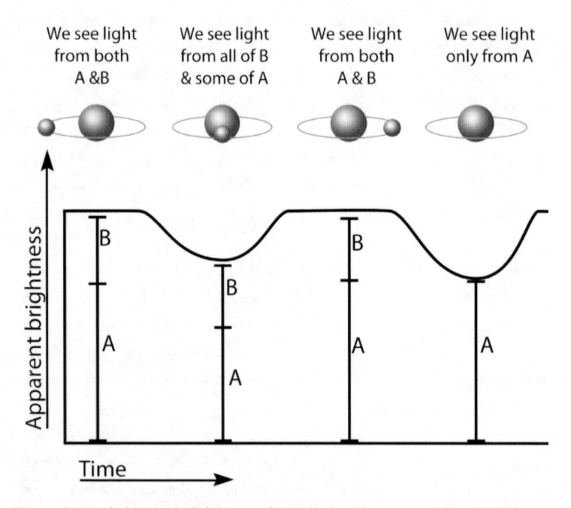

Figure 9.5 Variations in the brightness of an eclipsing binary are used to determine the period of the system then the masses of the stars.

Mass and Luminosity

Once astronomers were able to determine the mass of a number of stars, they began comparing the mass to the luminosity of the stars. Perhaps not surprisingly, it was found that for main sequence stars on the HR diagram, mass and luminosity are proportional. The cool, dim red dwarfs are low-mass stars, while the hot and bright blue giants are high-mass stars. Yellow stars like our Sun lie in between.

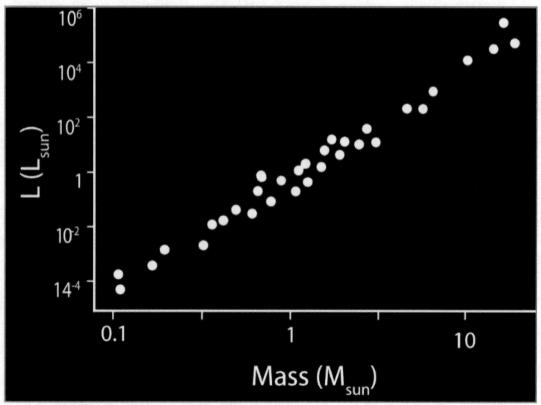

Figure 9.6 The Mass-Luminosity relationship.

In the next chapter, we study how the mass of a star controls just about everything that happens to a star, from if and when it will first start to shine, or is born, to when it collapses into a stellar corpse or dies. This process is known as *stellar evolution* or the lives of the stars.

Review Questions

1. Which star in Table 9.1 *really* is the brightest? Explain how you know. Why does it not *appear* to be the brightest?

2. If other stars on Table 9.1 are intrinsically brighter, how can *Sirius* appear to be the brightest star in our sky?

3. Which stars in Table 9.1 are among the hottest? What color will they likely be?

4. Which stars in Table 9.1 are among the coolest? What color will they likely be?

5. What is true about the apparent brightness of most of the stars in Table 9.2?

6. What it true about the actual brightness of most of the stars in Table 9.2?

7. *Proxima Centauri* has a parallax angle of 0.772 angular seconds. What should be true about the parallax angles of all the other stars on Table 9.2?

8. The Sun's absolute magnitude is about +4.8. Are most of the stars on Table 9.1 intrinsically brighter or dimmer than the Sun? What about the stars on Table 9.2?

9. What kind of star on the HR diagram is hot, but dim? Dim and cool? Bright and cool? Bright and hot? Kind of in the middle?

10. Describe in words the temperature and brightness of a red giant; a blue giant; a red dwarf; a white dwarf; the Sun.

11. Find the stars *Rigel* and *Betelgeuse* on Table 9.1. What kind of star is each on the HR diagram? Which is likely bigger? Explain how you know.

12. Find the stars *Wolf 359* and *Procyon B* on Table 9.2. What kind of Star is each on the HR diagram? Which is likely smaller? Explain how you know.

13. Explain how astronomers determine the masses of stars.

14. How does the mass of the stars on the upper-left of the HR diagram compare to the mass of the stars on the lower right?

15. Use data from Tables 9. 1 and 9.2 to list the following three stars in order of increasing mass; *Altair*, *Barnard's Star,* and *Spica*.

Tutorial-HR Diagram Plot

Directions

Use Table 9.1 to plot and label each star on the HR Diagram labeled "The Brightest Stars."

Use Table 9.2 to plot and label each star on the HR Diagram labeled "The Nearest Stars."

Plot the Sun on both diagrams; Absolute Magnitude +4.4; Spectral Type-G2.

Questions--To be answered after you have plotted the HR Diagrams

1. Do any stars other than the Sun appear on both Diagrams? If so, which?

2. In general what is true about the *absolute* magnitudes of most of the *brightest* stars?

3. In general, what is true about the *absolute* magnitudes of most of the *nearest* stars?

4. Are most of the brightest stars close or far away?

5. What do the answers of questions 1-4 suggest about how the numbers of brighter stars in the galaxy should compare to the numbers of dimmer stars?

THE BRIGHTEST STARS

Name _____

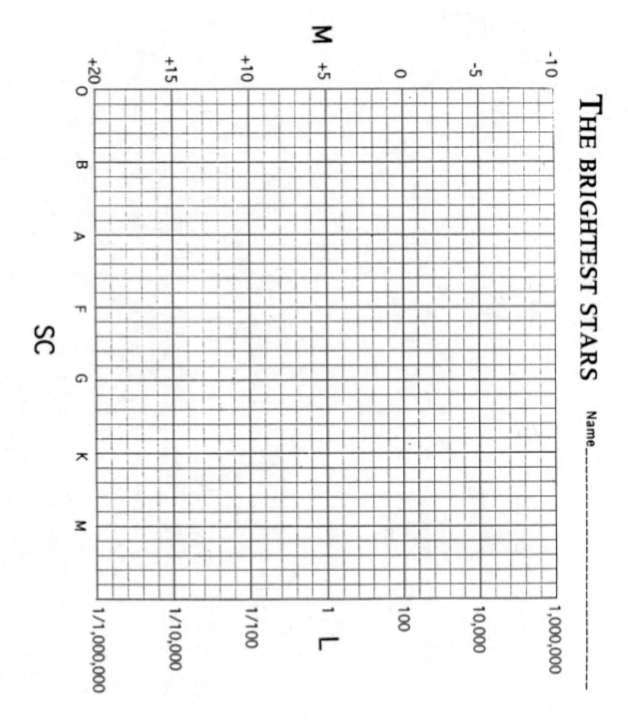

M

SC

273

THE NEAREST STARS

Name_____

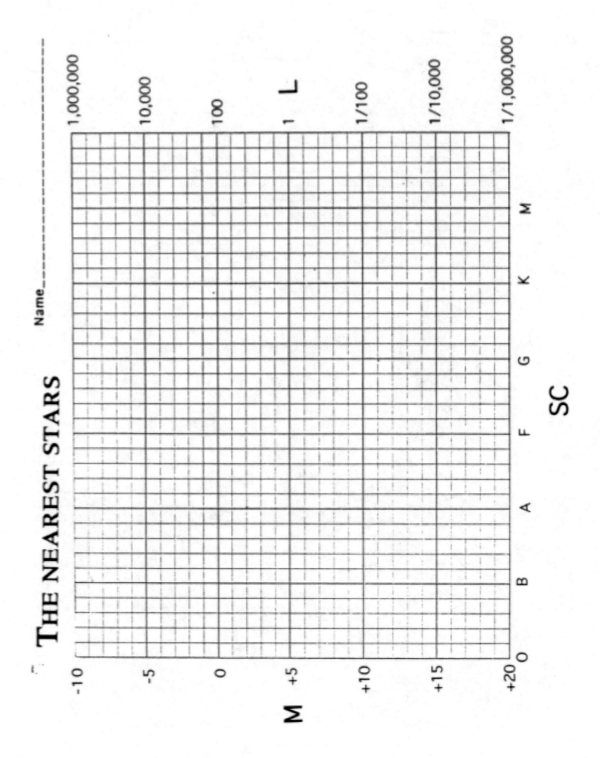

SC

274

Chapter 10 - The Lives of Stars

10.1 Introduction

In 1054 CE, Chinese astronomers witnessed what they called, "the guest star." In a region of the constellation of Taurus the Bull, a star appeared where there had not been one before. Over the course of about six months, the star got brighter and brighter until it was clearly visible during the day and gave off enough light that it could be read by at night. Then in about the same amount of time, it got dimmer and dimmer until it disappeared. Events like this were also observed much later by both Tycho and Kepler, and eventually were called *novae*, or *supernovae*, "nova," being Latin for *new*.

After stars were understood to be more than just points of light in the sky, that they are in fact, gigantic balls of hot, glowing gas, our Sun being just one among billions of them, these supernovae were recognized as not being new at all, but rather, the end of a star's cycle, or the death of a star. Since death implies life and life implies birth, astronomers began to piece together theories about the life cycle of stars.

Stars can last tens or hundreds of millions or even billions of years, so the life cycle of a single star obviously cannot be observed. Rather, astronomers, by observing countless numbers of objects and events and applying the laws of physics, have formulated theories about how stars are created, what happens during their life-cycles and how the cycles come to an end and what happens when they do. When events are witnessed, the theories can be tested. These theories about the lives of stars are collectively known as *stellar evolution*.

10.2 Star Birth

Stars are "born" out of gigantic clouds of mostly hydrogen gas and dust in interstellar space (the space between stars) called nebulae, the plural of *nebula*. Many nebulae have been observed by astronomers. If something stirs-up a nebula, such as a shockwave through space from a distant supernova explosion or other disturbance, the particles will begin to move faster and get closer to one another, close enough to gravitationally attract each other and form larger particles. When enough of these larger particles have formed, they will all gravitationally pull at each other and collapse toward a common center. Gravity is a force of attraction and always pulls objects toward a center. This *gravitational collapse* forms a large object in the nebula known as a *protostar*.

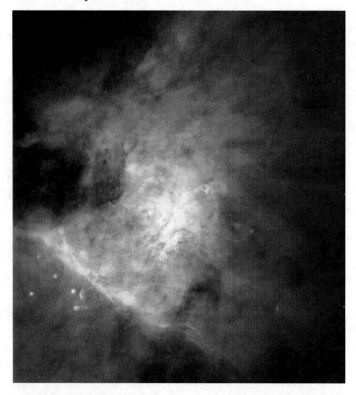

Figure 10.1 Star formation region in the Orion nebula.

When undergoing gravitational collapse, a nebula will form not one, but many protostars. Nebulae contain the mass of hundreds or even thousands or more stars. Protostars are not yet stars, that is what their name means, because they are not yet giving off light or shining. These protostars are the most massive objects in their area of a nebula, so they will begin to collect material and form a solar nebula, sometimes referred to as a cocoon, around themselves. Much of this material will become part of the protostar. As it collects more material, the protostar becomes more and more massive.

Figure 10.2 Material in a nebula gravitationally pulling together.

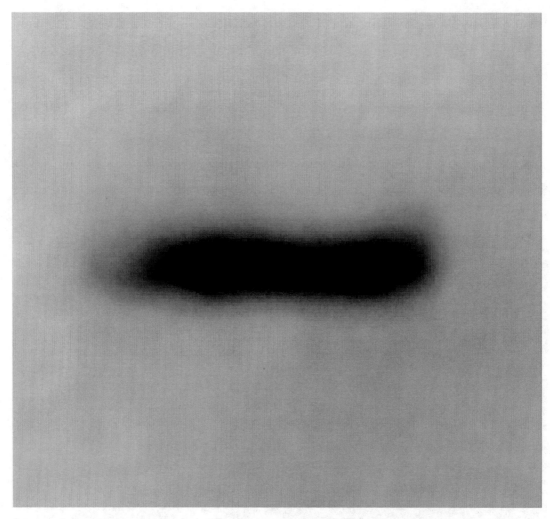

Figure 10.3 A solar or "cocoon" nebula around a protostar in a nebula.

10.3 Energy Production in Stars

As the mass of a protostar increases, the increased gravitational pull causes the object to collapse, or gravitationally contract. This gravitational contraction causes the temperature of the protostar to increase, especially in the core, which, because there is more mass pushing down on the core than on the layers above the core, is under more pressure from the mass than the outer layers. As the protostar collects more and more mass, there is more and more gravitational pressure on the core, causing the temperature to rise even higher. The higher the temperature rises, the faster the hydrogen atoms in the core move.

A hydrogen atom is composed of a single positively charged *proton*, its *nucleus*, being orbited by a much less massive, negatively charged *electron*. The two oppositely charged particles are held together by an *electromagnetic* attraction, similar to gravitational attraction, but actually much stronger. When temperatures get too high, the electrons are ejected from the atoms and all that is left are the protons. Normally when two positively charged protons get near each other, their like-charges will cause an electromagnetic repulsion of one another, but when they start to move very fast, they can come close enough to each other be held together by a force stronger than electromagnetic repulsion, the *strong nuclear* force.

As the name suggests, the strong nuclear force works only within the range of an atomic nucleus and is dominant at the scale of the nucleus. The electromagnetic force is longer range and is dominant at the scale of the entire atom. Gravity is also a long-range force that acts on large amounts of mass over great distances, but at the scale of the atom, the electromagnetic force is much stronger, and in the nucleus, the strong nuclear force is even stronger.

When a protostar becomes massive enough to put enough pressure on its core to raise temperatures high enough that the protons begin to move fast enough to get close enough to be held together by the strong nuclear force, the protons in the core begin to join together. This process of *nuclear fusion* is the energy source of stars.

Nuclear Fusion

Nuclear fusion is the process by which stars create the energy that allows them to give off light and heat. Once temperatures in the core are high enough, four hydrogen nuclei, protons, combine to form one slightly less massive helium nucleus that consists of two protons and two *neutrons*. Neutrons are particles similar in mass to protons, but with no electrical charge for, as their name suggests, they are electrically neutral. During the fusion process, two of the protons are stripped of their charges, releasing two *positrons*, particles with the same mass as electrons, but with a positive charge (anti-electrons). Two very low-mass, fast moving particles, called *neutrinos* are also released, as are two high-energy gamma rays. The positrons and neutrinos can be considered waste products of the reaction, while the gamma rays are the useable energy. The gamma rays eventually make their way from the core of the star to the surface and provide the necessary energy for atoms in the outer layer of the star to go through the process of emission, as discussed in the previous chapter, and give off light.

Neutrinos

Neutrinos are of such low mass and are so fast-moving that they can shoot out of the core of the Sun and arrive at Earth in just over the 8 minutes that it takes light to travel between Earth and Sun. This makes detecting neutrinos an ideal way for astronomers to use the Sun to test theories about energy production in stars. In order for the Sun to give off the energy that it does, fusion must be occurring in the core at a certain rate. If the number of neutrinos detected agrees with the number expected, this will verify that fusion in the core of the Sun is indeed going on at the predicted rate.

Neutrino detectors are gigantic underground pools of water. The intervening ground between Earth's surface and the detector will absorb most other particles that could cause reactions with the water that could be confused with neutrinos. For some time almost exactly one-third of the neutrinos expected were detected, which was interesting because there are actually three kinds of neutrino, the electron-neutrino being the type created during hydrogen fusion in the Sun. It was later discovered that during their lifetime, neutrinos oscillate, or change among the three types. This meant that solar-neutrino experiments not only verified the rate of nuclear fusion in the core of the sun, but they also provided experimental evidence for neutrino oscillation.

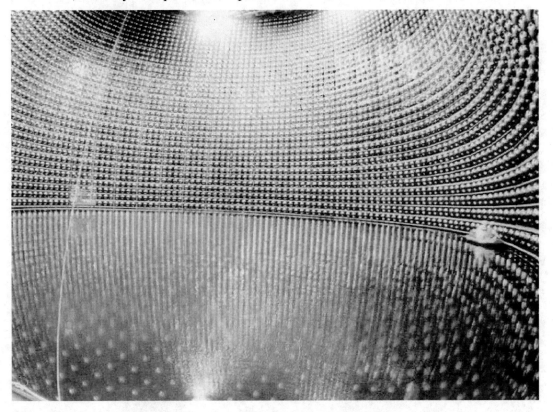

Figure 10.4 Underground neutrino detection experiment in Japan.

10.4 The Sun

Once nuclear fusion begins in the core, a protostar begins to shine and is a star. Before studying other stars that are much farther away, it makes sense to take a good look at our closest star, the Sun.

The processes occurring define the layers of the interior of the Sun. The *core* is defined as the region where nuclear fusion occurs. Energy is then radiated from the core; the zone where the energy is transferred by radiation is called the *radiative zone.* Just under the visible surface of the Sun, known as the *photosphere,* is the *convective zone.*

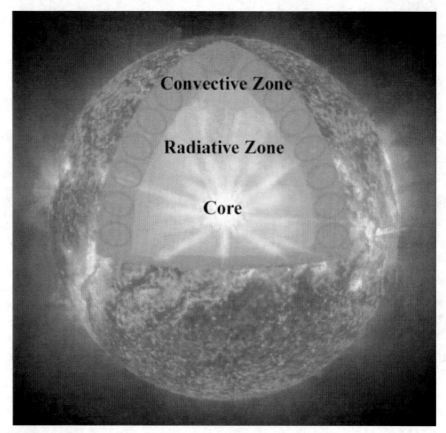

Figure 10.5 Layers of the solar interior.

Astronomers believe that convection is occurring under the solar photosphere, because the photosphere looks like it is made up of many convective cells, like the top of a pot of boiling water, as can be seen in Figure 10.5. The depth and processes occurring at the various levels in the solar interior have of course never been directly observed, but rather predicted by *solar models,* attempts to determine what occurs inside the Sun, based on what is observed, the amount and rate of energy emission and the known laws of physics.

The Sun's photosphere is relatively cool, about 6000 °C. At this temperature it radiates visible light, light that we can see. This is why it is called the surface of the Sun. The layers above the solar photosphere are known as the solar atmosphere. They are first, the chromosphere, a thin layer that is hotter than the photosphere and radiates energy in the ultraviolet. The outermost and hottest layer, the solar corona is even hotter than the chromosphere and emits x-rays. This layer of the Sun can be seen during a solar eclipse.

Figure 10.6 The solar corona imaged during a solar eclipse.

Solar Activity

The solar photosphere is often observed to have darker regions known as *sunspots*. Sunspots are areas that are as much as 1000°C cooler than their surroundings. They are believed to be poles of the Sun's complex and varying magnetic field. The number of sunspots varies in an approximately 11-year cycle that is an indicator of solar magnetic activity in general. At times when there are fewer sunspots, called a solar minimum, the Sun's magnetic field is not as active and the Sun is relatively quiet. During times of solar maxima, there are many more sunspots and the Sun is much more active. Recent Maxima were 1991, 2002, with another expected in 2013.

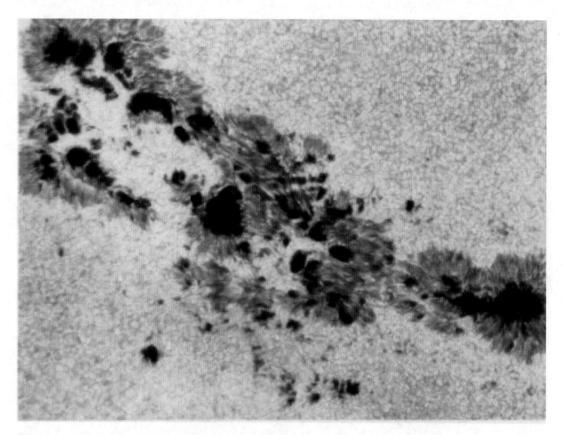

Figure 10.7 A close-up of a group of sunspots.

Two common types of solar activity are ejections of material, guided by the Sun's magnetic field, known as solar *flares* and *prominences*.

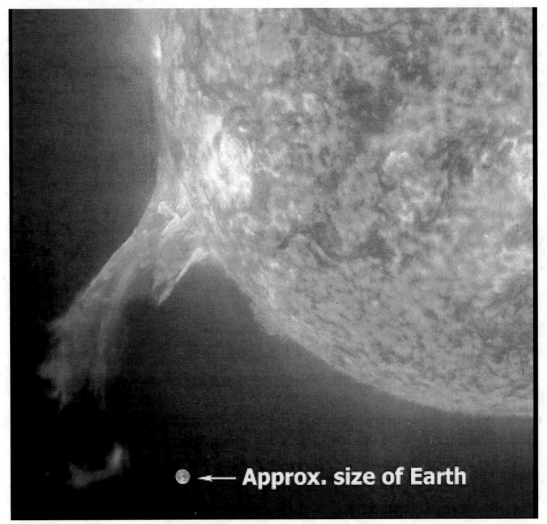

Figure 10.8 An eruptive solar prominence. Earth is much farther away than pictured, so although solar wind particles ejected from the Sun could have effects on Earth, such as interference with radio communication or overloading power grids, causing blackouts, an eruption cannot swallow up and vaporize Earth.

An ejection of electrically charged particles that streams out into the solar system is known as the *solar wind*. When these charged particles are pulled into Earth's atmosphere by Earth's magnetic field they interact with the gases and cause them to emit light. These light shows, more common near Earth's poles where the magnetic field is strongest, are called the *aurora*. The Aurora Borealis, as it is called when it occurs in the north (the Aurora Australis occurs in the south) is one of nature's most spectacular events. It can be seen as far south as the middle north latitudes of the United States and Europe near times of solar maxima. This is especially true shortly after the eruption of a large solar prominence or flare.

Figure 10.9 The Aurora seen from Alaska.

10.5 Stellar Maturity

Once a star begins fusing hydrogen into helium in its core, it will begin to give off light, or shine. Since it then has a luminosity, it will make its first appearance on the HR diagram, somewhere on the main sequence. Where on the main sequence it will appear depends on its luminosity and temperature. Both of these depend on the *mass* of the star. A star that is more massive will have more hydrogen to fuse, so it will burn hotter and brighter. As discussed in the previous chapter, hotter and brighter stars are found further up and to the left of the main sequence. Less massive stars that are cooler and dimmer are found lower and on the right of the main sequence.

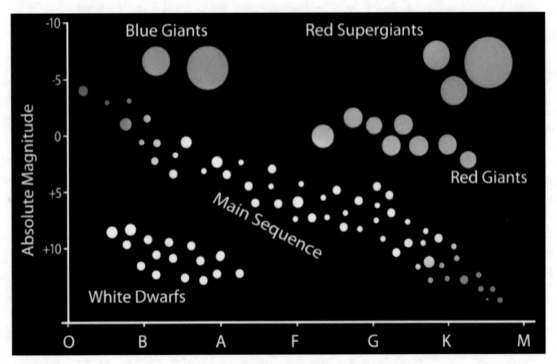

Figure 10.10 The more massive stars that are found on the hotter and brighter upper left end of the main sequence live shorter lives. The less massive stars that are found on the cooler and dimmer lower right live longer lives.

Perhaps contrary to intuition, the *less* massive stars have much *longer* main sequence lives. This is because the more massive stars, burning hotter and brighter, use up the hydrogen fuel in their cores much faster. Based on its mass and the rate it gives off energy, astronomers expect our Sun, which we believe to be about 5 billion years old, to last for about another 5 billion years, a total life span of 10 billion years. Stars more massive than the Sun are expected to have shorter life spans. Some very massive stars are expected to last only tens of millions or hundreds of thousands of years. Stars less massive than the sun may last up to 50 billion years. The hotter and brighter stars "live fast and die young"; they could be compared to gas-guzzling SUVs using up their fuel rapidly compared with much more fuel-efficient compact economy cars.

Recall that hydrogen fusion in a star's core begins because of the increased pressure from the mass of the star gravitationally collapsing and raising the temperature high enough for fusion to occur. Once this happens, the pressure from the fusing hydrogen gas pushes back and keeps the mass of the star from collapsing further. This balance, between gravity pushing downward and gas pressure pushing upward, is called *hydrostatic equilibrium*. This state will lasts as long as there is enough fusion occurring in the core to provide the pressure to balance or hold up the mass of the star pushing down. The star is in this state of *stellar maturity* throughout its main sequence life.

Stellar maturity, main sequence life, and hydrostatic equilibrium, are all ways to say the same thing; that the star is in its longest and calmest stage, its middle age. This is also the time when the leftover materials in the star's solar nebula are likely to be used to form a planetary system, as discussed in Chapter 3.

When there is no longer enough hydrogen left in the core for a fusion rate adequate to provide the gas pressure necessary to keep the star balanced, the star will again begin to collapse. The time of hydrostatic equilibrium is the thousands, millions or even billions of years, depending on the mass of the star, between the collapse that begins the hydrogen fusion in the core and the collapse that occurs at its end. This second collapse marks the end of main sequence life and the beginning of the final stages of the star's life cycle.

Star Clusters

When a nebula goes through star formation, not only one star is formed, but hundreds or thousands of stars are formed. The nebula becomes a *star cluster*. Just like there are many nebulae that have been observed, astronomers have observed great numbers of star clusters as well. The type of cluster that contains stars that formed together from a nebula is known as an *open star cluster*. The most famous example of an open cluster is the *Pleiades*, visible in the winter sky near the constellation of Taurus the Bull. Five of the stars are readily visible to the naked eye, but many more are revealed when the cluster is viewed through a telescope.

Figure 10.11 The Pleiades viewed through a telescope.

Figure 10.12 The Pleiades (top, left-center) photographed with Jupiter and Saturn on a winter's evening.

Astronomers know for two reasons that the Pleiades are relatively young. The cluster is still together; the stars have not drifted apart into different orbits around the center of the galaxy and broken up the cluster. Also, an HR diagram of the Pleiades shows that all the stars are still on the main sequence, none of them have moved off yet, which would indicate that they are still fusing hydrogen in their core, in hydrostatic equilibrium or middle age.

10.6 The Death of Light Stars

Eventually there will no longer be enough hydrogen fusing into helium in the core of a star to provide enough upward pressure to hold up the tremendous mass of the star. Gravity will cause the star to collapse. What will happen at this point, just as with how hot, bright, and long the star will burn, is determined by the mass of the star.

Low-Mass Stars

Stars less massive than our Sun will live very long lives, perhaps as long as fifty billion years, as relatively cool and dim red dwarfs. As will be discussed in coming chapters, the age of our universe is believed to be less than fourteen billion years, so it is possible that no red dwarf stars have yet died.

Red Giants

The hydrogen burning core of stars of similar mass as the Sun will be mostly converted to helium in about ten-billion years and the outer layers of the star will collapse. This contraction will heat the helium core that will in turn heat up the hydrogen in the surrounding layers. The star will then begin to expand and, as a result, cool. The increased surface area will make the star more luminous and on the HR diagram it will move up and, because the star is cooling, it will also move to the right. The upper-right of the HR-diagram is where the bright, but cool *red giant* stars are found.

How giant is a red giant? Figure 10.13 shows an image of the red supergiant star *Betelgeuse* compared to the size of Jupiter and Earth's orbits around the Sun. Our Sun is not massive enough to become a supergiant, but as a red giant, it will likely expand to a size large enough to engulf the orbits of the inner planets, including Earth. However, by this time, about five billion years from now, Earth will already have been rendered inhabitable, the atmosphere burned off and the oceans boiled by increasing temperatures of the Sun toward the end of main sequence life.

Figure 10.13 Hubble Space Telescope image of red supergiant star Betelgeuse.

Planetary Nebulae

During the red giant stage, the helium core will begin to fuse into carbon. When most of the helium has been converted to carbon the star will become very unstable actually varying in size and brightness, temporarily becoming one of several types of *variable stars,* until finally it throws about half of its mass out into space, forming what is called a.

When these objects were first discovered, it was suggested that they might be newly forming planets, thus the name *planetary nebula.* Unfortunately, despite the fact that these objects are now understood to have nothing to do with planets, the name stuck and can cause confusion.

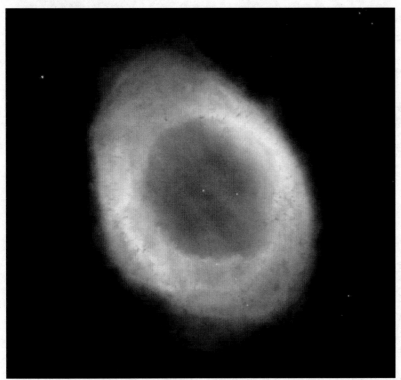

Figure 10.14 The *Ring Nebula*, a planetary nebula in the constellation Cygnus.

Astronomers have observed many planetary nebulae. Since they are the expanding outer shell of gas from a star, they will eventually dissipate to a point where they will no longer be visible.

White Dwarfs

After a red giant tosses off its outer layer and forms a planetary nebula the remaining carbon core will collapse, causing what is left of the star to get much dimmer, but very hot. This moves the star down and to the left on the HR-Diagram where the dim and hot *white dwarfs* are found. The collapse of a white dwarf will continue until the electrons in the atoms are packed as close together as their electromagnetic repulsion will allow. This results in a mass similar to the Sun packed into the size of the Earth, a spoonful of white dwarf material could weigh up to a ton. Astronomers have observed many white dwarf stars; this stellar-corpse of sun-like stars is a well-documented step in stellar evolution.

Figure 10.15 Sirius A and its white dwarf companion (the small dot on the lower left) Sirius B.

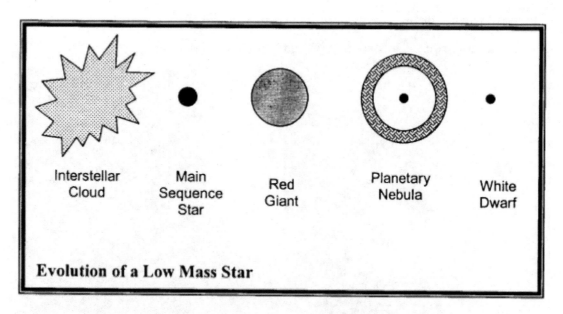

Figure 10.16 Stages on the life cycle of a low-mass star (the relative sizes of the object are not drawn to scale).

Black Dwarfs

It has been theorized that white dwarfs will eventually burn out and leave a mass mostly of carbon fused from the helium core, called a *black dwarf*. This could also possibly be the eventual fate of the long-lived main sequence red dwarf stars.

Brown Dwarfs

A *brown dwarf* is a protostar that never accumulates enough mass to exert enough pressure to raise the temperature in its core for hydrogen fusion, a protostar that never actually became a star. Brown dwarfs can be up to 80 times as massive as Jupiter and, being composed of mostly hydrogen and helium, could be considered similar to massive Jovian planets. However, since it would have had to be 80 times more massive than it is to force nuclear fusion in its core, Jupiter should *not* be considered a failed star. Brown dwarfs were also once theoretical objects, but have since been detected as companions to stars that presumably formed near them.

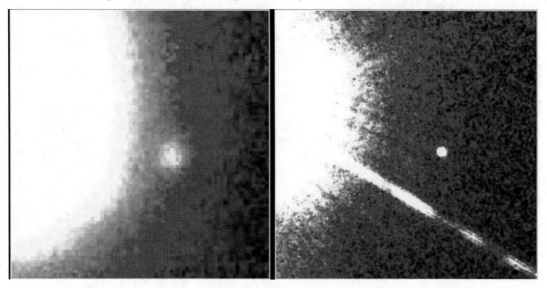

Figure 10.17 The smaller object in these infrared images is the brown dwarf companion of star Gliese 229.

10.7 The Deaths of Massive Stars

Neutron Stars

The Indian physicist Subramanyan Chandraskehar calculated that if the collapsing core of as star has a mass of more than 1.4 solar masses, then the mutual repulsion of the electrons would not be strong enough to stop the star from further collapse. The electrons would be smashed into the nuclei where they would combine with the protons, their opposite electrical charges canceling each other, and thus become neutrons. At this point the object would become a *neutron star*. This is more mass than the sun packed into the size of a mountain, a hundred million tons per teaspoon full. This *Chandrasekhar Limit* of 1.4 solar masses, the maximum mass that can still be a white dwarf, can be considered a dividing line between low-mass and high-mass stars.

Figure 10.18 Subramanyan Chandrasekhar

Supernovae

Another dividing-line between low- and high-mass stars is that the stars heavy enough to end their lives as neutrons stars go out with a bang rather than a whimper, in a *supernova* explosion. A massive star will go through main-sequence life and red giant stage similar to a lighter star, except it will be brighter, hotter and not last as long. By the end of the red giant stage the helium core in lighter stars has mostly fused into carbon. More massive stars put even more pressure on their cores and temperatures rise high enough to fuse carbon. As the core collapses, fusion continues into progressively heavier elements eventually ending with iron, the heaviest element that can be produced by nuclear fusion. The core can then collapse no further and rebounds with a supernova explosion.

Figure 10.19 A supernova explosion.

Supernova explosions are more than just the death of a star. They may also literally be the bringers of life. The shockwaves produced by a supernova explosion are what stir nebulae into star formation. Also, the explosions spray the heavy elements fused in the core of the massive star out into the galaxy to become parts of nebulae that will eventually form new stars. If not for supernova explosions, no carbon, oxygen, iron, or any other the other of the elements heavier than hydrogen and helium that are so abundant on our planet would have been available to be part of our Sun's solar nebula. Every atom on planet Earth, including those in your body, was synthesized in the core of a massive star, then blown out into the galaxy when that star went supernova. Since the most massive stars live much shorter lives, multiple generations of these stars have been born, lived to fuse heavy elements and then spread them throughout the galaxy when they died in supernova explosions. Elements heavier than iron all the way up to uranium are actually made by the supernova itself as subatomic particles are smashed together during the mayhem of the explosion.

Figure 10.20 The remnants of supernova explosions will become part of the material that forms new star systems like our own that are rich in heavy elements.

Pulsars

In 1967, Cambridge graduate student Jocelyn Bell detected unusual radio emissions that consisted of bursts of energy at unusually regular intervals. Since the bursts were so regular, it was suggested that they could be the first signs of extraterrestrial technology and therefore intelligence, perhaps lighthouses for flying saucers. The radio sources were jokingly referred to as LGMs (little green men) but later called *pulsars* due to their regular pulsing on and off.

Figure 10.21 Jocelyn Bell picture with the radio antenna with which she discovered the first pulsar in 1967.

Bell's thesis advisor, Anthony Hewish, took the lighthouse idea more seriously. The light at the top of a lighthouse appears to "blip" on and off because it is rotating. This is so ships can distinguish it from other lights that they see. Hewish suggested that pulsars were rapidly rotating neutron stars. Due to their incredible density, neutron stars should rotate at very high rates. This is like ice skaters that want to spin faster; they make themselves more compact by pulling their arms inward. The rotation rate of neutrons stars would be so fast that any energy they emit would not be in a steady stream, but appear to pulse on and off at the rate of the object's rotation.

Proof for this idea could come from finding another pulsar in a location where one would be expected to be present. Since neutrons stars are theoretically the end of the collapse of a massive star after it goes supernova, a *supernova remnant* nebula should be a likely place to find a pulsar. The most famous supernova remnant known to astronomers is the *Crab Nebula* in the constellation Taurus, the remnant left by the observed 1054 "guest star" supernova.

Figure10.22 Hubble Space Telescope image of the Crab Nebula.

Sure enough, a pulsar was detected in the Crab Nebula, verifying both the theory that neutrons stars do indeed exist and that pulsars are their signature. Controversy ensued in 1974 when Hewish was awarded a Noble Prize for his prediction that pulsars were neutrons stars and, in what many considered a sexist snub, Bell, the discoverer of pulsars, did not share in the prize.

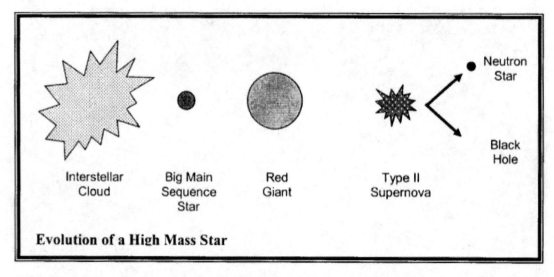

Figure 10.23 Stages on the life cycle of a massive star (the relative sizes of the object are not drawn to scale).

Black Holes

Recall that if a collapsing core of star is more massive than the Chandrasekar limit (1.4 solar masses) the electromagnetic repulsion between the electrons in the outer shells of the atoms cannot stop the collapse and the core will not become a white dwarf, but rather an even more dense neutron star. The collapse of a neutron star is ultimately stopped by the strong nuclear force limiting how close together neutrons can be packed in a fashion similar to the way the electromagnetic force limits the packing together of the atoms. However, if the collapsing core is more than about 3 solar masses, even the strong nuclear force, nature's strongest known force, cannot stop the collapse.

If the collapse cannot be stopped, the mass will eventually contract until it occupies no space. A mass taking up no space is infinitely dense. Clearly, this is not physically possible. When something is mathematically or theoretically possible but not physically possible it is called a singularity. A mass that cannot be stopped from collapsing and seems headed toward a singularity is on the verge of becoming a *black hole.*

Black holes can be understood, scientifically and rationally, without the need for any science fiction or fantasy. All masses have what is known as an *escape velocity*, the velocity that must be attained to escape the object's gravitational pull. As might be expected, the greater the mass of the object, the greater the escape velocity. A rocket must travel faster to escape Earth's gravity than the Moon's. If an object of a certain mass gets smaller, like the collapsing core of a massive star that already has a high escape velocity, the escape velocity will increase. It will become harder and harder to escape the object's gravitational pull. If a stellar core is about three solar masses, the minimum mass necessary to overcome the strong nuclear force, when it collapses down to a diameter of about 20 km (or 12 miles) across, the escape velocity will reach the speed of light.

Once the escape velocity reaches the speed of light, it becomes necessary to travel greater than that speed to escape the gravitational pull of the object. Since light travels at this speed, light from the object can no longer escape the gravitational pull and, as a consequence, the object can no longer be seen. It literally will disappear. This is the point where the object first becomes a black hole.

From then on there is a barrier or shield around the object through which no information about the object can pass. This boundary is called the *event horizon*. It is basically a sphere surrounding the object that is the size the object was when its escape velocity first became the speed of light, when it first disappeared from view and become a black hole. The distance from the center to the edge of the event horizon is called the *Schwarzschild radius*. First calculated by Karl Schwarzschild in 1916, this is the size the object was when it first became a black hole.

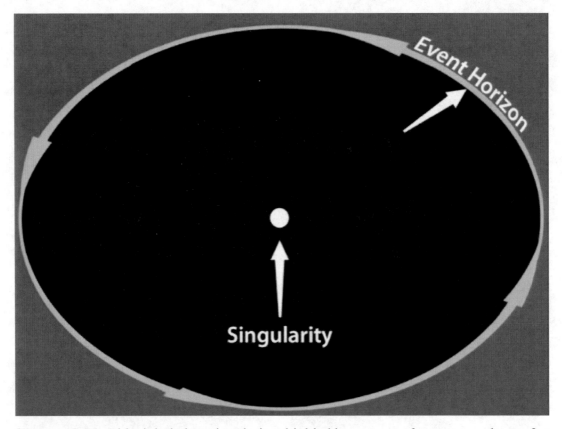

Figure 10.24 A black hole is a singularity shielded by an *event horizon*, a sphere of one *Schwarzschild radius*.

Once the collapsing object has shielded itself with an event horizon, it is no longer observable from the outside, so what happens, whether or not it ultimately does collapse to the point of singularity cannot be observed, cannot be known to an observer outside the event horizon. If an observer chose to cross the event horizon they would be ripped to shreds by huge tidal forces before they got there, but even if they somehow survived that, the trip would be one-way. To return would require traveling faster than light and, according to Einstein's theory of Special Relativity, that is not possible.

Even though it cannot be observed, a black hole can still be detected--by its gravitational pull. A stellar black hole will orbit the center of the galaxy just like any other star. If it should come in close enough to another star so the two form a binary system, the black hole will begin to pull mass from the star into its orbit. Material from the other star in orbit of the black hole is called an *accretion disk*. Material in the accretion disk will orbit faster as it gets closer to the event horizon and gives off high energy x-rays that can be detected. If a bright source of x-rays turns out to be a binary system, it is called a black hole candidate. Many binary x-ray sources have been observed, the first, called Cygnus X-I, in 1964. This was the first observational evidence of a black hole; like neutron stars, black holes were predicted theoretically before they were actually discovered.

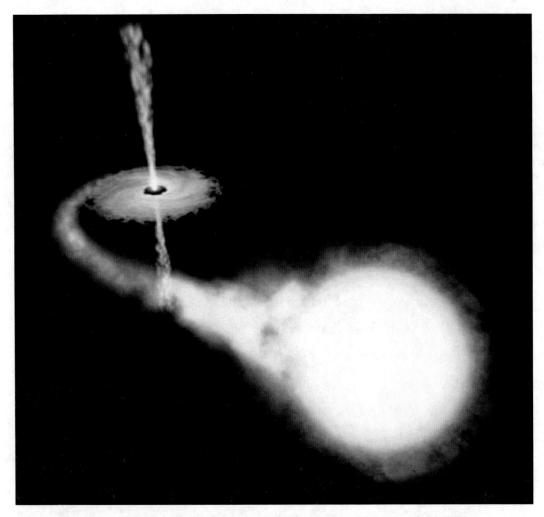

Figure 10.25 Artists conception of an accretion disk orbiting a black hole.

Relativity

In *Albert Einstein's Special Theory of Relativity,* the speed of light is a cosmic speed limit. He showed that objects can travel close to the speed of light but never reach or surpass it. The theory goes on to describe that as objects approach the speed of light, time for them actually slows down. If an object ever actually reached the speed of light, time from the object's perspective would stop, which is of course impossible. Experimental tests with the lifetimes of sub-atomic particles have verified this phenomenon, known as *time dilation*.

Figure 10.26 Statue of Einstein outside the *National Academy of Science* in Washington DC.

The *General Theory of Relativity,* also formulated by Einstein, is a new way to look at gravity. Rather than describing gravity as a force that pull masses together, as Newton did, Einstein described it as a curve in the fabric of space caused by mass. Think of a blanket pulled tightly at all four corners. The curvature of space caused by massive objects causes other objects to alter their paths when they pass near them. A small mass, like a marble, will bend the fabric of the blanket less than a larger mass like a softball, and the path of a marble rolling on the blanket will be changed by the *gravity-well* created by the softball. The more massive the object, the deeper its well and the faster another object would have to travel to escape. A black hole could be thought of as a bowling ball that rips the blanket so that another mass that falls through the hole cannot ever travel fast enough to come back out.

Figure 10.27 Gravity is described in General Relativity as a curvature in the fabric of space caused by the presence of mass.

Review Questions

1. What objects are considered the birthplaces of stars? How does star formation begin?

2. What is a protostar?

3. What provides the energy necessary for stars to give off light or shine? How is this energy created?

4. What is a star cluster?

5. What is the relationship between the mass of a star and how long the star will last?

6. What is hydrostatic equilibrium?

7. Name five stellar corpses, objects that are the last stage of the evolution of a star. Which were predicted theoretically before they were found? Which has not yet been found?

8. What type of object could be described as star that "did not make it?"

9. What is a planetary nebula? Does it have anything to do with planets?

10. What remains after a supernova?

11. What is a pulsar?

12. If we cannot see a black hole, how can we detect them?

13. What is an event horizon?

14. List the steps in the evolution of a low-mass star (like our Sun).

15. List the steps in the evolution of high-mass star.

Tutorial – Stellar Evolution Concept Map

Insert the following objects into their proper ovals or circles in the stellar evolution concept-map on the next page:

> *brown dwarf*
>
> *black hole*
>
> *main sequence*
>
> *nebula*
>
> *neutron star*
>
> *planetary nebula*
>
> *protostar*
>
> *pulsar*
>
> *red giant*
>
> *supernova*
>
> *white dwarf*

Hints: You may want to look at Figures 10.16 and 10.23.

The circles are where the *"stellar corpses"* go.

Since there are 11 objects and 10 ovals/circles, there is one place that two objects go.

Stellar Evolution Concept Map

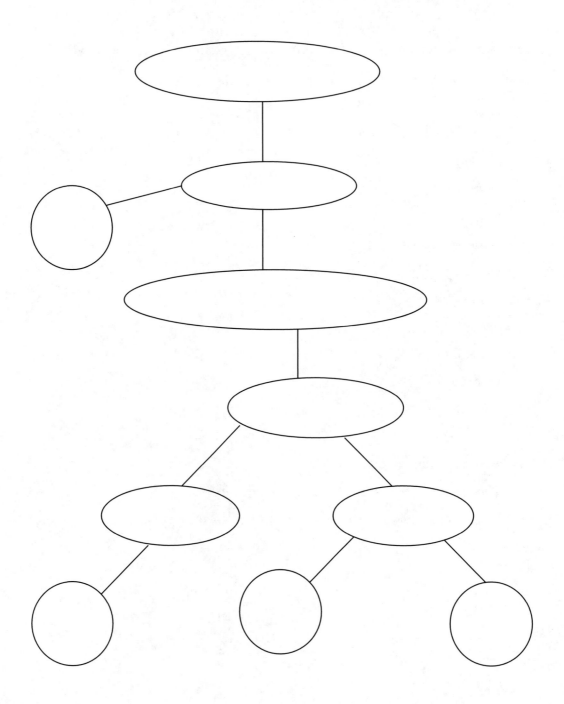

Chapter - 11 Galaxies

11.1 Introduction

The Sun is only one star in a spiral-shaped disk of several hundred billion stars called the *Milky Way* galaxy. The Milky Way galaxy and its two satellite galaxies, called the *Magellanic Clouds*, and our closest neighbor, the *Andromeda galaxy*, are part of a 25-30-member cluster of galaxies called the *Local Group*. The Local Group and uncounted other galaxies, some of very different types from our Milky Way, in other galactic clusters and super clusters and the intergalactic space between them make up the universe.

11. 2 The Milky Way

Originally, the *Milky Way* was the name used to describe a pale band of light that stretches all across the sky. It is less familiar nowadays, as it is often washed-out by urban light pollution and not visible from the most densely populated locations.

Figure 11.1 The *Milky Way*

The Galaxy

It was not until Galileo turned his telescope on the Milky Way, circa 1610, that the Milky Way was revealed to be the combined light from many stars that were all too dim to see as individuals. Presumably this was because they were farther away than most of the stars that we do observe as individual points of light. Later, in the late 1700's, William Herschel, who with his sister Caroline was the co-discoverer of the planet Uranus, suggested that this bright band of light was in fact a gigantic disk-shaped assemblage of stars, of which our Sun was one part. He tired to deduce the Sun's place in this "galaxy" of stars by counting the numbers of stars in different directions, thinking that there would be more stars in the direction of the center and less in the direction of the edge. The results of the Herschel's star-counts were always that there were about the same number of stars in all directions, so the Sun was at the center of the galaxy. Nobody, including the Herschels, wanted to believe this. It had taken over a thousand years for astronomers to move Earth out of the central position given to it by the ancients, so it did not seem likely that our solar system should be at the center of the galaxy we inhabit.

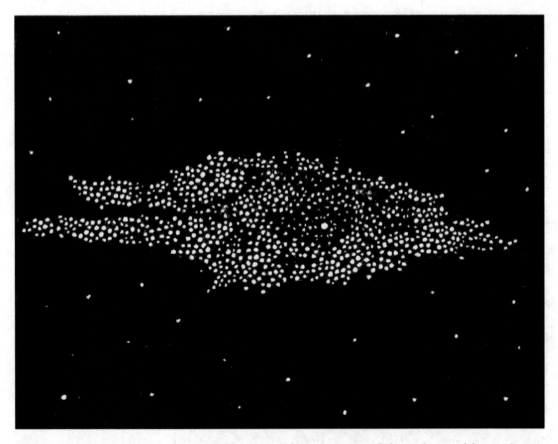

Figure 11.2 The Herschel's star-counts produced a map of the galaxy with our Sun nearly at the center.

Globular Clusters

It was not until the early part of the 20th century that the modern understanding of galaxies began to emerge. Astronomer *Harlow Shapely* estimated the Sun's position by observing objects called *Globular Clusters*. Unlike open star clusters, groups of young stars that formed together in the same nebula, globular clusters are groups of older stars that Shapley theorized form a *halo* around the outer edges of the galaxy.

Figure 11.3 *Globular Cluster* Omega Centauri.

Mutual gravitational pull between the several hundred billion stars holds the galaxy together. Since gravity pulls objects toward a central location, there are more stars near the center of the galaxy and less on the edges. Globular clusters are thought to form when stars in the outer edges of the galaxy exert as much gravitational force on one another as is exerted on them from the far-away galactic center and cluster together. Shapely found that there were more globular clusters located in some directions than others, and estimated the Sun to be in the main disk of the galaxy, but not in the center, rather, about two thirds of the way out from the center.

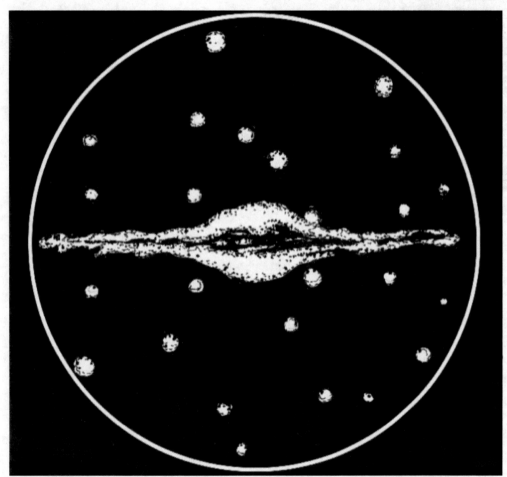

Figure 11.4 *Globular clusters* form a halo around the galaxy.

11. 3 The Shapely-Curtis Debate

The next question was whether the galaxy and its halo of globular clusters was everything, an *island universe*, as Shapely believed, or if our galaxy was only one of many galaxies in a much larger *universe*. This was the belief of astronomer *Heber Curtis*.

Figure 11.5 Harlow Shapely and Heber Curtis.

The *Shapely-Curtis Debate,* as the disagreement came to be known, centered on objects known as *spiral nebula.* The term *nebula* has already been introduced as a term to describe the large clouds of gas and dust in which stars form and then leave behind at the end of their life cycle. Around the time of the debate, 1920, the term nebula was used to describe any object in the sky that appeared as an indistinct patch or blob. Eventually some of the objects came to be known as star clusters and other galaxies, with the clouds of gas and dust retaining the name nebula, but at that time they were all called nebulae. The debate was whether the spiral nebulae were other galaxies like our own Milky Way galaxy, in which case Curtis would be right, or if Shapely was right, they were objects within our galaxy.

Figure 11.6 M 31, the great nebula in Andromeda; now know as the *Andromeda galaxy*.

The answer would only come if the distance to spiral nebulae could be compared to the distance to other objects already known to be part of our galaxy, such as Shapley's globular clusters. The debate was finally resolved when astronomer *Edwin*

Hubble determined that a variable star in the Andromeda nebula was over a million light years away, much farther away than any of the objects in our own galaxy.

Figure 11.7 Edwin Hubble.

11.4 The Distance Ladder

Determining the distance to stars by parallax only works with stars that are close enough to show enough parallax to be measured, stars within 100 parsecs or just over 300 light years away. Star farther away can be compared or *fit* with stars on the HR diagram having distances already known from parallax. If the two stars on the main sequence are of the same spectral type, they can be assumed to have the same luminosity. How far away the star of known distance would have to be to have the same apparent magnitude as the other star can be calculated and can be assumed to be the distance to that star. This technique, called *main sequence fitting,* can be used to determine distances up to about 10,000 pc or over 30,000 ly, the maximum distance to objects in our galaxy.

Outside our galaxy, the rate at which the brightness of certain types of variable stars change can be used to compare such stars in our galaxy to those in other galaxies, and to determine distances of up to 15 million pc, or almost 50 million light years. Hubble used a method developed by astronomer *Henrietta Swan Leavitt* to determine the distance to a *Cepheid variable* star in the Andromeda galaxy. Other rare objects like supergiant stars, certain types of supernovae, and globular clusters, can be compared in a similar fashion. Even galaxies, once their distance is known by one of these methods, can be compared to similar galaxies even farther away. These methods can be used to measure distances up to hundreds of millions of parsecs to almost a billion light years.

Figure 11.8 Henrietta Swan Leavitt.

The final step of the distance ladder, used to determine distances to the farthest objects in the universe is known as *Hubble's Law*. Hubble's Law will be discussed in the next chapter.

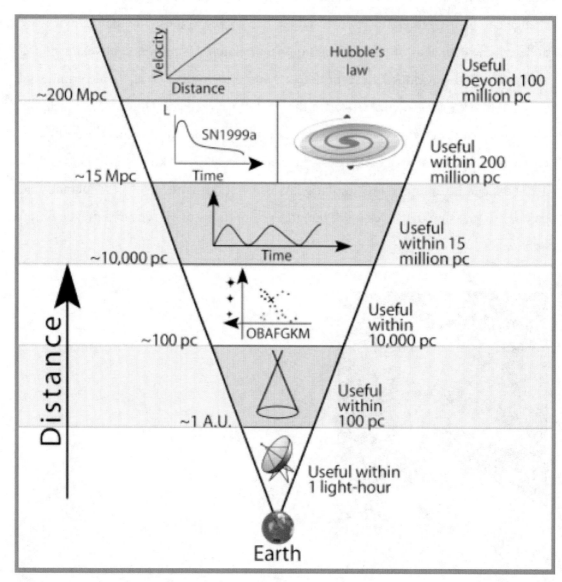

Figure 11.9 The distance ladder.

11.5 Other Galaxies

Hubble's discovery verified that our galaxy was only one of many in the entire universe, and gave birth to galactic astronomy. Hubble began observing and determining the distance to many galaxies. He discovered that there are only a few different types; he called them *spirals, barred-spirals and elliptical* galaxies, and he featured them on his *tuning fork diagram* seen in Fig. 11.10. The few remaining galaxies that do not fit in these classifications are called *irregular* galaxies.

The great galaxy in Andromeda (Fig 11.6), as it began to be called, is a spiral galaxy and, at almost 3 million light years away, is the nearest neighbor to our own Milky Way galaxy. Our Milky Way's satellite galaxies, the Magellanic Clouds (Fig. 11.11) are examples of irregular galaxies.

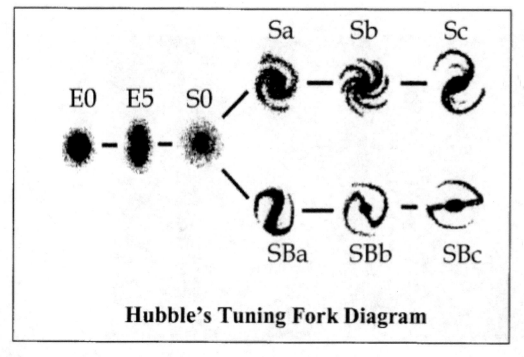

Figure 11.10 Hubble's *Tuning Fork Diagram.*

Figure 11.11 The *Magellanic Clouds*.

Figure 11.12 M51 The *Whirlpool galaxy*, a *spiral* galaxy.

Figure 11.13 A *barred-spiral galaxy*.

Figure 11.14 An *elliptical galaxy*.

11.6 The Shape of The Milky Way Galaxy

The shape of our own Milky Way galaxy had been thought to be a spiral similar to that of M 51 shown in Figure 11.12, but this was hard to establish, since astronomers and their telescopes were on the inside looking out, not on the outside looking in as with all other galaxies. Also, much of the view inside our galaxy is obscured with dust that visible light could not penetrate. It was not until the 1950s when radio telescopes become more common, due to surplus radio equipment available after World War II, that radio maps verified the Milky Way's spiral shape. More recently there have been some observations that have suggested that the Milky Way may be more of a barred spiral similar to the galaxy shown in Figure 11.13.

11.7 Galactic Centers

More recently, it has also been suggested that the central objects in galaxies are *supermassive black holes*. The stellar blackholes described in the previous chapter are very small objects, but a blackhole is not required to be small. Any mass that has a size such that the escape velocity is greater than the speed of light is a black hole. For example, the minimum, 3 solar mass blackhole is almost 20 km across. This means that a 3000 solar mass blackhole would be 20,000 km across and a 30,000 solar mass black hole would be 200,000 km across. If enough stars gravitationally pull close enough together, the center of a galaxy could indeed be a huge back hole. Evidence for this is that the centers of most galaxies, including our own Milky Way, are super-bright x-ray sources as would be expected from a massive accretion disk surrounding a supermassive blackhole.

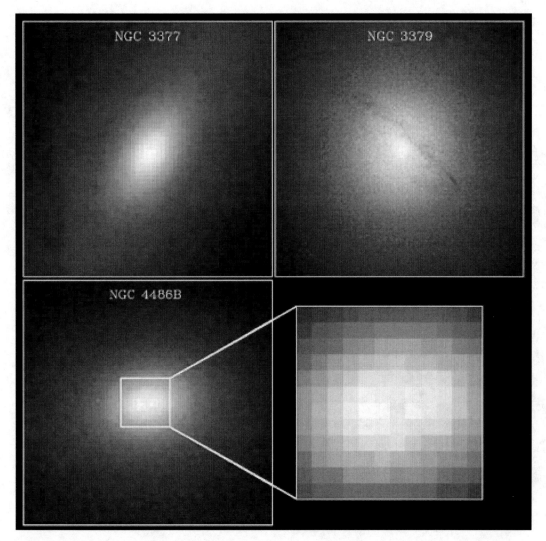

Figure 11.15 *Supermassive blackholes* at the center of several distant galaxies.

11.8 Clusters of Galaxies

The Milky Way and the Andromeda Galaxy and 25 to 30 other smaller galaxies make up the *Local Group*, a cluster of galaxies about 10 million light years across. A cluster of galaxies, or *galactic cluster,* is a group of galaxies that are gravitationally bound together. The *Virgo Cluster*, that contains over 1000 galaxies, is the nearest galactic cluster to the Local Group, at a distance of almost 60 million light years away. It is named after the constellation Virgo that it appears to be behind, or is seen through. Other nearby clusters, again named after the constellations they appear to be in, are the *Coma* and *Fornax* clusters.

Figure 11.16 Galaxies in the *Virgo Cluster*.

The Local Group and the Virgo Cluster are part of the Local or Virgo *Supercluster* of nearly 100 groups and clusters of galaxies that is 100 million light years across. A *supercluster* is a group several of galactic clusters. Galaxy clusters and superclusters and the vast voids of intergalactic space between them are the *universe*. The study of the universe as a whole, its origin, current state, and ultimate fate is called *cosmology* and is the subject of the next chapter.

Review Questions

1. What are the two uses of the term Milky Way?

2. Where was the Sun located in the first maps of the galaxy. [?]Was this believed to be accurate?

3. Where relative to the center of the galaxy is the Sun currently thought to be located? How was this first determined? By whom?

4. What was the Shapley-Curtis Debate about? How was it resolved? Who ended it? Who won the debate?

5. What four types of galaxies did Edwin Hubble identify? Which type was not on his tuning fork diagram? Which type is our Milky Way galaxy?

6. Since astronomers are "on the inside looking out," of our Milky Way galaxy, how was its shape determined?

7. Describe the steps of Hubble's *distance-ladder*.

8. What are found at the centers of most galaxies?

9. Of what cluster is our Milky Way galaxy a part? How many galaxies are in this cluster? Of what supercluster is our cluster a part? What other cluster is in this supercluster?

10. How large is the galactic cluster of which our Milky Way galaxy is a part? How large is the supercluster of which our cluster is a part?

Tutorial-Galaxy Classification

Part 1 –Classify the pictures of galaxies 1-18 on the following two pages into up to four different categories defined *by the members of your group*. List which galaxies are in each category, and define your categories in the table below.

Category	Galaxy ID Numbers	Defining Characteristics
I		
II		
III		
IV		

Part 2 –After completing **Part 1,** refer to Figure 11.10 Hubble's Tuning Fork Diagram and classify galaxies 1-18 according to Hubble's Categories.

Hubble's Category	Galaxy ID Numbers	Defining Characteristics

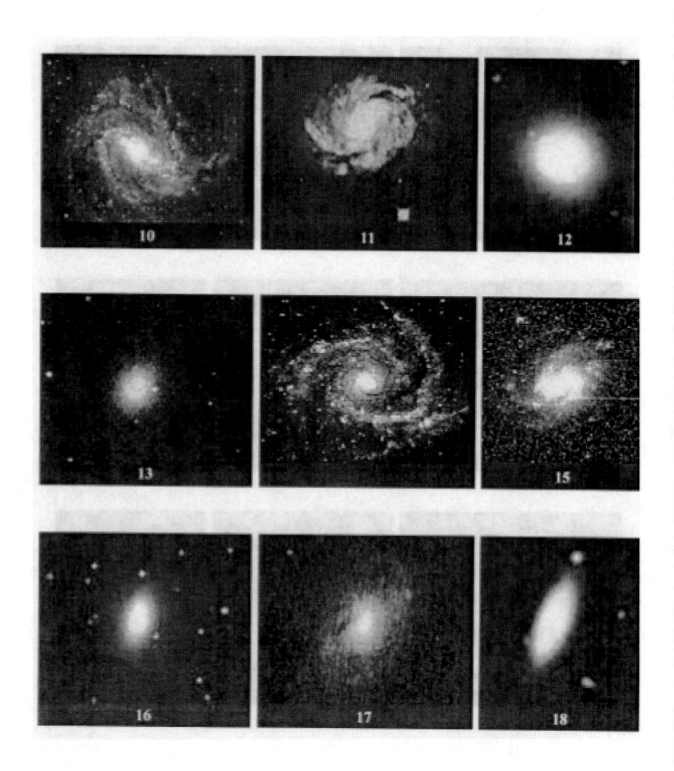

Chapter 12 - Cosmology

12.1 Introduction

Astronomy is the study of the universe. *Cosmology* is the branch of astronomy in which the universe, its origin, current state and ultimate fate, as a whole, single entity is studied. On this universal scale, the composition of the universe is basically large amounts of empty space interspersed with points of mass. These points of mass are galaxies. In the large scale of the universe, all objects within the galaxies and the space between them can be considered essentially microscopic.

12.2 Theories about the Universe

Throughout most of the history of astronomy, planets, stars, and galaxies were all studied. But the *universe*, of which all these objects are a part, was considered immense in both size and age, perhaps infinite in both and, as a whole, unchanging. Any ideas about the beginning or end of the universe were left to religion. The original scientific theory about the universe was that it was in a *steady state,* that on its large scale, the universe was unchanging. This changed in 1929 when *Edwin Hubble* made observations that suggested that the universe is expanding.

12.3 The Expanding Universe

When examining the spectra of light from more distant galaxies, Hubble noticed that the spectra were all *redshifted*. According to the *Doppler effect*, discussed in Chapter 4, since red is the color of the longest visible wavelength of light, a shift toward the red end of the spectrum means that the waves coming from the source are being left behind and stretched out as the object moves away from the observer. So, if a galaxy shows a redshift in its spectrum, it is moving away from us in our Milky Way galaxy.

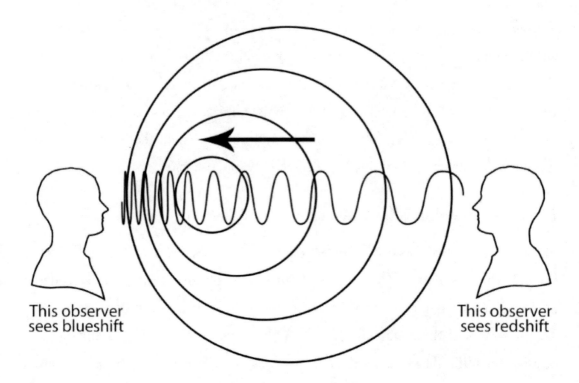

Figure 12.1 The *Doppler effect.*

American astronomer *Vesto Slipher* had noticed this shift before Hubble, and observed that some closer galaxies, such as our nearest neighbor, Andromeda, show blueshifts, meaning that they are moving toward us, but any beyond our local cluster show redshifts and are moving away from us. Hubble used this data and made more observations that also showed that the further away a galaxy was, the more redshift was present, meaning that it was moving away, or receding, even faster. Hubble showed that the amount of redshift, or the rate a galaxy is receding is in proportion to its distance. This relationship soon became known as Hubble's Law or the *Hubble Law*. From this, Hubble deduced, that since all distant galaxies are moving away from us and the farther away they are, the faster they are moving, that the universe must be expanding.

Figure 12.2 Vesto Slipher.

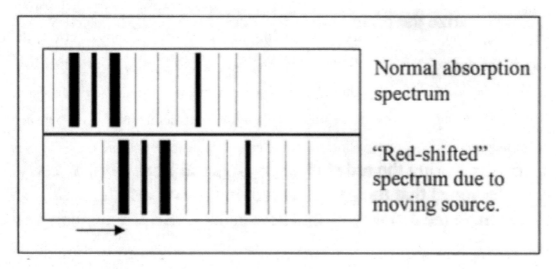

Figure 12.3 The spectra of an object moving away from an observer is shifted toward longer wavelengths, or *redshifted*.

The theoretical idea of an expanding universe had been first suggested in 1922 by a Russian, *Alexander Friedman*, based on solutions of Einstein's General Theory of Relativity. Einstein himself was a believer in a steady-state universe but thought that mutual gravitation between galaxies would cause the universe to collapse. To *fix* this, he inserted a term he called the cosmological constant, a repulsive force that balanced the pull of gravity to stabilize his theoretical steady-state universe. Hubble invited Einstein to California to see the data. When Einstein realized that Hubble's observations did indeed show that the universe was not in a steady state, Einstein called the addition of the cosmological constant "the greatest blunder" of his scientific career.

The Cosmological Redshift

An important distinction to make when discussing the expanding universe is that the galaxies are not rushing out into space that is already there, but rather it is space itself that is expanding. Although recognized with knowledge of the Doppler effect, the *cosmological redshift* is actually caused by the space between galaxies expanding. As a result, the wavelengths of light traveling through that space expand *with* the space. Think of drawing two dots that represent galaxies on a balloon and a wave between them that represents light traveling from one galaxy to the other before the balloon is inflated. Then blow up the balloon. The distance between the dots or galaxies will increase and the length of the wave will also increase.

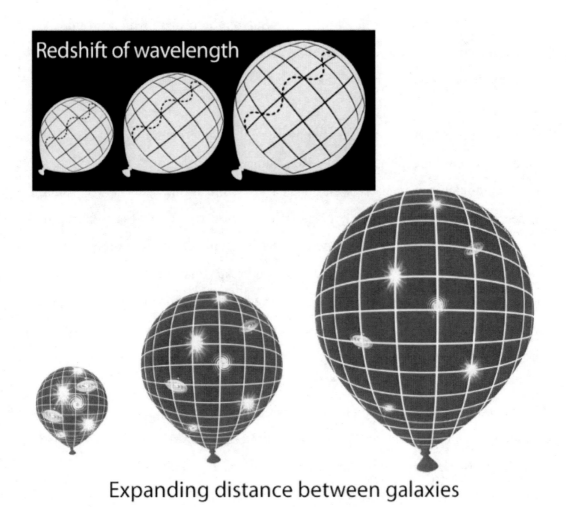

Redshift of wavelength

Expanding distance between galaxies

Figure 12.4 The *Cosmological Redshift* and the expanding distances between galaxies.

Are We at the Center of the Universe?

The interpretation that the redshift indicates that all distant galaxies are receding, could suggest that the observer is at a central point in the universe. Proving that this was *not* the case was of course, what the Copernican Revolution was about (Chapter 2), and early attempts at mapping our Milky Way Galaxy (Chapter 11) were not taken seriously because they seemed to show our Sun as the center, which ultimately did not turn out to be the case either. Both of these points suggest that it is unlikely for our own galaxy to be the center of the universe.

The reason that observations seem to show our location as central is that observations would show *any* location as central. Returning to the example of the balloon, this time imagine drawing many dots on its surface before inflating it. As the balloon is inflated all the dots would move away from each other, so an observer on *any* dot would observe all the other dots moving away from them. A common example used by cosmologists is that of a rising loaf of raisin bread. Imagine the raisins as galaxies and the bread as the fabric of space. As the bread rises, or expands while being baked, the distance between all raisins will increase, and observers on any raisin will see all other raisins moving away from them.

A common misconception about the expanding universe is that if everything is expanding then the expansion should not be noticeable. Everything is *not* expanding. Only space is expanding, not the matter in the space, and only on the scale of the immense distances between galaxies is this expansion noticeable. It is not noticeable in the space between stars within in galaxies or planets within solar systems like our own.

What Is the Size of the Universe?
Another idea about the universe that should be discussed is its size. Often, the size of the universe is considered to be infinite. This does solve one problem, the problem of where the center is. This is because if the center is defined as a point that is equally

distant from all edges, then any point in an infinite universe could be considered the center, just as with the balloon or raisin bread analogies.

However, a universe infinite in size brings up perhaps an even worse problem. Physically, something *cannot* be infinitely large. This problem can be discussed with an analogy as well. Even though we all know that Earth is spherical in shape, locally it looks flat because it is so large. Now imagine a tiny insect walking along Earth's surface. The insect is so small that no matter how far it walks it cannot detect the curvature of Earth's surface. To that insect, Earth (its universe) will appear as a very, very large two-dimensional flat sheet. Now imagine Earth was being blown up like a balloon, causing the insect's universe to expand at a rate faster than the insect can walk. To that insect Earth's surface would appear as an infinitely large flat two-dimensional sheet.

According to General Relativity, on the large scale of the entire universe, the mass in the universe has curved space into four physical dimensions. The universe is so large however, that it appears locally flat in three dimensions. So, by bumping up the dimensions of the tiny insect's story by one, we are three-dimensional creatures living in a four-dimensional universe that, because it is expanding faster than we can travel through it, appears locally flat in three dimensions and infinite in size.

12.4 The Age of the Universe

Hubble's Law is a relationship between the rate at which galaxies are receding (their speed) and how far away they are (their distance). Very basic physics tells us that the distance something travels divided by the amount of time it took to travel that distance is the velocity (technically speed, but in this example the two are interchangeable). So if distance divided by time is velocity, it follows that distance divided by velocity is time. So, the distance to a galaxy divided by it recessional velocity would be the amount of time the galaxy has been moving away from us. If the average of the recessional velocities of and distances to many galaxies were used, the time would be an estimate of how long the universe as a whole has been expanding, the age of the universe.

Hubble's law often appears in the form of a graph of the recessional velocity of galaxies as a function of their distance. Since according to Hubble's Law, the two quantities are proportional, the graph is a straight line. How steep the line is, or the line's *slope,* is referred to as *Hubble's constant* or the *Hubble constant.*

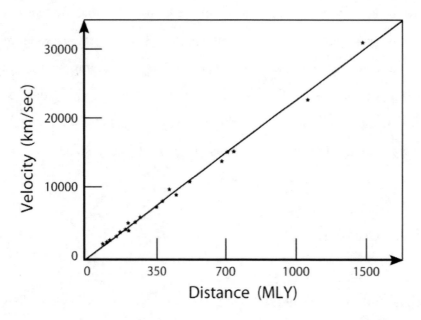

Figure 12.5 Hubble's Law in graph form.

The slope of a line is defined as its rise divided by its run, how far up it goes divided by how far over. So the Hubble constant would be the recessional velocity of the galaxies divided by the distance to them. This is the opposite or reciprocal of the time that is distance divided by velocity, so the time the galaxies have been receding, the age of the universe, is the reciprocal of, or simply one divided by Hubble's constant. The current estimate of the age of the universe, based on Hubble's constant is about 13.7 billion years.

The age of the universe sets a limit on the size of the *observable* universe. If the Universe is just under 14 billion years old, than nothing farther than 14 billion light-years away can be seen. The light from anything farther away than that would not yet have had time to reach us. The universe could be larger than that, but just less than 14 billion light years is our *cosmic horizon,* the farthest distance to which we can see.

12.5 The Big Bang Theory

If the universe has been expanding for almost 14 billion years, this means that over that time, as it has been getting larger, the universe would be getting more spread out or *less* dense and because of this, the overall temperature of the universe would be getting *lower*. This also suggests that in the past when the universe was smaller, it was *more* dense and because of this, the overall temperature was *higher*.

What follows from the above, is that a very long time ago, the universe would have been very dense and very hot and that the universe actually may have began expanding from an infinitely dense and infinitely hot singularity. This theory, first suggested in 1927 by a Belgian Priest *Georges Lemaitre,* based on his study of the universe using General Relativity, has become known as the *Big Bang Theory.*

Figure 12.6 Einstein and Lemaitre.

Ironically, the term "Big Bang" was coined by astronomer *Fred Hoyle*, who was one of the originators of the Steady-State Theory, in an attempt to diminish the idea. The basic idea is, that just under14 billion years ago (the age of the universe as estimated from Hubble's Law) the universe began with an expansion from a singularity. Temperatures were so high that the universe was pure energy. As the universe got larger, temperatures dropped, first allowing fundamental particles to condense from pure energy, then cooling further causing these fundamental particles to be confined into larger sub-atomic particles, then these particle formed atoms and great numbers of atoms eventually formed the beginnings of galaxies. Ultimately, within the galaxies, stars formed, leftovers from stars formed planets, at least one of which gave rise to the life that now studies the universe.

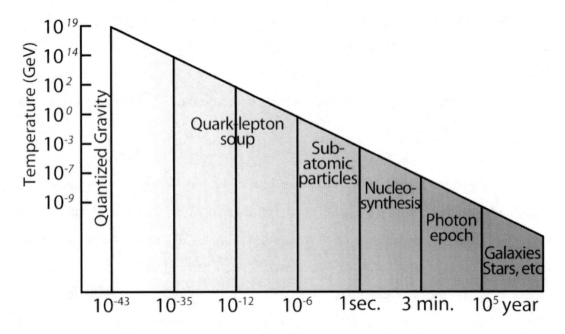

Figure 12.7 The cooling universe from the time of the Big Bang.

What the Big Bang Theory *Cannot* Tell Us

Before any further discussion, a few important points must be made about the Big Bang theory. First, the Big Bang did not occur at a certain point in our current universe; at the time of the Big Bang the singularity *was* the universe. The singularity did not begin expanding into empty space that was already there, rather all the space that is now in our universe was contained by the singularity, just as the space is inside our universe now. Also, although the question "What happened before the Big Bang?" is certainly a viable question to ask, it is not a question that the Big Bang theory can answer. Scientific theories only answer questions they are designed to answer. The Big Bang is a theory about the creation of our universe, and our measurement of time began when our universe began, at the Big Bang. So the theory contains no description about what happened before that. Another viable question is "What was outside the singularity?" The answer is that, since the singularity was the universe, the answer to that question then is the same as it is now; since the theory is about our universe it does not describe anything outside our universe. Lack of answers to either of these questions does not invalidate the theory; the theory is just not designed to address the question.

It has been suggested that, not unlike the black holes in our universe that we are outside of and unable to look into, the universe can be thought of as a blackhole that we are on the inside of and unable to look out. Estimates of the mass and size of the universe fit the black hole criteria. The mass of the universe is contained within a size that makes the escape velocity greater than the speed of light, so to leave our universe, one would have to travel faster than light, something that, according to Einstein's theory of Special Relativity, is not possible.

Once again, the fact that the Big Bang theory does not answer these questions does not invalidate the theory. What will validate or invalidate the Big Bang, or any other scientific theory, is whether or not its explanations and predictions agree with the evidence that can be gathered about our universe through observations.

12.6 Evidence for the Big Bang Theory

The Cosmic Background Radiation

The first observational evidence for the Big Bang theory came in 1963. It had been theorized by Robert Dicke of Princeton University that the universe should be filled with a *background* of radiation or *after-glow* of the original energy from the Big Bang. The energy would have originally been very short wave when the universe was young and hot, but due to the expansion of space it has since been stretched to much longer microwave wavelengths and cooled to a very cold temperature of just under 3 Kelvin, only 3 degrees above absolute zero. Dicke was building an antenna to search for this *cosmic microwave background* (*CMB*) radiation when radio astronomers *Arno Penzias* and *Robert Wilson* of nearby Bell Labs discovered it accidentally while testing an antenna designed for satellite communication. Dicke later verified that what they discovered was indeed what he had predicted. In what many considered to be yet another injustice by the Nobel committee, Penzias and Wilson, but *not* Dicke, shared the 1965 Nobel Prize for their discovery of the 3K cosmic microwave background, the first observational evidence of the Big Bang theory

Particle Physics

Evidence for the conditions in the early universe can come from the theories and the experiments of *particle physics*. Particle physics is the study of the fundamental particles of matter and the interactions or forces between them. Every time a particle accelerator is used to observe what happens to particles and their interactions at higher and higher energies and temperatures, physicists come closer to simulating conditions at the time of the Big Bang.

Figure 12.8 Wilson and Penzias in front of their horn antenna.

Quasars

These objects were first observed in the 1950s as radio signals that had no visible source. Many more were found in the 1960s. One appeared to be coming from what looked like a small blue star, but was emitting as much energy at radio wavelengths as *an entire galaxy*. They were named *Quasars,* an acronym for; *QUAsi Stellar Radio Sources.*

The spectra of quasars was one that no one had ever seen before. Some astronomers thought that they were made of an entirely new substance until it was suggested that their spectrum was that of hydrogen, but with an extreme redshift, greater than had ever been observed. If indeed this were true, then, by Hubble's Law, quasars would be the farthest objects yet observed, farther than any known galaxies.

Because looking out into space is also looking back in time, quasars have the greatest look-back time of any objects. This means that they are being observed as they looked when they were very young. This brought about the hypothesis that quasars represent the early stages of galaxy formations; that quasars are *infant galaxies* being observed at a time when the supermassive black holes at their centers were first forming and gravitationally collecting the tremendous amounts of hydrogen gas that would soon begin to form the stars.

It is an intriguing possibility that quasars observed from our Milky Way galaxy today may now be much more like our own galaxy, but being billions of light years away, the light from their infant stages is just now reaching our galaxy. It follows from this, that if beings are observing from a galaxy that is seen from our Milky Way galaxy as a quasar, they may observe our galaxy as a quasar.

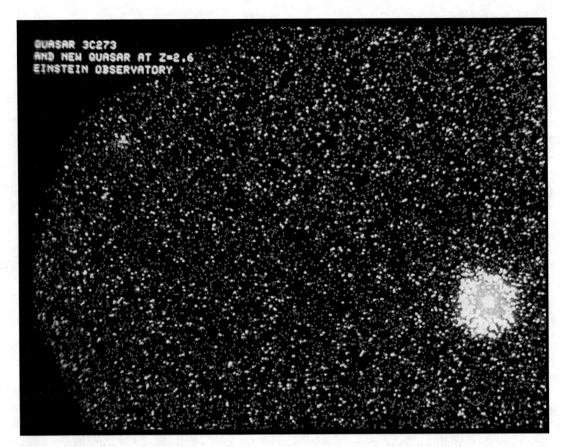

Figure 12.9 An image of a *quasar*.

12.7 Inflation

Despite the observational evidence, the Big Bang theory did have some problems. The Big Bang did not satisfactorily explain why the universe was overall, on its vast scale, so uniform, why areas of the CMB so far away from each other had exactly the same temperatures, just under 3K. Also, among other problems, there was no satisfactory explanation for why matter, galaxies, clumped together in only certain places and why the rest of the universe is empty space.

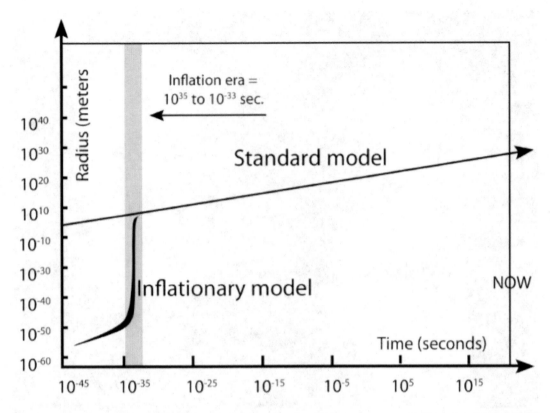

Figure 12.10 Expansion of the universe in the *Inflationary* and *Standard* Big Bang Models.

In 1980 MIT physicist *Alan Guth* when investigating some of these problems discovered that if very early on, at a time of only about 10^{-35} seconds, the early universe experienced an epoch of very rapid expansion driven by a mechanism known as *vacuum energy*, all of these problems would be solved. This era of rapid expansion became known as the *inflation* era and the idea, the *inflationary model*. Russian physicist, Andrei Linde, now at Stanford University, independently proposed similar ideas.

Figure 12.11 Alan Guth and Andrei Linde.

Observational evidence of inflation came from the *Cosmic Background Explorer (COBE)* satellite in 1992 when it was used to map the CMB (Figure 12.13). The map showed slight variations in the temperatures of the early universe. The lighter areas in Figure 12.13 were areas of slightly higher temperature and therefore energy that eventually would become galaxies, and the darker areas of slightly lower temperature would become the empty space. These *ripples in the cosmos,* as they have been called, could have been caused by an early, sudden rapid expansion of the universe, providing proof that inflation *could* have happened. Project leaders *George Smoot* and *John Mather* shared the 2006 Nobel Prize for the COBE results. More recently the *Wilkinson Microwave Anisotropic Probe (WMAP)* verified the COBE observations in even more detail.

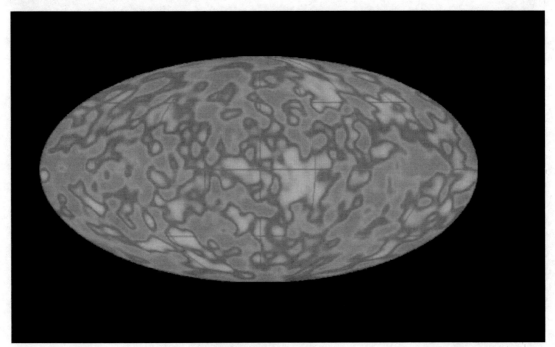

Figure 12.12 COBE map of the CMB showing areas of slightly higher (lighter) and lower (darker) temperature that eventually become the universe's matter (galaxies) and empty space.

12.8 The Fate of the Universe

Questions about the ultimate fate of the universe hinge on whether the universe will continue to expand as it is now, or whether there is enough mass in the universe to provide the gravitational pull necessary to stop the universe from expanding and possibly even cause it to begin to contract. Considering only regular matter, matter detectable by electromagnetic radiation, there is barely 10 percent of the matter necessary to provide the gravity necessary to stop the expansion, so it would seem that the universe will continue to expand and cool until it ultimately reaches the temperature absolute zero. Energy naturally flows from where there is more to where there is less. At absolute zero everything will be at the same temperature, so no more energy will flow; there will be no more natural processes, and the universe will be dead.

Dark Matter

Regular observable matter is not the only kind of matter that exists. In the 1930s Swiss astrophysicist, *Fritz Zwicky* proposed that there was unseen mass providing the gravity that caused unaccounted for motions in galactic clusters. In the 1960s astronomer *Vera Rubin* made measurements of the orbital velocities of stars around the center of our own Milky Way galaxy and showed that their speeds *did not* decrease with distance from the center as expected, verifying that there was unseen or missing mass at work providing gravity in our galaxy. This solution to this *missing mass problem* as it was called was dubbed *dark matter*.

Soon it was estimated that up to 90 percent of the mass in the universe could be this dark matter. If this were true, it was then possible that the universe would someday stop expanding. Among the candidates for dark matter are unaccounted-for fundamental particles, *weakly interacting mass particles (WIMPS)* and large, dark, rogue planetary objects in interstellar and even intergalactic space, *massive compact halo objects (MACHOS)*.

Figure 12.13 Fritz Zwicky and Vera Rubin.

Dark Energy

Recent observations using Type I supernovae, white dwarf stars that accumulate accretion disks from binary companions and then explode when they reach the Chandrasekhar limit, as standard candles (objects of known brightness) to measure the distance to faraway galaxies more accurately than ever before suggest that the rate of the expansion of universe is actually increasing.

The likely agent for this acceleration is the vacuum energy first suggested as the mechanism for inflation, now called *dark energy*. This energy of empty space is repulsive, thus causing expansion, and is currently considered the dominant factor, being much stronger than the influence of dark and regular matter, in the overall dynamics of the universe. It may also turn out that dark energy can be represented by Einstein's cosmological constant, which would mean that when he made what he called his "biggest blunder," he might have been right all along.

12.9 Is the Universe Fine-Tuned for Life?

It has been observed that if the values of some of the fundamental constants of nature, the mass of certain particles or the strengths of interactions were just a little bit different, life as we know it would never have been possible in our universe. This brings up the question that, since life is what possesses the consciousness to observe and understand the universe, is the universe is indeed somehow *fine-tuned* for life? In the next and final chapter, questions about what is necessary for life to come about, survive, and even thrive in our universe will be discussed and ultimately, whether or not there is life elsewhere in our galaxy and universe and whether it can be detected or contacted from Earth.

Review Questions

1. What is the cosmological redshift? What does it suggest about the universe?

2. Why is the observation that all galaxies seem to be moving away from our galaxy not considered problematic by cosmologists?

3. How is the age of the universe estimated? What is the current estimate for the age of the universe?

4. What is the cosmic horizon?

5. According to the Big Bang theory, how do the density and temperature of the universe in the past compare to the density and temperature now? In the future?

6. According to the Big Bang theory, what happened before the Big Bang? What is outside our universe?

7. What evidence is there for the Big Bang theory?

8. What are quasars?

9. What problems are there with the Standard Big Bang Model?

10. What is inflation? Why was inflation proposed? What evidence is there for inflation?

11. What is dark matter? Why was it proposed?

12. What is dark energy? What is it considered to be causing the universe to do?

13. Based on current data, what will the ultimate fate of the universe be?

14. Why do some believe that the universe is fine-tuned for life?

Tutorial--Hubble's Law

Distance to Galaxy	Redshift
(Megaparsecs)	(km/s)
19	1210
300	15000
430	21600
770	39300
1200	61200

1-Plot the Distance vs. Redshift data in the above table on the graph below.

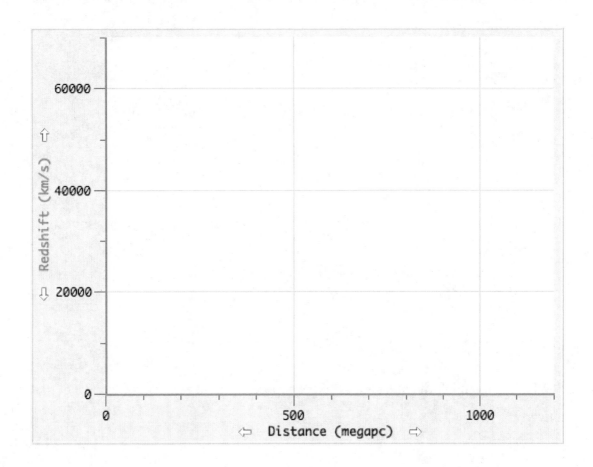

2-The value of the Hubble constant is the slope of the graph. Since the line is very straight, taking any one of the galaxies velocities and dividing by it the corresponding distance can determine this.

H= _____ km/s/Mpc

3-The age of the universe in billions of years can be estimated by dividing the Hubble constant into 1000.

Age of the Universe= _____ billions of years.

4-Is this estimate higher or lower than the recent estimate of the age of the universe reported in the chapter ?

5-What do you think might be a way to get a more accurate estimate of the age of the universe?

Chapter 13 - Life in the Universe

13.1 Introduction -Are We Alone?

The question of whether or not life on Earth is unique in our galaxy, or even the universe, is perhaps the most profound question that could ever be asked by the human species. A scientific attempt to answer this question begins with asking how life came to be on Earth. Then the question is whether what happened on Earth could have happened elsewhere. Then if it did, would we be able to detect or even recognize and/or contact this life?

13.2 The Miller-Urey Experiment

Experiments have shown that life could possibly have arisen naturally from conditions thought to have prevailed on Earth when the atmosphere was first forming. In 1952, *Stanley Miller*, then a graduate student, performed just such an experiment in the laboratory of Nobel-laureate chemist, Harold Urey. He simulated conditions on the primeval Earth by mixing water, methane, ammonia, and hydrogen, heating up the mixture and sending electric sparks through it to simulate lightning. After a week, much of the carbon (from the methane) in the mixture had become solid and formed amino acids. Amino acids form proteins, which are the building blocks of life. The experiment, that has been replicated many times, did not actually create life, but it showed that the potential for life to arise did exist in the conditions prevalent early on in Earth's development.

Since the time of Miller's experiment, life has been found to exist and even thrive in more extreme environments such as the deep freeze underneath Antarctic ice-sheets and in hot, undersea volcanic vents. Microbes on the Apollo spacecraft even survived a trip to the moon and back. This could make the possibility of life existing elsewhere even more promising than initially suggested by the Miller-Urey experiment.

Figure 13.1 Stanley Miller and his experimental set up.

13.3 Life Elsewhere in Our Solar System?

If we accept that life arose naturally on Earth, the next question is: could it have happened elsewhere in our own solar system? By far the planet with the most Earth-like conditions is our neighbor, Mars.

Mars

Life on Mars has been the subject of much speculation and even fantasy. In 1877, before he began the search for the "planet-X" that eventually became Pluto, Percival Lowell heard that Italian astronomer Giovanni Schiaparelli had observed *canali*, which is Italian for *channels*, on Mars. Lowell made an incorrect translation and convinced himself that Martians were building *canals* to move ice from the polar regions of the planet to the equator to melt it to supply water for the dying jungles. This scenario was part of the inspiration for H.G. Well's 1898 novel *War of the Worlds*, an early work of science fiction about a Martian invasion of Earth. In 1938, actor Orson Wells panicked much of the nation with a radio dramatization of the story that many, likely because of the United States' impending entry into World War II, mistook for an actual news report of a real-life Martian invasion.

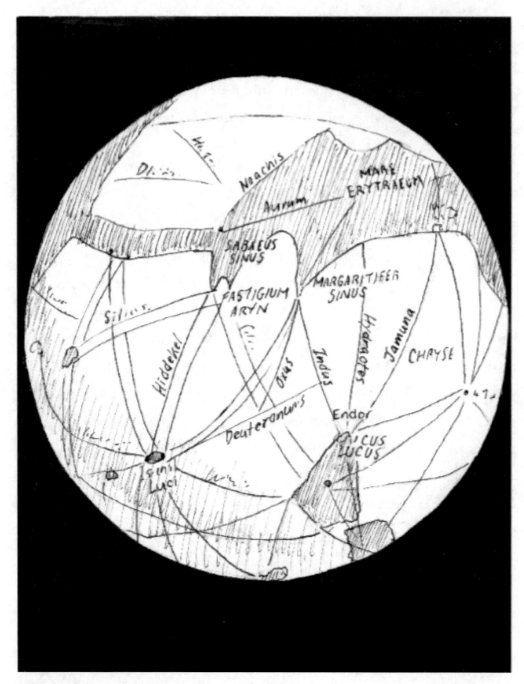

Figure 13.2 Lowell's Mars.

In real life, it is Earth that has invaded Mars, having sent more unmanned spacecraft there than anywhere else in our solar system. None of them, even landers that analyzed soil samples, have found any traces of life. In 1996, evidence of a Martian "invasion" was announced in the form of a meteorite that was found in Antarctica.

Figure 13.3 The *Viking* lander on Mars in 1976.

The meteorite, know as ALH-84001, is of a type known, due to its chemical composition, to have originated on Mars and was found to contain a microscopic structure that resembles fossilized bacteria.

Knowing how an object originally from Mars could end up on Earth is the simple part. Being only about a tenth as massive, Mars has only 38 percent the gravitational pull of Earth, so a meteor collision on Mars can send debris from the planet flying out of orbit and heading toward the Sun. Since Earth is between Mars and the Sun, it can intercept some of the material. The real debate is about whether the object found in the meteorite is organic or geological in origin and, if it is indeed organic, if it is from Mars or whether it contaminated the meteorite after the meteorite landed on Earth.

Figure 13.4 The Martian meteorite.

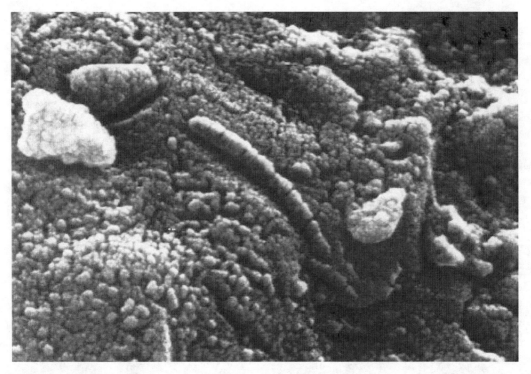

Figure 13.5 The microscopic "organism" inside ALH84001.

Titan and Europa

Other candidate locations in the solar system to harbor life are Jovian Moons. Some, being as large as the planet Mercury, are viable worlds in their own right. Titan of Saturn is the only moon in our solar system with a substantial atmosphere, and scientists have speculated for a long time that it has chemistry similar to that on Earth at the time of the formation of life.

Recall from Chapter 7 that the surface of Europa (Fig. 13.6) of Jupiter is covered with ice. In fact, Europa's surface appears very similar to the ice cap that covers Antarctica on Earth. Astronomers have speculated that it may be warm enough underneath the ice on Europa's surface for a liquid water ocean. Since water is essential for the existence of life, this makes Europa's ocean a promising environment for life to develop. The surface of Titan has already been visited by the *Huygens* probe, and there are future plans for a *Europa Astrobiology Lander.*

Figure 13.6 Europa imaged by the *Galileo* spacecraft.

13.4 Life Beyond OurSolar System?

When considering whether or not life exists beyond our solar system and whether or not contact is possible, it becomes necessary to think in terms of probabilities--the probability that stars have planets, that planets have life, that life will survive and evolve to intelligence and eventually develop technology. *Frank Drake* of Cornell University recognized this. In 1961 he devised a way to estimate how many planets there may be in our galaxy that harbor life with which we may be able to communicate. This is known as the *Drake Equation*.

Figure 13.7 Frank Drake and the *Drake Equation*.

The Drake equation is not meant to give a precise answer, but to encourage thought about all the factors that go into whether or not life has developed elsewhere and if we might communicate with it. It starts with how many stars there are in our galaxy, then an estimate of what fraction of those stars have planets, then how many planets per solar system are "Earth-like" or capable of supporting life. It goes on to consider that if a planet is able to support life, whether or not life will develop. If life does develop, will intelligence evolve? Does intelligence necessarily mean civilization and then technology? And finally, how long do technological civilizations last. Do they destroy themselves with warfare? Do disease or other natural disasters wipe them out? Or do they find a way to endure? Each factor gets more and more difficult to estimate, as they involve things that are harder and harder to know for sure. But again, Drake never intended that his equation would tell us exactly how many civilizations with which we could communicate are out there, just that it would get us thinking and talking about it.

13.5 SETI

Frank Drake founded the *Search for Extra-Terrestrial Intelligence (SETI)* in 1960 when he used a 26-meter radio telescope at the

National Radio Observatory in Green Bank, West Virginia to search areas of the sky near certain stars for radio signals that were possibly of non-natural, or technological, origin. His reasoning was that, since our civilization uses radio transmissions for communication, we have announced our presence in the galaxy, and others may be doing the same and it might be possible to detect their signals.

Since radio waves are electromagnetic waves, they travel at the speed of light and are considered by far the most likely method for possible communication with life elsewhere in our galaxy. Civilization on Earth has been using radio communication for over 100 years now, so the first radio waves broadcast from Earth have now traveled over 100 light-years in all directions out into the galaxy. Travel by spacecraft would take tens of thousands of years to reach even the nearest stars, so radio is currently accepted as the only technology by which there is any reasonable chance of contact.

In what has now been 50 years of searching, SETI has had a few exciting moments, but has not yet found a signal that can be verified as technological in origin. But as even the most enthusiastic of SETI's practitioners will admit, amongst the several hundred billion stars in our galaxy and the immense distances between them, the chance of looking precisely in the right place at the right moment is very remote.

It is important to know that there is not a tremendous amount of time and money spent on SETI, and that most time on radio telescopes is spent observing natural radio-sources like pulsars, quasars, and galaxies. However, the belief in how important a discovery by SETI could be has kept the program going for 50 years now, and at present seems to be strong enough to allow SETI to continue into the foreseeable future.

Figure 13.8 Radio Telescopes at the Very Large Array (VLA) in New Mexico.

In 1974 astronomers working on SETI decided that since we were listening, maybe we should broadcast, too--the logic being that if other technological civilizations were searching for signals, maybe it would be nice to find one meant for them rather than just one of our many random broadcasts that had escaped out into space. Initial public reaction was negative. Concern was expressed about what would happen if hostile aliens found the message and that maybe Earth should remain quiet. The truth is however, that the minute humans began using radio for communication, we announced our presence in the galaxy, and there is no way to take those first radio waves back. Also, maybe it would be desirable to send a more intelligent message than some of the radio and television broadcasts that have already come from our planet!

The next question is, of course, what do we say? Anyone receiving a message is unlikely to speak any verbal language spoken on Earth. But if they have the technology to receive a radio transmission, they are likely to have a knowledge of certain universal ideas, like mathematics, and will know about stars and planets and the hydrogen atoms of which most of the universe is made. Figure 13.9 shows a representation of a FM-radio broadcast that was beamed in a binary-code for 3 minutes from the Arecibo radio telescope in 1974 toward the globular cluster M13, a distance of about 25,000 light- years away.

Figure 13.9 The Arecibo message. See the representation of a person with the solar system (Earth elevated) below (to the right in the figure) and below that the radio dish from which it was sent. Also, above the person (to the left) DNA and representations of some chemical formulas associated with DNA and the numbers 1-10.

Figure 13.10 The giant radio telescope at Arecibo, Puerto Rico.

Section 13.6 Other Messages

The message from Arecibo was not sent with any real hope that it would be received by any living being. Nor are the chances that SETI will detect an alien transmission any time soon considered high. Rather, there are those that believe that since we *can* attempt to communicate beyond our own world we should at least *try*. This was also the thinking with messages that were included on the Pioneer and Voyager spacecrafts. Launched in the 1970s, these were the first spacecraft from Earth sent to explore the outer planets. Now over 30 years since the launch of the Voyagers and almost 40 years since Pioneers several of these spacecraft have actually left our solar system.

Figure 13.11 shows a plaque, designed by astronomers Frank Drake and *Carl Sagan*, that was affixed to the Pioneer 10 and 11 spacecrafts before their respective launches in 1972 and 1973. Figure 13.12 shows a phonograph record that was affixed to the Voyager I and II spacecrafts. Also included was a packet of pictures that included instructions for playing the records on a player in the spacecraft. Titled *Murmurs of Earth,* it includes greetings in 55 different languages, recordings of common sounds, both natural and technological, and 90 minutes of music from many different cultures and eras. The pictures included, among other things, landscapes, sunsets, cities, and people of many different cultures and races.

Like the Arecibo message, no one really expects that these messages will ever be found. Rather, they represent a symbolic statement that we humans are, or at least were, present in the galaxy and that we wish to communicate to any others with whom we may share its vastness, that they are indeed *not* alone.

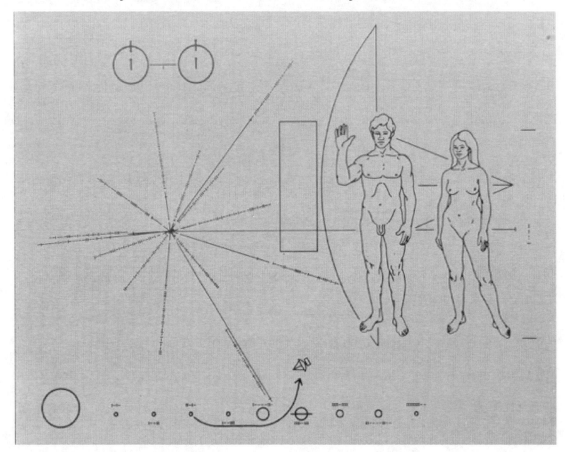

Figure 13.11 The Pioneer Spacecraft's *"Message from Earth."* Behind the man and woman is the outline of the spacecraft on the same scale. Along the bottom, the spacecraft can be seen on its trajectory through, and eventually out of, the solar system. The figure in the upper left is a depiction of a diatomic hydrogen molecule, the "1's" representing the number of protons and the electrons orbiting them.

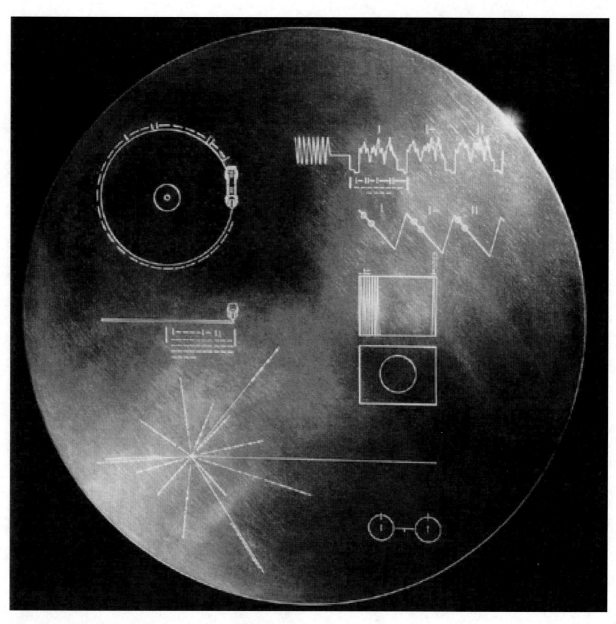

Figure 13.12 The *Voyager* record.

Figure 13.13 Co-designer of the Pioneer Plaque, chairman of the *NASA-Voyager* record committee, *SETI* enthusiast and astronomy popularizer, the late Carl Sagan.

Review Questions

1. What was produced in the Miller-Urey experiment? What is the significance of the experiment?

2. What is the current status of the answer to the question "Is there life on Mars?"

3. Other than Earth and Mars, what are considered the most promising places in our solar system for life to develop? Briefly describe each environment and why it is believed to have the potential to harbor life.

4. What is the purpose of the Drake Equation?

5. What is considered the most likely way that communication with extra-terrestrial life could occur? Why is this mode of communication in particular considered the most likely?

6. How long has the project SETI been going on? What are its results thus far? How does this affect the prospect of continuation of the project?

7. What is the primary purpose of radio astronomy?

8. What are the chances that radio transmissions from Earth or messages on robot spacecraft will ever be received by living beings? Based on your answer, what is the reasoning behind sending them?

Tutorial--The Drake Equation

Go to the website:

http://www.activemind.com/Mysterious/Topics/SETI/drake_equation.html

Read the description of the Drake Equation at the site and use the tool at the site to make your own estimate for N, the number of communicating civilizations in our galaxy.

Record *your* estimates for each factor in the equation and give the reasoning behind each estimate.

N_* = the number of stars in the Milky Way galaxy = _____

f_p = fraction of stars with planets around them = _____

n_e = number of planets per star ecologically able to sustain life = _____

f_l = fraction of those planets where life actually evolves = _____

f_i = the fraction of f_l that evolve intelligent life = _____

f_c = the fraction of f_i that communicate = _____

f_L = the fraction of the planet's life during which the communicating civilizations survive= _____

$$N = N_* \, f_p \, n_e \, f_l \, f_i \, f_c \, f_L$$

N = the number of communicating civilizations in the galaxy

$$N = \text{\underline{\hspace{3cm}}}$$

APPENDIX 1 - OBSERVATION ACTIVITIES

Star Observations

Daily Motion: Go outside on a clear night about an hour after sunset. Find the *Big Dipper* and use it to find the North Star, *Polaris*. To review how to do this, see **Figure 1.3**. In the space below on the left, draw the *Big Dipper* and the *North Star*. Now wait three hours and do the same thing in the space on the right. Note any changes you see.

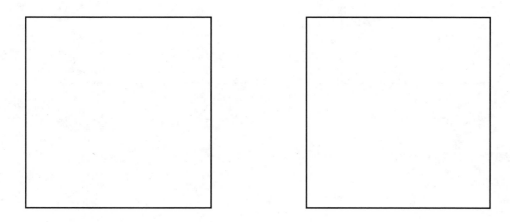

Big Dipper and North Star

Date-   Time-

Big Dipper and North Star

Date-   Time-

What changes do you notice?

Star Observations

Annual Motion: Go outside on a clear night about an hour after sunset and look in the southern sky. In the space below, draw a constellation that you can see. Use the seasonal star maps in **Appendix 2** for help identifying constellations. *Do this activity once near the beginning of the semester and once near the end.*

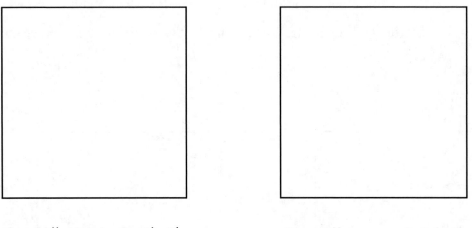

Constellation in South Sky

Date-   Time-

Constellation in South Sky

Date-   Time-

Sun Observations

Observe the Sun four times throughout the semester, preferably spaced out about once per month. Choose either *sunrise* or *sunset,* and make all four observations at the time you chose. They must also all be made from the same location. In the spaces on the **Sunrise/Sunset Observations** page, draw a picture of the horizon and any nearby landmarks (trees, buildings, etc.) and draw the Sun in its position on the horizon. The only thing that should be different in the four drawings is the location of the Sun.

Moon Observations

On every clear night for two weeks, beginning with the date of the *New Moon*, go outside, face due south, and find the Moon. In the spaces provided on the **Moon Observations** page, record the date and time of four (4) of the observations you make during the two weeks and draw the Moon, showing both its *phase* and its position relative to the Sun. Try to space out the observations you record as evenly as you can over the two weeks. You should be facing south for all your observations, so east would be on the left of the drawing and the setting Sun in the West on the right. Your instructor will provide the dates of New Moon during the semester. A new Moon occurs about once per month, so you should have at least three and maybe four chances to complete this exercise in a semester.

Sunrise / Sunset (circle one) Observations

Date of Sun Observation-

Date of Sun Observation-

Date of Sun Observation-

Date of Sun Observation-

Moon Observations

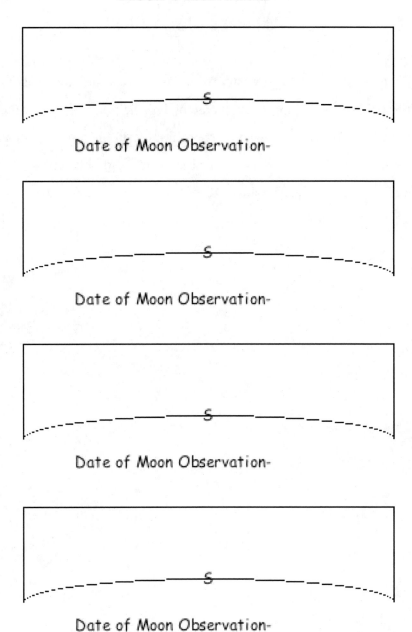

Date of Moon Observation-

Date of Moon Observation-

Date of Moon Observation-

Date of Moon Observation-

Planetary Observations

Planet positions in the sky vary from year to year, and their visibility varies as they and Earth orbit the Sun. Your instructor will help you decide which planets to look for, as well as where and when. Also, monthly publications such as *Astronomy* or *Sky and Telescope* and many websites keep track of planetary positions. Draw what you observe in the space below. Record the date and time, label each planet and the direction you are facing.

APPENDIX 2-SEASONAL STAR MAPS

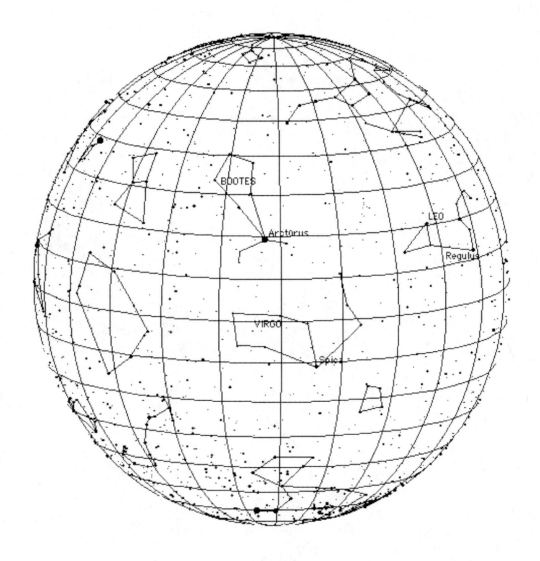

(Looking south at mid-evening)

Spring

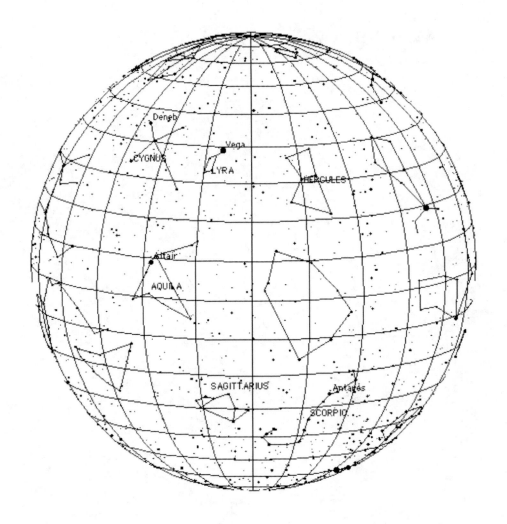

(Looking south at mid-evening)

Summer

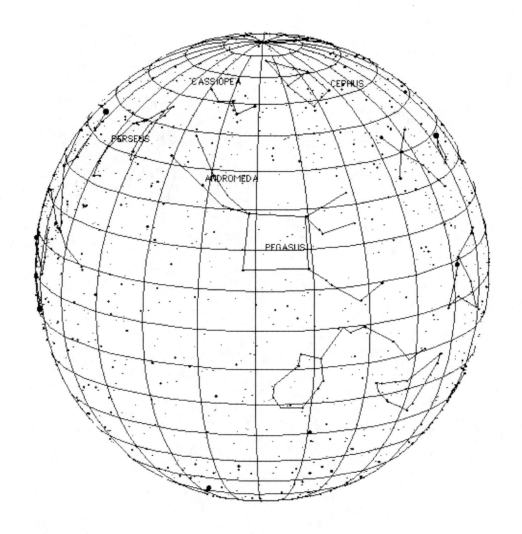

(Looking south at mid-evening)

Fall

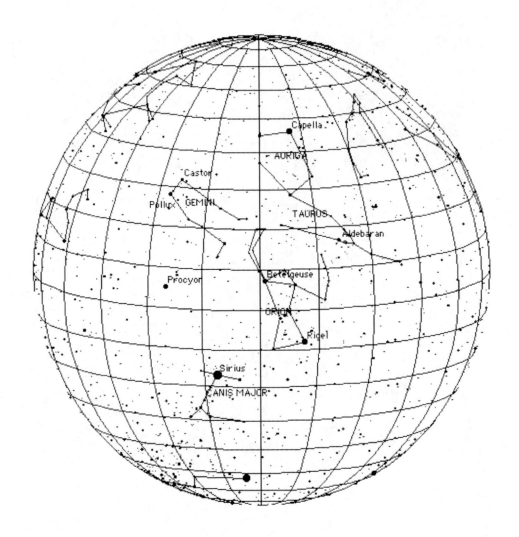

(Looking south at mid-evening)

Winter

APPENDIX 3 –TELESCOPE ACTIVITIES

Deep Sky Telescopic Observations--Fall Term

Note: Some of the suggested objects may not be observable depending on when during the semester you visit the observatory.

1-There are three types of "Deep Sky Objects":

Nebulae (plural of Nebula)--gigantic clouds of gas and dust

Star Clusters--groups of hundreds or even thousands of stars

Galaxies--Assemblages of 100s of billions of stars

It is also interesting to observe double stars, which, as the name suggests, are stars that either appear to be, or really are, very close to one another.

2- The summer sky is full of many interesting deep sky objects:

Nebulae--M57, M27 are planetary nebulas

Star Clusters--M13, M 92 are *globular clusters*
M 52 and The Double-Cluster in Perseus are *open clusters*

Galaxies--M31, M 32, M33 are galaxies

Double stars--Alberio, the Double-Double in Lyra

Ask the instructor running the observing session which of these objects you will be able to observe tonight.

Deep Sky Telescopic Observations--Winter Term

Note--Some of the suggested objects may not be observable, depending on when during the semester you visit the observatory.

1-There are three types of "Deep Sky Objects":

Nebulae (plural of Nebula)--gigantic clouds of gas and dust

Star Clusters--groups of hundreds or even thousands of stars

Galaxies--Assemblages of 100s of billions of stars

It is also interesting to observe double stars, which, as the name suggests, are stars that either appear to be or really are very close to one another.

2- The summer sky is full of many interesting deep sky objects:

Nebulae--M42, M43 are star formation regions
　　　　M1 is a supernova remnant

Star Clusters--The Hyades, M45 (the Pleadies)
　　　　　　and M 44 are *open clusters*

Galaxies--M81, M 82, M51 are galaxies

Double stars--Mizar/Alcor

Ask the instructor running the observing session which of these objects you will be able to observe tonight.

Deep Sky Telescopic Observations--Summer Term

Note--Some of the suggested objects may not be observable, depending on when during the semester you visit the observatory.

1-There are three types of "Deep Sky Objects":

Nebulae (plural of Nebula)--gigantic clouds of gas and dust

Star Clusters--groups of hundreds or even thousands of stars

Galaxies--Assemblages of 100s of billions of stars

It is also interesting to observe double stars, which, as the name suggests, are stars that either appear to be or really are very close to one another.

2- The summer sky is full of many interesting deep sky objects:

Nebulae--M57, M27 are planetary nebulas
        M8, M16 and M20 are star-formation regions

Star Clusters--M13, M 92 are *globular clusters*
        M 29, M39 are *open clusters*

Galaxies--M81, M 82, M51 are galaxies
        Virgo cluster of galaxies

Double stars--Alberio, the Double-Double in Lyra, Mizar/ Alcor

Ask the instructor running the observing session which of these objects you will be able to observe tonight.

Deep Sky Telescopic Observation Sheet

Signature of Instructor Present -_____

Date-
Time-

Object Observed-
Type of Object-

Draw a picture of the object in the space below

Familiar Name of Object-
Where object was in the sky-
Constellation Object is in-
Magnitude of Object-
Distance to Object-
Look the object up in your textbook or another reference, and explain the nature of the object. Include your impressions when viewing of the object.

Telescopic Observations--Planetary Objects

Note--Some of the suggested objects may not be observable, depending on when during the semester you visit the observatory.

1--If the Moon is out, you should be able to get a close observation of its surface features, including craters and mountains.

2--If any of the following planets are out, you can make special observations for each one:

Venus--What phase is it in?
Jupiter--How many moons do you see? Can you see any surface features?
Mars--Can you see any surface features?
Saturn--Can you see its rings?
Mercury--What do you see?
Uranus--What color is it? How does it look different from the stars around it?
Neptune--What color is it? How does it look different from the stars around it?

3--Are there any asteroids out tonight?

Ask the instructor running the observing session which of these objects you will be able to observe tonight.

Planetary Telescopic Observation Sheet

Signature of Instructor Present -_____

Date-
Time-

Object Observed-
Type of Object-

      <u>Draw a picture of the object in the space below.</u>

If you have observed any of the following objects, answer the question that goes with it:

      Venus--What phase is it in? Do you see any surface features?
      Jupiter or Saturn--Include and label any moons you see in your drawing. Include any Surface Features you see in your drawing.
      Mars--Include any Surface Features you see in your drawing.
      Mercury--Just describe what you saw.
      Uranus or Neptune--What color is it? How can you tell it is different than a star?
      If you observe an asteroid, draw the star field around it and label which object is the asteroid.

Sun or Moon Telescopic Observation Sheet

Signature of Instructor Present -_____

Date-
Time-

Object Observed-

<u>Draw a picture of the object in the space below.</u>

Include and label any surface features you observed.

Telescope Activities
Laboratory or Independent Study

Observing the Moon

Observe a portion of the Moon's surface close up. Obtain an image of your observation and find a reference that has a detailed labeled map of the Moon. Attempt to identify the name, type, and size of several of the features in your image.

Observing Venus

Note--This project can only be done during a semester when Venus will be east of the Sun and therefore visible above the western horizon during the early evening.

Observe Venus as many times as possible during the semester; keep track of the date and time of each observation. Carefully note Venus' phase each time you image it. Compare the changes in phase to the changes in Venus' angular distance from the Sun. Is there a relationship between Venus's phase and its apparent distance from the sun during the time of your observations? What conclusion (s) can you draw from this relationship?

Observing Jupiter & Its Moons

Note--Jupiter must be within the part of the sky visible to the telescope in the evening for a significant portion of the semester for this project.

Observe Jupiter as many times as possible during the semester; keep track of the date and time of each observation. Carefully note the position of the visible moons each time you image Jupiter. Use your images to attempt to estimate the orbital period around Jupiter of any of the satellites that you observe. Look up the orbital periods in your textbook or another reference. How accurate are your estimates? Can you think of any reasons for discrepancies between your estimates and the actual figures?

If possible, observe Jupiter and its visible moons multiple times in one evening. Carefully record the time of each observation. Can you make any estimates based on these observations?

Did you make observations where there were fewer moons visible than at other times? Can you think of the reason for this?

Observing Saturn

Note--The only constraint for this activity is that Saturn be visible in the night sky at some time during the semester.

Observe Saturn and obtain a copy of the image. On the image carefully measure both the diameter of the planet and the diameter of the rings.
Divide the diameter of the rings by the diameter of the planet.

Diameter Rings/Diameter Planet = _____

In your text book or another reference, look up the "*Roche-Limit*." Compare your calculation to the accepted value of the *Roche Limit*. Explain what the *Roche Limit* is and any discrepancies between your value and the accepted value.
If possible, obtain an image of Saturn in which one or more of its moons are visible. How are moons involved with the *Roche Limit*? Are the moons you observed in agreement with this?

Observing Asteroids

Choose one asteroid and attempt to image it as many times as possible during the semester. Compare successive images and attempt to draw a map showing the asteroid's apparent motion through the nearby "fixed" background of stars. This is how asteroids are discovered. What is the reason for this apparent motion?

Observing Pluto?

It may be possible to identify Pluto in the field of view of an image similar to the way it was done for asteroids.

Galaxy Types

Note--The "Virgo-Cluster" of Galaxies is only visible from the observatory at certain times of the year.

Observe a number of galaxies within the Virgo Cluster. Attempt to identify the type of each galaxy you observe. Try to find at least one example of each major galaxy type. Save images of your examples; identify the galaxy and the type in each image. You may have to do some research in your textbook or another reference to determine the different galaxy types and which ones you are observing.

Observing *Deep Sky Objects*

Nebulae, Star Clusters, and *Galaxies* are collectively known as *Deep Sky Objects*. The two basic types of *nebulae* are star-formation regions and *planetary nebulae* or *supernova remnant* nebulae. *Star clusters* are either *open clusters* or *globular clusters*. Throughout the course of the semester, observe one example of each type of *nebula*, one of each type of cluster, a galaxy, and a double star. Use your textbook or another reference to research each object you observe. Submit along with an image a report on the nature of each object.

Devise Your Own Observation Activity

Design an observation project yourself that you would like to undertake. Since you only have a semester, make sure it is not too complex and is also within the capability of the observatory. Discuss possible ideas with your astronomy or observatory instructor(s).

APPENDIX 4 –CELESTIAL GLOBE ACTIVITIES

*Note--These activities are designed for use with a standard Celestial Globe. They should be useful for any number of different models.

Celestial Globe Activity 1--STARS

1.)   Set the Celestial Globe for your Latitude. You do this by moving the top of the globe (90° Declination), the *North Celestial Pole*, (*NCP*) toward the North so that the *Latitude* you want is at the *Zenith*, the point directly overhead. Your *Latitude* =_____°.

a.)   Find the four *Constellations* in the table below. Classify them as stars that either: *rise and set* (R/S), *never set* (NS), or *never rise* (NR) at your *Latitude*. Also give the name of a bright star in the *Constellation* (if one is labeled).

Constellation	R/S	NS	NR	Bright Star
Canis Major				
Cassiopeia				
Crux				
Cygnus				

b.)   Leave the globe set at your *Latitude*. Determine whether the *Transit Altitudes* (the *Altitude* at which they cross the *Meridian*) of the stars named in your above table are high-h, medium-m or low-l. High would be close to the *zenith*, low would be close to the *horizon*. Also, determine the *Azimuths* on the *Horizon* when they rise and set. Are they rising in the NE, E, or SE? Are they setting in the NW, W or SW?

Star Name	Transit Altitude (h/m/l?)	Rise Azimuth (NE,E,SE?)	Set Azimuth (NW,W,SW?)

2.)   Use the Celestial Globe to answer the following questions:

a.) Is the *Altitude* of the *North Celestial Pole* as seen from your *Latitude*

h / m / l (circle one)?

b.) Now set your Globe to 90° N *Latitude*. Your geographic location is
(where on the Earth are you observing from?) _____. The *Altitude* of the
NCP is

h / m / l (circle one).

c.)   Find the same four *Constellations* you found in 1-a.   In the table below,
classify each of them as stars that either: *rise and set* (R/S), *never set* (NS), or *never
rise* (NR) from 90° N *Latitude* (a constellation can only be ONE of these choices
from a given location). Also, transfer your results from part 1-a to complete the third
column.

Constellation	90°N	Your Latitude =____°	0°	90°S
Canis Major				
Cassiopeia				
Crux				
Cygnus				

d.)   Now set your Globe to 0° *Latitude*. Your geographic location is (where on the
Earth are you observing from?) _____. The *Altitude* of the *NCP* is h / m /
l (circle one). In the table above, classify each of the four *Constellations* as stars that
either: *rise and set* (R/S), *never set* (NS), or *never rise* (NR) from 90° N *Latitude*
(again, a constellation can only be ONE of these choices from a given location).

420

e.)   Compare the *Altitude* of the NCP in parts 2-a, 2-b, and 2-d. <u>How does the *Altitude* of the NCP seem to be related to the observer's *Latitude*?</u>

f.)   Now set your Celestial Globe to 90° S *Latitude*. Your geographic location is (where on the Earth are you observing from?) _____. In the table above, classify the four *Constellations* as stars that either: *rise and set* (R/S), *never set* (NS), or *never rise* (NR) from 90° S *Latitude*. Can you see the NCP from here?

g.)   Of the locations you visited, which has the most *never-set* (or *never-rise)* stars? Which location has the least *never set* or *never-rise* stars?

h.)   Which location that you visited has the *most rise-and-set* stars? Which location has the *least rise-and-set* stars?

i.)   About what percentage of the stars visible from your location are *rise-and-set* stars?

j.)   As you travel from the equator to a pole the number or *never-rise* and *never-set* stars

                    increases/decreases   (circle one)

and the number of *rise-and-set* stars

                    increases/decreases   (circle one).

*After you have completed this activity, you should be able to:

     1-Set the Celestial Globe at any *Latitude*.

2-Determine the approximate *Altitude* **(h /m /l) and** *Azimuth* **(i.e. N, NW, SW etc.) of an object.**

Celestial Globe Activity 2--THE SUN AND THE SEASONS

1.) Set the Celestial Globe to your *Latitude*. You do this by moving the top of the globe (90° Declination), the *North Celestial Pole* (NCP), toward the North so that the *Latitude* you want is at the *Zenith*, the point directly overhead. Your *Latitude* =_____°.

> Now move your Sun to the current date on the *Ecliptic.*

2.) The Sun is in the *Constellation* _____ .
The Sun rises in the   NE / E / SE   (circle one).

The *Transit Altitude* is h / m / l ?
What time of day is this? -

The sun sets in the   NW / W/ SW (circle one).

3.) Name a *Constellation* that will be visible high overhead:

shortly after *sunset-*

around *midnight-*
Explain how you can tell it is *midnight-*

shortly before *sunrise-*

4.) Record on the table below the rise and set *Azimuth* (example-NE, E or SE) for the Sun, the *Transit Altitudes* (h / m / l) and the approximate number of hours the Sun is up. Do this for each date given.

Date	Rise/Set Azimuths (i.e. NE, E, SE etc)	Transit Altitude (h / m / l)	Hours Up**
March 21			
June 21			
September 21			
December 21			

Note-You can count the <u>HOURS UP</u> by counting how many lines of *Right Ascension* pass under the *Meridian* during the time the Sun is up.

Based on the above table, give two reasons that summer is warmer than winter.

March 21 and September 21 are called the *Vernal* and *Autumnal* _____ s. Based on the table above, explain the reason for this name.

5.) Classify each *Constellation* as either seasonal or *circumpolar* by placing a check mark in the appropriate box. A *Constellation* will be named after the season you *can* see it best. This is the season that it is high at *midnight*. So, put the *Constellation* on the *Meridian* then move the Sun to *midnight* and see what date on the *Ecliptic* the Sun is on. The *season that date is in is the season you will best see the constellation. Circumpolar Constellations* can be seen all year around, so they are not seasonal.

	Cepheus	Leo	Lyra	Pisces	Orion
Spring					
Summer					
Fall					
Winter					
Circumpolar					

*After you have completed this activity, you should be able to:
3-Correctly place the Sun on the *Ecliptic* for any day of the year.
4-Determine the approximate number of hours an object is up.
5-Determine the season in which a *Constellation* will be best seen.

Celestial Globe Activity 3--AROUND THE WORLD

1.) To set the Celestial Globe for any *Latitude*, move the top of the globe (90° Declination), the *North Celestial Pole (NCP)*, toward the North so that the *Latitude* you want is at the *Zenith*, the point directly overhead.

Place your Sun under each of the dates on the *Ecliptic* in the tables below and record the information for each of the given *Latitudes*.

TRANSIT ALTITUDE
(h / m / l)?

Date	40°N	80°N	20°N	40°S
March 21				
June 21				
September 21				
December 21				

HOURS UP**

Date	40°N	80°N	20°N	40°S
March 21				
June 21				
September 21				
December 21				

Note-You can count <u>HOURS UP</u>, by counting how many lines of Right Ascension pass under the Meridian during the time the Sun is up.

RISE AND SET AZIMUTHS
(E, NE, SE; W, NW, SW)

Date	40°N	80°N	20°N	40°S
March 21				
June 21				
September 21				
December 21				

2.)   Answer the following questions about the Sun based on the tables above.

Which *Latitude* has the greatest variation in <u>HOURS UP</u>?

The least variation?

Was the Sun ever (close to) directly overhead (near the *Zenith*)? If so, where and when?

Did you ever observe "Midnight Sun" (the Sun up all night or close to it)? If so, where and when?

Did you ever observe a day with (little or) no sun at all? If so, where and when?

Explain what reasons **you observed** for the *Polar* Regions of the world always being so cold and the *Tropical* Regions being so warm.

Based on what **you observed**, does the length of time the Sun is up seem to be a primary or a secondary effect on both latitudinal and seasonal variations in temperature?   Explain your answer. Hint: compare <u>HOURS UP</u> and <u>TRANSIT ALTITUDES</u> at 20°N and 80°N.

*This Activity introduces no new skills with the Celestial Globe, but reviews almost all of those previous learned.

Celestial Globe Activity 4--THE MOON

1.) To set the Celestial Globe for any *Latitude*, move the top of the globe (90° *Declination*), the *North Celestial Pole (NCP),* toward the North so that the *Latitude* you want is at the *Zenith*, the point directly overhead. <u>For this activity, set your globe to the *Equator*</u>.

2.) Now move the Sun to the date of March 21 on the *Ecliptic* (along the 0 hour of *Right Ascension* line).   A *New Moon* occurs when the Moon, at the same *Right Ascension* as the Sun. Place your Moon on the same location on the *Ecliptic* as the Sun. Record the Date and the *Rising*, *Setting*, and *Transit* times of the Moon on the table below.

3.) The Moon will move completely around the *Ecliptic* in about one Month. This is 24 hours of *Right Ascension* (*RA*) So, the Moon will move about _____ hrs of *RA* in one week. The Sun will move completely around the *Ecliptic* in one year, so in one month it will move _____ hrs of *RA* and in one week it will move about _____ hrs.

Now advance the Sun one week along the *Ecliptic* and advance the Moon one week. The Moon is always within 5° of the *Ecliptic*; so for this activity it can be considered to move along the Ecliptic too. Record the approximate Date and the *Rising*, *Setting*, and *Transit* times of the Moon on the table and the name of the *Lunar Phase*. Hint for the Phase-What fraction of the way around the *Ecliptic* has the Moon moved since *New Moon*?

4.) Now, advance the Sun another week and the Moon another week. Record the Date and the *Rising, Setting,* and *Transit* times of the Moon on the table and the name of the *Lunar Phase*. Hint: Is the side of the Moon facing the Earth, facing toward or away from the Sun?

5.) Advance the Sun and the Moon one more week. Record the Date and the *Rising, Setting*, and *Transit* times of the Moon on the table and the name of the *Lunar Phase.* Hint: What fraction of the way around the *Ecliptic* has the Moon moved since *New Moon*?

6.) Finally, advance the Sun and the Moon one more week. Notice that the Moon has NOT returned to the *New Phase*. The Moon is about _____ hrs of *RA* "behind" the Sun. It will take about _____ days to "catch up" and return to the *New Phase* (divide the number of hours of RA the Moon is behind by the number of hours of *RA* in a week then divide the answer into the 7 days in a week).

The time for the Moon to move all the way around the *Ecliptic* is about _____ days, this is called a *sidereal* month (this is the time the Moon takes to orbit Earth). The time between two *New Moons* is about _____ days and is called the *synodic* month (this the time the Moon takes to go through its cycle of phases).

Moon Table

Record the *Phase,* the Date, and the *Rising*, *Setting,* and *Transit* times of the Moon from questions 2-5 above. Enter each times as either sunrise, noon, sunset, or midnight (use whichever one is CLOSEST).

Phase	New			
Date	March 21			
Rise Time				
Transit Time				
Set Time				

7.)   Answer the following questions based on the table above:

During which *phase* will you see the Moon mostly at night?

During which *phase* will you see the Moon first during the day, then at night?

During which *phase* will you see the Moon first at night, then during the day?

During which *phase* is a *Lunar Eclipse* most likely? Explain your reasoning and what happens during a *Lunar Eclipse*.

During which *phase* is a *Solar Eclipse* most likely? Explain your reasoning and what happens during a *Solar Eclipse*.

During which *phase* will the Moon not be visible? Explain your reasoning.